Informing Interwar Internationalism

Histories of Internationalism

Series Editors: Jessica Reinisch, Professor in Modern History at Birkbeck, University of London, UK, and David Brydan, Senior Lecturer of 20th Century History and International Relations at King's College London, UK.

Editorial Board: Tomoko Akami, Australian National University, Australia
Martin Conway, University of Oxford, UK
Adom Getachew, University of Chicago, USA
Sandrine Kott, University of Geneva, Switzerland
Stephen Legg, University of Nottingham, UK
Su Lin Lewis, University of Bristol, UK
Erez Manela, Harvard University, USA
Samuel Moyn, Yale University, USA
Alanna O'Malley, Leiden University, The Netherlands
Kiran Patel, Ludwig Maximilian University Munich, Germany
Tehila Sasson, Emory University, USA
Frank Trentmann, Birkbeck University, USA
Heidi Tworek, University of British Columbia, Canada

This book series features cutting-edge research on the history of international cooperation and internationalizing ambitions in the modern world. Providing an intellectual home for research into the many guises of internationalism, its titles draw on methods and insights from political, social, cultural, economic and intellectual history. It showcases a rapidly expanding scholarship which has begun to transform our understanding of internationalism and the modern world.

Cutting across established academic fields such as European, World, International and Global History, the series critically examines historical perceptions of geography, regions, centres, peripheries, borderlands, networks and connections across space in the history of internationalism. It includes both monographs and edited volumes that shed new light on local and global contexts for international projects; the impact of class, race and gender on international aspirations; the roles played by a variety of international organizations and institutions; and the hopes, fears, tensions and conflicts underlying them.

The series is published in association with Birkbeck's Centre for the Study of Internationalism.

Published:

Organizing the 20th-Century World, ed. by Karen Gram-Skjoldager, Haakon Andreas Ikonomou, Torsten Kahlert

Placing Internationalism: International Conferences and the Making of the Modern World, ed. by Stephen Legg, Mike Heffernan, Jake Hodder, and Benjamin Thorpe

Inventing the Third World: In Search of Freedom for the Postwar Global South, ed. by Jeremy Adelman and Gyan Prakash

Internationalists in European History: Rethinking the Twentieth Century, ed. by Jessica Reinisch and David Brydan

International Cooperation in Cold War Europe, Daniel Stinsky

Socialist Internationalism and the Gritty Politics of the Particular, ed. by Kristin Roth-Ey

Relief and Rehabilitation for a Postwar World, ed. by Samantha K. Knapton and Katherine Rossy

Dismantling the League of Nations, Jane Mumby

Cosmopolitan Elites and the Making of Globality, Leonie Wolters

Forthcoming:

Socialism, Internationalism, and Development in the Third World, ed. by Su Lin Lewis and Nana Osei-Opare

Dam Internationalism, ed. by Vincent Lagendijk and Frederik Schulze

The War for Anatolia and the Unmaking of International Order ed. by Georgios Giannakopoulos, Joseph A. Maiolo and Gonda Van Steen

International Organizations and the Cold War ed. by Sandrine Kott, Elisabeth Röhrlich and Eva-Maria Muschik

Poland and the Making of Transnational Social Science, Olga Linkiewicz

Student Internationalism and the Global Cold War, Mikuláš Pešta

Informing Interwar Internationalism

The Information Strategies of the League of Nations

Emil Eiby Seidenfaden

BLOOMSBURY ACADEMIC
LONDON • NEW YORK • OXFORD • NEW DELHI • SYDNEY

BLOOMSBURY ACADEMIC

Bloomsbury Publishing Plc, 50 Bedford Square, London, WC1B 3DP, UK
Bloomsbury Publishing Inc, 1359 Broadway, New York, NY 10018, USA
Bloomsbury Publishing Ireland, 29 Earlsfort Terrace, Dublin 2, D02 AY28, Ireland

BLOOMSBURY, BLOOMSBURY ACADEMIC and the Diana logo are trademarks of
Bloomsbury Publishing Plc

First published in Great Britain 2024
This paperback edition published in 2026

Copyright © Emil Eiby Seidenfaden, 2024

Emil Eiby Seidenfaden has asserted his right under the Copyright, Designs and
Patents Act, 1988, to be identified as Author of this work.

For legal purposes the Acknowledgements on p. xi constitute an extension
of this copyright page.

Cover image © United Nations Archives, Geneva

All rights reserved. No part of this publication may be: i) reproduced or transmitted in any form, electronic or mechanical, including photocopying, recording or by means of any information storage or retrieval system without prior permission in writing from the publishers; or ii) used or reproduced in any way for the training, development or operation of artificial intelligence (AI) technologies, including generative AI technologies. The rights holders expressly reserve this publication from the text and data mining exception as per Article 4(3) of the Digital Single Market Directive (EU) 2019/790.

Bloomsbury Publishing Plc does not have any control over, or responsibility for, any third-party websites referred to or in this book. All internet addresses given in this book were correct at the time of going to press. The author and publisher regret any inconvenience caused if addresses have changed or sites have ceased to exist, but can accept no responsibility for any such changes.

A catalogue record for this book is available from the British Library.

A catalog record for this book is available from the Library of Congress.

ISBN: HB: 978-1-3503-8212-1
PB: 978-1-3503-8215-2
ePDF: 978-1-3503-8213-8
eBook: 978-1-3503-8214-5

Series: Histories of Internationalism

Typeset by Deanta Global Publishing Services, Chennai, India

For product safety related questions contact productsafety@bloomsbury.com.

To find out more about our authors and books visit www.bloomsbury.com and
sign up for our newsletters.

Contents

List of figures	ix
List of tables	x
Acknowledgements	xi
Introduction	1
The League and its audience: Some conceptualizations	7
Locating 'information' in League archival records	13

Part I

1   Centre of world information: Creating an information section, 1919–21   19
    Founding an Information Section   20
    The politics of nationality in the Information Section   26
    Internationalism in the Information Section   31
    The propaganda spectre   35
    Conclusion   37

2   More than a press bureau: The Information Section at work, 1920–32   39
    From the gallery down to the floor: Working with the press   41
    Secrecy and transparency   45
    Moral disarmament and management of the press   48
    Cooperative publicity   51
    Would-be diplomats   59
    Conclusion   62

3   Confidence and cynicism: League public information material, 1919–32   64
    Publications of the Information Section   65
    Target audiences   66
    Four strategies, 1919–33   67
    Action and progress   69
    The moral force of public opinion   73
    Confident indirect legitimization   80
    More than the legacy of war   83
    Conclusion   85

Part II

4 Downscaling ambitions: Reorganization of the Information
   Section, 1933–40 89
   The Secretariat in the shadow of crisis 90
   Exit diplomacy? 101
   The collapse 106
   Conclusion 108

5 Crisis and retreat to aesthetics: League public information, 1933–40 ... 110
   Enter the technical 114
   Crisis rhetoric 117
   Retreat to aesthetics 124
   Conclusion 131

6 Exit Geneva: League legacies in UN publicity planning, 1942–46 ... 133
   Crossing the Atlantic or the channel 134
   Planning for the UNDPI 143
   The silent League presence 144
   The UNDPI 148
   Conclusion 152

Conclusion 153
   Public opinion 155
   Internationalism 157
   Propaganda 159
   The message from Geneva 161

Notes 165
Bibliography 194
Index 204

Figures

1	Total number of staff appointments of the six largest sections of the Secretariat, 1919–25	25
2	Citizenship of Information Section officials 1919–23 and 1928–32	27
3	Palais Wilson in the 1920s	28
4	Pierre Comert, director of the Information Section 1919–32	33
5	A group photo of the Information Section in 1923 or 1924	41
6	The Salle de la Réformation during the 8th General Assembly of the League of Nations	43
7	A group of students at the League summer school, organized by the IFLS visiting the Secretariat in 1922	56
8	Arthur Sweetser, assistant director of the Information Section 1919–32, director 1933 and independent director of the Secretariat 1934–40	61
9	Gustav Stresemann, addressing the League General Assembly in 1929	79
10	A meeting of the League Council in the brand-new Palais des Nations, April 1936	128

Tables

1	Salary Budget of the Section throughout the 1920s Compared to the Complete Salary Budget of the Secretariat	25
2	Share of the Information Section in the League's Overall Publication Activities between 1931 and 1939	66
3	Share of Salaries and Allowances of the Secretariat Taken up by the Information Section 1931–40	96
4	Development of size of Information Section	96

Acknowledgements

THANK YOU

A great number of people helped me in the research behind this book and in the framing and planning of the book itself. I would like to express my heartfelt gratitude to those among them who gave most of their time.

Karen Gram-Skjoldager, Aarhus University, brought me on the League of Nations adventure in the first place as part of her Aarhus University research group of the collective project the *Invention of International Bureaucracy (…) 1920-1960*. Karen took a deep interest in the project, shared her immense knowledge and guided me, always constructively, into academic adulthood.

Daniel Laqua, Northumbia University, gave patient advice and invaluable comments and feedback for the framing of the book proposal.

Haakon A. Ikonomou, University of Copenhagen, offered much help and feedback for several parts of the manuscript.

Patricia Clavin, University of Oxford, encouraged me to pursue a book on the subject and gave excellent advice on the process.

Jacques Oberson, United Nations Archives, Geneva, with his knowledge, coolness and creativity, is everything historians could ask for in an archivist.

Finally, I would like to thank the two anonymous peer reviewers both of whom offered excellent points and suggestions for the manuscript.

Thank you all.

Introduction

This book is about internationalism in practice. It tells the story of how international officials worked together to communicate with the public on behalf of the first global intergovernmental organization tasked with facilitating world peace. It unpacks how the League of Nations forged lines of communication with the press, with civil society and with common citizens of the interwar world and explores what rhetorical strategies its officials employed to argue that these people needed an organization to commit their governments to the prevention of war. On a more overall level, it asks how the League conceptualized and instrumentalized this public as a source of legitimacy. Finally, it discusses what lessons the officials of the disintegrated League passed on to the nascent United Nations during the Second World War – and how their understanding of the public became transformed in the process.

Thus, the book delivers the first systematic, historical examination of how the League of Nations sought to implement its ideals of forging a new powerful bond with public opinion, how this work developed across the interwar period and what lessons from it were transferred into the rising UN organization during the Second World War. It illuminates how the League, in a certain sense, preached to the choir. The audience that came to be constructed by officials of the Information Section of its Secretariat was an educated elite public which were largely already supporters of the organization. However, it also shows how this construction cannot be reduced to a reflection of a naïve or narrow understanding within the League of who counted as relevant members of the public. It came about as the result of a careful navigation of dangerous waters, the nature of which the League's information officials only gradually realized. When the international atmosphere started to change in Geneva after Japan, Italy and Germany's defections from the organization, the Information Section was one of the prime victims, as the Secretariat tried desperately to salvage its credibility by ridding itself of 'propagandists'. When the world war was over, the lessons drawn from the debacle by the former information officials was that a future information policy would have to be much bigger, better funded and more diverse in its communication.

It all began more than a quarter of a century before that, with the Treaty of Versailles, signed in 1919. Attached to this document, the most significant of peace treaties produced by the Paris Peace Conference, was a plan for an intergovernmental body to eventually include all the nation states of the world. Besides a new Permanent Court of International Justice there would be the League of Nations, the main pillars of which would be an assembly of delegates from all member states and a council in which only the Great Powers of the world were to regularly deliberate to maintain international stability. These two bodies were to be served by a permanent League Secretariat.

During the war, ideas for a League of Nations had flourished among thinkers and writers who drew on vocabularies of pacifism and liberalism in civil movements of the nineteenth century, sometimes described as the earliest 'internationalisms'.[1] However, the specific catalyst for the implementation of such a thing into the peace agreement came from America. US president Woodrow Wilson had called for a new global commitment to disavowing secret alliances, respecting the principle of national self-determination and establishing a 'concert for peace'. It was his vision to replace the agreement between the great European powers often referred to as the Concert of Europe which had been established a century earlier in 1815 but had long ceased to be effective as a guarantor of peace by 1914.[2] Wilson's vision collided with, and became reshaped by, a more concrete French wish to keep defeated Germany in check as well as both French and British ambitions of preserving European imperialism, a phenomenon epitomized in the enthusiasm of British South African Jan Smuts for the establishment of the League.[3]

The result materialized in 1919. Despite the League's composite nature, constrained as it was by political compromise, it demonstrated how during the interwar period radical political experimentation took place at the international level just like it did at the national. The war had escalated a corrosion of traditional sources of political legitimacy. Ideologues fought for the control of hearts and minds, and the eyes of the world were being opened to the violent potential of the political exploitation of national identities.

The League project soon found its enemies. Critics in the United States and Britain claimed that instead of a replacement, it represented a continuation of the logic that had spawned the Concert of Europe. Only, whereas the Concert had existed to contain defeated Napoleonic France, the new machinery, dominated by Britain and France, targeted Germany. To the French, conversely, the League appeared as a vague, liberal project. The French feared its machinery was not backed by the necessary force to guarantee their country's security *vis-à-vis* the threat of a future vengeful Germany.⁴ Yet the organization enjoyed substantial support from dedicated internationalists too, particularly in the United States, Great Britain and France, who sensed that here was a first step towards lasting peace among nations and a link between the man (and woman) in the street and the world's most powerful decision-makers. They hoped that it would eventually commit all nations to settle peacefully their disputes and thus preventing them from turning into new wars. The toolkit would include the provision of a transparent diplomacy and the principle of collective security and the aim to make the League a forum for the management of the vast transnational challenges facing the postwar world.

In the summer of 1919, while the newly appointed secretary general of the embryonic League was setting up its provisional Secretariat in London, observers in Western metropolises eagerly discussed the emergence of the organization. Raymond Fosdick, a young American lawyer, who had been named the League's first deputy secretary general, corresponded with his countryman, the journalist Walter Lippmann, who would later become a renowned thinker on media and the nature of public opinion in democracies. This was before President Wilson's failure to commit the United States to join the League, and it was generally expected that the United States would assume a leading role in the organization. Lippmann, who had been among Wilson's closest advisors, was a staunch critic of the final Versailles Treaty, in particular its punitive measures against the defeated Germany. He predicted that the League would become a *de facto* instrument of France and Britain. Fosdick acknowledged his countryman's criticism but was now respectfully asking Lippmann's advice: since it was settled that the League would materialize, 'how', he asked him, could it 'humanize the treaty' and become 'an instrument of lasting peace?'⁵ Lippmann responded:

> There is no mystical power whatever in this covenant. It consists of a group of governments, and the error which it seems to me affects certain liberals today is their enormous desire to believe that the covenant is greater than the great powers. It would be if there was any popular representation in it, but that has been rigorously excluded. I think if I were in your position, I should make publicity my whole aim.⁶

Lippmann's words echo today. They convey a fundamental doubt about the value of international institutions, which still haunts us and probably will continue to do so. At the moment of writing, the 2023 UN General Assembly is convening in New York City with only one out of five head of governments among the permanent members of the Security Council present.⁷ However, since 1945, whenever the

UN has been criticized (often in the context of helpless paralysis in the Security Council, brought about by the veto of a permanent member) a typical response from a believer in the system has been that despite their weaknesses, international institutions are valuable because they deliver a stable diplomatic framework which buys time, calms tempers and sheds light on things that would otherwise remain hidden. Lippmann's response to Fosdick encapsulated both attitudes. However, on top of his scepticism as to the political muscle of the League, he was open to the possibility that publicity could be a vital help to the organization. The organization stated in its Covenant – its constituting document – that 'open diplomacy' was of supreme importance in preventing the disaster of the war from happening again.[8]

The aim of this book, then, is to show how this vision of open diplomacy and the idea that the public was the League's most important ally came together in the League's information practices. It combines the disciplines of intellectual history, international history and the history of communications to examine the work of a group of officials within its Secretariat who were given the task of legitimizing the League to the public. Their challenge was complex, and they faced it at a time when not only traditional models of diplomacy but also of governance were being redefined by the emerging idea of the masses as a political force in society. In the words of Jan-Werner Müller mass democracy increasingly 'imposed the need for what we might call mass justification (or mass legitimation) – the need that is, to justify forms of rule and institutions'.[9]

The emergence of this vision of a more open diplomacy would coincide with – and come to be seen as a vitalizing force in – the novel experiment of an international bureaucracy. Therefore, it paradoxically laid the groundwork for public suspicion directed against international civil servants which has existed in different shapes and guises ever since. It has been surfacing in recent decades, when for example European nationalists incite suspicion against what political scientist Ivan Krastev has called the disloyal elites employed in intergovernmental institutions, or when US president Donald Trump at the 2019 UN General Assembly criticized 'global bureaucrats'.[10] It is thus worthwhile examining the public relations of the League as the first globally aimed international organization for peacekeeping. Could such an institution engage in propaganda and defend itself against defamatory agitation? How did one explain its workings to the public? And, seen from the office of an international official, who was this public exactly? The book confronts these questions by mapping the development of the public legitimization strategies of the League of Nations Information Section 1919–40 and sketches the transfer of these experiences into the United Nations 1940–46.

Arguably, to understand the species of internationalism that came to be produced and disseminated from Geneva is to observe how the organization's own information officials planned and executed its public legitimization effort – and, notably, what obstacles they encountered along the way and how they adapted to these. Before the turn of the millennium not many scholars engaged with the League's relation to the public. In 2007, Susan Pedersen summarized some main historiographical trends on the League.[11] She pointed out an emerging avenue of research on its 'complex relationship with various "mobilized publics".[12] Common in much of this research is that it has discussed the interactions of local and regional actors external to Geneva with the Secretariat, and rarely put the League headquarters themselves under the microscope. Of course, there are many good reasons for studying League activities outside Geneva. Despite recent warnings about writing the history of its internationalism exclusively from the Palais Wilson (or later from the Palais des Nations) an examination of the institutional strategizing made *by* the Secretariat *vis-à-vis* its 'international public' must focus on the halls of Geneva, because that is where this strategizing took place.[13] Despite the visible surge of interest in the interactions between the League and the 'private associations' surrounding it, no historian has made a thorough empirical study, across the interwar years, of the principal institutional unit *in* the Secretariat tasked with public relations, its Information Section.

The only significant recent examination of the Information Section has come from a group of media scholars, who evaluate the section as part of a site in which different kinds of agents came to together in a an 'epistemic project' of promoting the League. Erik Koenen, Arne Gellrich and Stefanie Averbeck-Lietz demonstrate how a 'journalistic' way of thinking came together with what would today be called a 'strategic communication' way of thinking, and how League officials needed to speak the language of open diplomacy but often came to enable the opposite. These are important findings that also play a role in this work. Although their work does not make historical change across the two interwar decades their ambition, even so their findings appear regularly in the historiographical dialogue of the present book.[14]

Thus, until recently, scholarship on this field of League activity has been pursued either by League officials themselves as part of the institution's commemoration of its effort during the war- and postwar period or the Information Section has been a side-show in another story.[15] In the only clear-cut historical analysis of the League's public relations practices until recently, Tomoko Akami, in an examination of the activities of the Information Section in Japan, asserted that the League pursued its public legitimization in a narrowly expert-oriented way, which failed to appeal to the public. Deeming that this failure laid the roots for contemporary populist revolts against international organizations and their sympathizers, she calls the League's work 'a lost opportunity for interwar liberal internationalists in adapting an alternative method to reach the emerging masses as serious political actors'.[16]

This book shows that these strategies were not static but were shaped continuously by the constraints laid on the section's work from above, which in turn stemmed from the climate of political resentment between the Great Powers at the time. Perceiving them as inherently expert-oriented misses the point that the League *attempted* to promote the new organization to people who were not knowledgeable about it already. Looking at the progress of the League's publicity policies throughout the interwar period one sees that the conceptualization by the organization of the public changed slowly from one which mainly considered it as consisting of liberal, well-educated sympathizers of the League to a broader one resembling more closely the 'whole' public with the birth of the United Nations.[17] The book assumes an organizationally focused approach because it seeks to place the Information Section in its bureaucratic setting showing how it pursued its activities not only in accordance with its own ideas of how to do a good job but also firmly steered by the secretary general as well as the political bodies of the League. This hitherto unexplored perspective shows how its conceptualization of its own role *vis-à-vis* public opinion was shaped by the administrative and political infrastructure it operated within.

Throughout the twentieth century, information officials in national governments or international administrations have grappled with whether to aim 'broadly' to engage a 'general public' or to focus on elites, powerful stakeholders or experts.[18] The question of target audiences related to another one of how to balance aggressive information campaigns, which risked being labelled 'propaganda', and more restrained, neutral types of communication.[19] Since several League officials had prior experience within war propaganda and government publicity strategy this temptation and principal discussion was not new to them.[20] It is important to understand that although the concept of propaganda was generally understood as an illegitimate practice during this period it was still acknowledged as a necessary practice if one wanted to efficiently engage with the public. Public opinion was ascribed a kind of mythical power by European diplomats at the time who felt that information needed to be used strategically.[21]

This book, therefore, combines an empiricist ambition of mapping the League's information work with consistent attention to how ideas have been expressed in the practices of international institutions. It collects the strands of the vast and promising area of research which reaches into diplomatic history as well as media history and the history of communications and provides a point of departure for further specialized studies. It engages the emerging historiography of the League's interactions with the public and of the role of news and information in the fight for peace, but it employs a different lens than existing research by concentrating on the Secretariat and its officials as agents of internationalism.[22] It takes inspiration from new literature on the public diplomacy of international organizations during and after the interwar period to move inside the international bureaucracy of the League and study it in its political context.

The League and its audience: Some conceptualizations

When the first League officials were planning the international Secretariat they were keenly aware that such a thing was a genuinely new idea. Thus, experience could not offer a blueprint for the kind of public information policy that was needed.[23] At the time, Western governments had begun to devote resources and personnel to propaganda or 'information' domestically and in foreign states, to influence opinion in general or to campaign for specific causes. However, with the establishment of an Information Section in the League Secretariat, such activities, hitherto pursued by states alone, had to be reinvented and adjusted to the purposes of an international organization. Understanding what challenges the League faced when going about this task requires us to discuss some concepts that officials were obliged to engage with in their work and which will therefore act as analytical lodestars in the book, namely *public opinion*, *internationalism* and *propaganda*. I shall show that each of these phenomena related to a 'tension' that came to be inherently present in the League's efforts to promote itself during its entire lifetime.

League officials were not convinced that the League could base its authority simply on its member states tolerating its existence and using its diplomatic channels. To them, it needed the support of the 'man on the street' to strengthen its moral claim.[24] To understand how they went about legitimizing the League one needs to reflect on the way in which a set of new ideas could be legitimized by an agency which could not explicitly advocate its own policy and thus had to refer to and 're-forge' commonly accepted tropes and arguments that were used in other contexts. Intellectual historian Quentin Skinner argues that historical evolution is steered by rhetorical legitimization of new ways of thinking or acting. Ideologists need to 'show that at least some of the terms used by their ideological opponents to describe what they admire can be applied to include and thus to legitimize their own seemingly questionable behavior'.[25] He argues that public speech is best understood as social action rather than simply communication. This approach to political communication is useful when analysing a body of text like that emerging from, what we shall see was a cautious, restrained information department. The Information Section stuck to a strict dogma of neutrality and rarely argued any cause openly, just as it rarely defined public opinion or spoke of the League as an agent. However, in effect it demonstrated how it approached these concepts through its actions. I therefore draw on Skinner's assumptions in this book, but I go further and invert it, so that I consider not only its rhetoric as social actions but also, conversely, its social actions as rhetoric. This enables us to look at the restrained utterings and actions of the League and its Information Section as subtle communication. Including or omitting certain pictures or certain phrases, re-forging arguments normally used in other contexts all contribute to an understanding of how the League legitimized itself as well as, more indirectly, what kind of relationship it imagined between itself and the public. Let us look closer at this 'triangle of tensions', relating to respectively public opinion, internationalism and propaganda.

The League and public opinion

'In no other respect', wrote a former official of the Information Section, 'did the creation of the League mark a more complete break with the habits of the past than in the new kind of relationship between a diplomatic body and public opinion that was established at Geneva.'[26]

The official, Egon Ranshofen-Wertheimer, was describing the way the Secretariat sought to realize a vision of an open diplomacy. This vision was based on the assertion that the world war of 1914–18 could not have occurred had 'secret diplomacy' not been customary in the international system of the early twentieth century. The new internationalism that Ranshofen-Wertheimer believed in considered secrecy in diplomacy dangerous and irrational in an age of rapidly shifting power balances, growing nationalism and an aware public.[27] In his well-known Fourteen Points Address, US president Woodrow Wilson called for a new world doctrine of 'Open covenants of peace, openly arrived at, openly agreed after which there shall be no private international understandings of any kind, but diplomacy shall proceed always frankly and in the public view'.[28]

After a heated domestic US debate, Wilson failed to convince Congress to ratify the Versailles Treaty and join the League of Nations. This was the beginning of the interwar era of what has been called American isolationism. Although, as recent scholarship highlights and this book will also discuss, the United States was far from absent in Geneva, its government remained outside the League of Nations throughout the organization's existence.[29] Yet the planners of the League went on to fuse Wilson's ideas with their own and implemented them into the Covenant of the League of Nations. Article 18 stated:

> Every treaty or international engagement entered into hereafter by any Member of the League shall be forthwith registered with the Secretariat and shall as soon as possible be published by it. No such treaty or international engagement shall be binding until so registered.[30]

To the League's founders, transparency was at the heart of the organization's *raison d'être*. But the publication of treaties and meeting minutes was not all that officials like Ranshofen-Wertheimer thought of when they spoke of a new kind of public relations. They foresaw that the Great Powers would not acquiesce to unlimited public scrutiny of diplomatic negotiations. Indeed, as we shall see, journalists were never admitted full access to meetings of the League Council. The Secretariat therefore did not consider its job completed by simply registering treaties. The League needed more from public opinion and worked to *inform* it of what took place in the new international forum. This task fell exclusively on the Information Section. The section oversaw the dissemination of information to the press and the public and operated based on a principle of *publicity* – an obligation to make sure the public had the information it needed to understand international diplomacy. Indirectly, there was also a goal to gain legitimacy for the League by increasing its standing among public opinion. This mission was not unproblematic. Indeed, historical research suggests that when the League managed to really get the public's attention this could backfire. For example, Haakon A. Ikonomou has shown how the buildup of expectations for League action among activists and interest groups in the period leading to the big Disarmament Conference in 1932 undermined the organization's attempts to secure a deal among the Great Powers.[31]

Yet, the League placed its stakes on public opinion. In 1919, during the ratification debate of the League Covenant in the British House of Commons, Lord Robert Cecil, a prominent Conservative politician and League proponent, stated:

> there is no attempt to rely on anything like a superstate; no attempt to rely upon force to carry out a [League] decision. . . . That is almost impractical as things stand now. What we rely upon is public opinion . . . and if we are wrong about it, then the whole thing is wrong.³²

Public opinion thus became a concept of key importance to the Secretariat, and some historical context on this key concept is useful to grasp the point(s) of departure for the work of the League and its Information Section.

By the start of the interwar period, public opinion had existed as a moral reference point since at least a century earlier, when it had been invoked against the conservative order upheld through the Concert of Europe. Following the post-Napoleonic restauration, the protected ideal of European 'free' states referred not to the freedom of populace but that of the sovereigns, but this notion became contested with the rise of the idea of 'a new power called opinion' in the words of the French writer and clergyman Abbé de Pradt.³³ References to this phenomenon increased during the period leading up to the First World War, in the Anglophone and Francophone world.³⁴

Looking back on the League at the end of what would be known as the interwar period, historian E. H. Carr blamed an uncritical faith in public opinion on the legacy of the philosopher Jeremy Bentham's utilitarianism. Carr argued that the utilitarian school of thought had given rise to a two-step liberal misunderstanding: First, that 'public opinion is bound in the long run to prevail' and, second, that 'public opinion is always right'.³⁵ He concluded that League proponents had uncritically operationalized these beliefs in a sphere that they did not belong in – that of international politics.³⁶

The popular understanding of public opinion was in flux during the whole interwar period. Since political polling did not become widespread until after the Second World War, differing ideas coexisted regarding what exactly was the meaning and potency of the concept. Walter Lippmann and others expressed scepticism as to the rationality of the public, invoked by prewar intellectuals such as Lawrence Lowell who in turn had leaned on a sometimes-implicit premise, that the public should not be expected to rule unchecked but would have to be carefully guided by elites and experts.³⁷ It was thus a widespread sentiment that public opinion consisted of the opinions of exclusive, qualified strata of society. However, going into the 1930s others would begin to argue a more radical understanding. As this book will show, a broadening, or democratization of the concept started to emerge among officials and sympathizers affiliated to the League, during the Second World War, when the legacy of the information policies of the old organization were drawn on in the planning of the UN. The League's understanding of its audience – the public – moved decisively from sometimes describing the 'right people' who were educated and already committed to League internationalism via transnational civil society, to a broader mass-focused understanding.

The League and internationalism

The League of Nations is generally understood to have been an internationalist project or, in the words of Sandrine Kott, a 'site of internationalization', where internationalism 'happened' as much as was expressed or performed.[38] How should we understand the slippery concept of the international and the more ideologically loaded 'internationalism'? Patricia Clavin notes that the 'etymology of "internationalism" lies in the aspiration for world peace, in the notion of world citizenship inscribed in institutions like the League of Nations which for some of its advocates lay in aspirations for democratic globalization through the creation of world government'. However, Clavin notes elsewhere, interwar internationalism was not cosmopolitan in a twenty-first-century understanding of 'anti-national', but inextricably linked to the idea of the nation state, without which it would have little meaning, a point theorized further by Glenda Sluga, and by Sluga and Clavin in their introduction to *Internationalisms – a Twentieth Century History*.[39]

While socialist organizations of the late nineteenth and early twentieth centuries have been described as 'internationalist' the ideological tenets of the League were commonly associated with the vision of President Wilson.[40] This is what we today call 'liberal internationalism', a set of ideas which embraced the right of nations to national self-determination and emphasized the duty of independent states to commit to a system of so-called collective security. Collective security was the principle in international relations that an aggression against one member of an alliance was to be considered the concern of all its members.[41] As Carsten Holbraad has shown there were (and are) several, if not many, internationalisms, mirroring the domestic political left and right.[42] A key assumption and point of departure of this book is that the League Secretariat initially attracted people who were devoted to a liberal internationalist vision of world peace brought about through a community of nations working together to ensure free trade and travel and cooperating to confront a wide range of transnational issues. Whenever I mention internationalism in this book, it can be assumed, unless something else is specified, to describe such a liberal internationalism. However, as is well-known, the liberal species was not the only internationalism – indeed the most well-known internationalism is probably the socialist version. In addition, in League historiography the last phase of its existence, under the secretary general Joseph Avenol, has been described as shaped by other 'darker' versions of internationalism.[43] As in the case of public opinion, the question of exactly how we should understand internationalism is part of our investigation into the work of the League and its Information Section. As will be seen from the attention paid by the book to the rhetorical strategies of the League, shifting political tides inside and outside the Secretariat constantly impacted the internationalism it expressed. Internationalism was practised as well as articulated (to take inspiration from Daniel Laqua's distinction between internationalism as 'narrative', 'practice' or organization'), and the book seeks to unpack how these practices and articulations happened.[44] The values that the Information Section attributed to the League and the extent to which it considered the organization something 'more' than the sum of its parts shaped the way the section legitimized the League. Just like the League's understanding of public opinion reflected its understanding of its audience, its understanding of the international connected to the question of itself: who or what was the League?

The League and propaganda

League information officials were obliged to engage with the, at the time, compromised word 'propaganda', which, like 'public opinion' and 'internationalism', is not easily defined. Historian Philip M. Taylor used the NATO definition (1999) which defined it as 'any information, ideas, doctrines or special appeals disseminated to influence the opinion, emotions, attitudes or behavior of any specified group in order to benefit the sponsor, either directly or indirectly'.[45] Nowadays, we tend to suppose that the word became disgraced after the Second World War because it became associated with Nazi Germany's ministry of propaganda under Joseph Goebbels. However, scholarship suggests that the word already became increasingly labelled as an illegitimate activity in peacetime during the interwar period and might even have been so since the nineteenth century.[46] What we should take away from this is not that propaganda was despised by all public officials during the period. Rather, we shall see that League officials hesitated to use the word in public to describe their work, but that they still did use it internally on a regular basis. This reflected not only the struggle of an international organization to grasp its own mandate but also a slow, gradual return to peace conditions, propaganda having been taken for granted between 1914 and 1918 as a necessary weapon of war. Should the League, a peacekeeping organization but one that had grown out of a world war, completely refrain from 'getting its hands dirty'? A conviction was developing that public information would become increasingly important as mass society expanded, and when officials of the Secretariat used the word 'propaganda', they used it almost synonymously with 'information' often alluding to the overall activity of informing the public through a pamphlet, a news communiqué or later through radio or cinema. When in this book the author uses the word 'propaganda' it echoes the words of the officials themselves and does not imply a value judgement of their activities. As with 'public opinion' and 'internationalism', the conceptualization of propaganda is part of the book's object of study. It relates to the question of how the League could 'speak' – how and through what channels it could address its audience.

Locating 'information' in League archival records

Despite a magnificent recent digitization project, a challenge awaits historians of the Information Section in the League of Nations Archives in Geneva: there is no substantial collection of sources there that belonged exclusively to the Information Section. Instead, one relies on correspondence and working memos from the archive's Registry that passed through the section and referred to its work.[47] The work behind the book is therefore based partly on *discerning strategy from practice*.

More specifically, the book combines two investigations that complement each other.

On the one hand, it explores the practices of the Information Section and the developments these underwent by studying its organizational setup, priorities, financial framework and the development of its functions and terms of reference. Special attention is given to three senior officials, Pierre Comert, the director of the Information Section 1919–32, Arthur Sweetser, his second-in-command 1919–32 and acting director during 1933, and Adrianus Pelt, director during 1934–40.[48]

On the other hand, it identifies and discusses the rhetorical strategies and messages the League sought to convey to its audiences in its news material and the publications it produced.

Every historian knows that periodization affects the way in which we go about interpreting events. This is bound to present a challenge when studying the

League of Nations. For example, the year 1933 saw a series of radical changes in world politics, and these reverberated inside the Secretariat and the Information Section. Japan and Germany resigned from the League. National disagreements over the purpose of an international civil service had consequences for the Secretariat. The Frenchman Joseph Avenol became secretary general. Inside the Information Section, a change of leadership directly sparked by high politics took place, and its working conditions and terms of reference changed. These developments justify perceiving the two periods as worth discussing each in their own right. Still, dividing the interwar period into a 'before and after' the politically highly dramatic year of 1933 obviously involves the risk of exacerbating a simplistic impression of a set of binary opposites (optimism/despair) between these two periods. Altogether, the book covers a period of a quarter of a century. This means there are gaps as well as details and actors that do not get the attention they deserve, a fact which is hopefully compensated for by my attention to general trends and shifts over a longer time span.

Another limitation that should be addressed is that this book does not study in depth the actual impact of the League's information strategies on its target groups. The book is an 'inside out'-study of the Secretariat, and the effect of the League's information policies, directed as they were towards the press and publics of more than thirty different countries each with different political situations, cultures and relations to the League, cannot be the object of study in a book of this scope. Even though, as Linda Risso has observed in her survey of the NATO information policies, impact is notoriously difficult to measure and even though the League existed (mostly) before the broad introduction of opinion polls, an attempt could be made to examine the reception of its messages throughout the world.[49] However, such an endeavour would become a project of its own which would overtake the story of what was planned in the halls of Geneva. Moreover, it is a finding in its own right that League officials largely envisioned their audience as consisting of people who were already devoted to its cause through membership of pro-League civil society groups and the like. In the following chapters the narrative therefore regularly goes into dialogue with the question of the Secretariat officials' relationship with these groups which formed an important part of its *raison d'être* and through which much of the actual as well as perceived impact of the League's strategies was felt. This included negative impact, such as the buildup of unrealistic expectations for the League as exemplified by Ikonomou.[50]

The book is organized into two parts, each consisting of three chapters.

Chapter 1 presents the main actors, their coming together and planning the organization of the League's Information Section between 1919 and

1933. It sketches the setup of the Secretariat, the role played in it by national representation and to the idealism of its officials, as factors that shaped the construction process of a section such as this. It shows that the section became a well-funded and integrated part of the Secretariat's work led by officials of a genuine internationalist persuasion. At the same time, they shared a vision of embedding the section in the distinct national publics of the member states of the League through a broad, multinational staff of which each official would connect to his or her own public. They came to affirm the importance of the nation as a prime source of legitimacy in the League and attempted to reproduce a proportional representation of the League's hierarchy of Great Powers.

Chapter 2 turns to the section's activities during that same period. It outlines the section's trajectory from its cautious beginnings and the turf battles to define its role and onto the late 1920s when it enjoyed a very strong position in the Secretariat. It shows how at this point it could begin to take more initiative in creating a voice for the League in international press cooperation and inventing new ways to spread the League's message in national contexts. Its officials strived to secure a 'collaboration' between the League and public opinion by means of liaising with an 'elite' of influential people in their home countries. Some even pursued semi-diplomatic liaison towards national governmental elites in competition with the diplomatic service of the Secretariat. Arguably, this strategy rested on an assumption that the best way of legitimizing the League was to target educated circles because a 'taboo of propaganda' in the Secretariat made the secretary general prefer cautious, informal legitimization strategies.

Chapter 3 delves into the news and publications released by the section during that period and the rhetorical strategies to legitimize the League to the public these reflected. It argues that the section operated on a 'base line' of neutrality, of sticking to the facts and even being deliberately boring in order to imitate the dull workings of state power. This was always the most important underlying public legitimization strategy that could be seen in the material released from Geneva. However, other strategies ran as undercurrents below this implicit argument during 1919–32, as do a subtle shift in how one may think about the League's relation to public opinion. Initially, the section deemed it necessary to occasionally speak in moral language to bolster the League's authority. However, as its presence on the international stage became more consolidated it settled for a more dignified and neutral style, letting prominent political leaders speak its cause on its behalf.

Chapter 4 gives an account of how the Information Section and with it the League's information policy came to be rethought after 1933, when political disagreements between member states and the global economic crisis combined to cause the League Assembly to question the section's hitherto prominent position and generous allowance. It shows that the Information Section was dramatically reduced in size and had its terms of reference changed. The Commission was empowered by a changed political atmosphere in the League's Council and Assembly due to the rebellion of Germany and Italy against the dominance of Britain and France. The section resisted the implications of its reorganization. However, it ceased to regard itself as a competitor to the Political Section in terms of traditional diplomacy, and it disassociated itself somewhat from its private 'collaborators' in civil society. Since the weakening of the section paralleled the breakthrough of new communication technologies, its new director, Adrianus Pelt (from 1934), became increasingly convinced that the future of information policy must lie in genuine mass communication rather than 'collaboration' with national elites.

Chapter 5 revisits the League's public message of that final period of the League's peacetime existence and thus traces how these changed after the upheavals in international politics and in the League's information policy. It demonstrates that the League tried to redraw rhetorically the battlefield by avoiding topics deemed political and by 'retreating' to the League's aesthetics; its buildings, its history and the leaders associated with it, and thereby indirectly mimicked a state apparatus in an attempt to preserve the feeling of stability associated with a national government.

Chapter 6 traces the footsteps of the leading officials of the section during the Second World War and immediately after it as they took part in evaluating the League experience and making suggestions for future international cooperation in the exile metropolises of London and Washington DC. It argues that the legacy of the League's public legitimization strategies consisted first and foremost in a realization that the limited, cautious and indirect ways in which the Information Section had disseminated League information made for an insufficient strategy. An information department in an intergovernmental organization would always run the risk of being subdued by sceptical member states no matter how cautiously it went about its work, and the section's doctrine of primarily addressing elite audiences was outdated. A future organization would have to aim broader and work more unashamedly to promote its internationalist project. These were the lessons, highly shaped by the interwar climate of international tension, unaddressed war grievances and appeasement, which survived the twenty years of experimental public relations that began in London in 1919 and ended in Geneva in 1940.

Part I

1

Centre of world information
Creating an information section, 1919–21

'As the League will be the center of world government', wrote a young American, Arthur Sweetser, in May 1919, 'so it must be the center of world political information.'[1] Sweetser was reflecting on how the League should engage with what he perceived as the crucial force of public opinion. A former war correspondent, he was increasingly convinced that the League's Information Section, which he had been given a key position in, needed to be instrumental in informing and mobilizing the public to the support of the new organization.

In this chapter, a closer look is taken at the earliest (and therefore important) ideas and principles laid down in the ambitious new Secretariat for how to practice League information policy. The chapter discusses the organizational setup of the Information Section, its status and function in the League Secretariat and the vision behind it, focusing on its first director Pierre Comert and his second-in-command Arthur Sweetser. It shows how the early decisions made by Comert and his section, under scrutiny by the secretary general, laid the foundation for its activities and the ideas underlying its functions for the next dozen years. Comert and Sweetser shared internationalist convictions and together built a large section based on the idea that the League's relation to public opinion was key in securing its democratic legitimacy. Its characteristic multinational composition played a double role, as it not only reflected demands for representation by member states but also, in the eyes of the section, fused it closer together with public opinion. Comert, and with him his strong belief in the primacy of the traditional political press and his light favouring of a French outlook, assumed a dominant role in the early Information Section, yet he allowed Sweetser, with his strong bonds to US stakeholders, to be his second-in-command. Comert's ability to align rhetorically the interests of 'public opinion' with those of French official opinion contributed to a fusing of the two functions of nationality in the section; the representation of state interests and the rhetorical appeal to public opinion. The result was an ambiguity about the nature of the public reflected in the ways section officials spoke of their mission. They regularly dismissed the use of 'propaganda' and yet often discussed in internal correspondence how to do the best 'propaganda'. This signalled an early indication that two underlying ideas of who the public was coexisted in the section, one focusing on masses and the 'man on the street' and another (which would come to dominate as the years went by) focusing on cultural and political elites. Thus, already the section's triangle of tensions regarding its audience, the League's international nature and the means by which it could be advocated was at stake from day one.

Founding an Information Section

On 28 April 1919, the Commission on the League of Nations, which consisted of representatives of the Great Powers attending the Paris Peace Conference – the United States, Great Britain, France, Italy and Japan – appointed Eric Drummond secretary general. The appointment took place about four months into the conference, but since the League was part of the Treaty of Versailles the institution would not formally come into existence until 10 January 1920, when the treaty had been ratified. In the meantime, Drummond, a Scot and former high official in the British Foreign Office, spent those first nine months organizing the Secretariat and appointing its senior staff. In this preparatory work, Drummond worked together with an Organizing Committee of representatives of the Great Powers. However, the Committee left the first secretary general considerable freedom in his mission. In fact, he asserted later that with the exceptions of the appointment of his deputy secretaries general and undersecretaries general he was given free hands in picking his staff.[2] Drummond drafted his first plan between the close of the Peace Conference and his official appointment in April. He famously decided that the Secretariat's staff should be 'truly international', representing the League rather than their respective national governments. He also formulated a plan to organize it into 'sections', similar to ministerial departments.

Among these sections one group would work as secretarial units to the League's various specialized organizations (e.g. the Health Organization and the Economic and Financial Organization), while a second group served the secretary general – and thus the League's Permanent Secretariat itself. Drummond's scheme included an Information Section, which would belong to the second group, although it would act as the press service not only of the Secretariat but also of the League's Council and Assembly and as an information department in a broader sense, tasked with disseminating trustworthy information about the new organization. The first terms of reference for this section said that it would be charged with 'the Publicity work of the League of Nations'.[3] Like most sections it would be headed by a director, who acted under the authority of the secretary general. During this planning phase there was some uncertainty about what would be an appropriate name for such a section. Raymond Fosdick, the deputy secretary general (soon to resign, when the United States withdrew from the League) suggested changing the name from the initially proposed 'Publicity Section' to the 'Public Information Section' which soon after became simply the 'Information Section'. Fosdick felt that 'publicity' bore connotations of propaganda, and that it had been 'used so dishonestly during the war that the very name will arouse suspicion'.[4]

By the time of the change of name, which signalled a political sensitivity about the section, built in from the very start, the section had been operational for one week, since 7 July 1919, when Drummond appointed the Frenchman Pierre Comert as its director.[5]

Directors constitute a good lens when studying the workings of the Secretariat, because they were present at most levels of the work of the Secretariat. They operated within and outside their departmental turfs, associating with members of national elites, foreign correspondents as well as with the secretary general and diplomats from all over the world – Geneva elites. In a way, the directors were politically observant bureaucrats (or 'bureaucrats with visions' with Jan-Werner Müller).

Pierre Comert was the main architect of the Information Section, and his impact would be felt long after his resignation (more on that later). He was born in 1880 in Montpellier in southern France and had served as correspondent for *Temps* in Vienna and Berlin, and as press officer to the French diplomatic mission in London during the war.[6] These credentials, and his presence in the French delegation in Paris during the Peace Conference, made him an obvious candidate to a high post in the League Secretariat.[7] His compatriot Jean Monnet, Fosdick's colleague as deputy secretary general, seemingly facilitated his appointment.[8]

Arthur Sweetser was born in Boston, Massachusetts, and, like Comert, came from a career in journalism. He had spent 1915 as an independent war correspondent, crisscrossing the European Western front on a bicycle (!) and was taken prisoner twice on suspicion of espionage, first by German then French forces. He later published a journalistic memoir-book about his observations at the front.⁹ He returned to serve as State Department correspondent for the Associated Press. Drawn back to European affairs, he boarded a ship to Europe to attend the Paris Peace Conference where he served as press attaché at the American delegation.¹⁰ Expecting US membership of the League to be certain, State Department accepted Sweetser's appointment to the Information Section 7 September 1919.¹¹ Private letters indicate that the two men met each other for the first time and discussed the section they were to build on a summer's evening a few days after the signing of the Versailles Treaty, at 'l'Ane Rouge', a café on the edge of the city's legendary Montmartre district.¹²

Soon after this, Comert had the first working plan for the section approved by Drummond, and by December he had its first staff list ready. This list, which was to be formally approved by the Council at its first convening in 1920, foreboded a section staffed with people who shared an important characteristic with Comert and Sweetser: they were foreign affairs journalists with some diplomatic experience.¹³

Organization of the section

Comert organized his section into what he called a press office, a liaison office, a publications office and an office for the review of the press. Many of his officials would rotate and share several of these functions.¹⁴ He was keen to set up a system of external branch offices in places deemed important as permanent points of contact with Geneva. Accordingly, the section set up offices staffed with 'correspondents' in the capitals of the member states of the Council, namely London, Paris, Rome, Tokyo (later, after Germany's entrance in 1926, Berlin too, and in the early 1930s, offices were added in Delhi and in Nanking).¹⁵ Most branch offices operated as extensions of the Information Section. However, the two largest ones, in London and Paris, initially worked as field offices of the entire Secretariat, staffed with high-ranking officials and capable of hosting Committee meetings and screening applicants for positions in Geneva.¹⁶

In addition to the sparsely staffed branch offices, the section employed more loosely affiliated correspondents who assisted with local press relations and distribution of information material in countries like Hungary, the Netherlands, China, Haiti, the Dominican Republic, and a string of countries in Mesoamerica and South America.¹⁷

Comert appointed about three-quarters of the 200 officials who would come to work in the section during the League's existence. Of the many typists, translators, messengers, correspondents and so on who worked in any given section of the Secretariat, a principal group of officials have our main interest, namely the so-called members of section. They reported to the director, Comert, who in turn reported to the secretary general.[18]

Comert hired predominantly foreign correspondents or foreign affairs journalists.[19] He deemed these well suited for the job, because he needed people who were capable of writing and editing League press material in several languages, and also since he expected them to travel regularly 'for the purpose of promoting relations with the Press [sic] and public opinion' and to remain in contact with 'their former *milieu*'.[20] The preference given by him and others in the Secretariat to journalists is worth reflecting on for a moment. In the absence of a consolidated field of public communication in many countries, journalist seem like an obvious choice for the League, but it is worth noting that the change from the emerging professional ethos of journalism into a job as a promoter of the League of Nations was not an obvious one from the journalists' perspective. First, the prestige and career advantages were not obvious. In 1921, officials of the section noted as a potential structural problem of the section's in attracting talent was that a journalist might face difficulties securing a job back home after leaving the Secretariat.[21] The League was a new and unknown phenomenon which did not come with the prestige and promise of useful international experience such administrations may be said to entail today. Second, the professional self-image of journalists at the time did not fit seamlessly with working in the Information Section. From the beginning, it was obvious that speaking on behalf of the League would be a cautious, restrained voice with little or no space for a personal voice, flavour or even analysis. Talbot Imlay has noted how US foreign affairs journalists who began their careers during the 1920s did so during a 'Golden Age' of foreign correspondence and constructed (between themselves and in their writings) an image of the travelling reporter as an audacious figure with a mission to see things clearly and use analysis to make the public understand political issues at stake.[22] At the same time, French journalists were protesting about a professionalization gone 'too far', with emerging demands for objectivity ruining the freedom of journalists as analysts and opinion-makers.[23] Taking on work in the League could be an awkward fit for a foreign affairs journalist who wanted to save the world.

However, while this dynamic risked impacting negatively the quality of staff in the Information Section it meant, at the same time, that the officials that were taken on were often devoted to the League's internationalism rather than motivated by money or prestige, even if they would be disappointed later when their ideals turned out to be unrealistic.[24] Media scholars have recently argued that League information policy evolved as an 'epistemic project' in which both Information Section staff and the most devoted members of the Geneva press corps were stakeholders – committed to a common Wilsonian mission of creating the new kind of diplomacy. These fuzzy boundaries between journalism and a diplomacy, argue Gellrich, Koenen and Averbeck-Lietz, mirrored the historical co-development of professional journalism and the modern public relations branch.[25] What is clear in these early years is that Comert's staffing of his section with journalists (and the secretary general's accept of this) clearly demonstrated a conviction that the press had the potential to be League allies and collaborators and neither enemies nor a passive audience.

The centrality of the Information Section

The apparent paradox of a section staffed with former journalists who were only gradually adjusting to a world of professionalized values of objectivity also relates to another 'hidden function' of the Information Section and of Pierre Comert, namely that of talent-spotter and selector of a cohort of Secretariat veteran officials who could receive their training in the section to acquire a general knowledge of the League and then move on to specialized work. As Torsten Kahlert has shown, a remarkable number of long-serving and high-ranking officials, including Salvador de Madariaga, Egon Ranshofen-Wertheimer and Benjamin Gerig, started their career in the Information Section. That many such officials were 'only' journalists did not prevent them from moving from the 'generalist' Information Section and onto specialized sections, in particular since foreign affairs journalists during the first half of the twentieth century often had academic backgrounds anyway.[26]

During the 1920 the League's commitment to publicity was reflected in the section's size. In terms of the number of personnel it was consistently the largest section of the Secretariat, and it would remain the largest or second largest throughout the League's lifetime[27] (see Figure 1).

A salary budget of the section throughout the 1920s compared to the complete salary budget of the Secretariat shows that the Information Section was consistently given a high priority, culminating in 1932 (Pierre Comert's last year in office) when it took up almost a fifth of Secretariat salary budget (the Secretariat included more than ten sections).

The sections of the Secretariat existed 'below' the level of what the League accounted for in its annual budgets or the confidential audits the Secretariat produced after each year. The funds controlled by the section were therefore

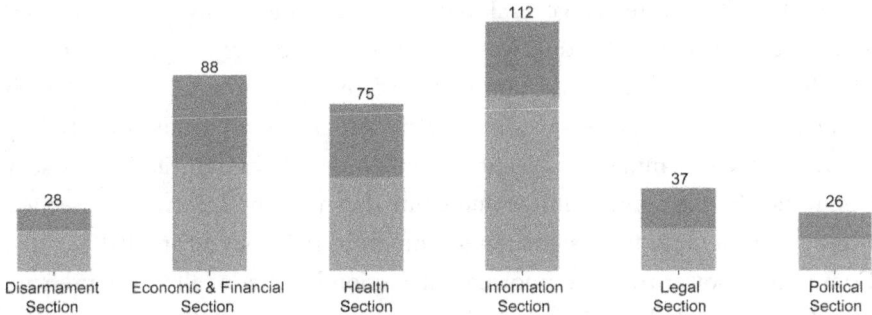

Figure 1 Total number of staff appointments of the six largest sections of the Secretariat, 1919–25.

Figure generated using digital research tool: Ikonomou, Yuan Chen, Obaida Hanteer, Jonas Tilsted 'Visualizing the League of Nations Secretariat – a Digital Research Tool' (Copenhagen: University of Copenhagen, 2023), https://visualeague-researchtool.com/ (25 May 2023).

Table 1 Salary Budget of the Section throughout the 1920s Compared to the Complete Salary Budget of the Secretariat

Year	Salaries budget, Secretariat	Salaries, Information Section	Share, Information Section (%)
1921	3,255.000*	450,000*	13.8
1922	3.906,300*	606,300*	15.5
1923	4,309,635**	657,083**	15.2
1924	4,074,674**	652,726**	16
1925	4,194,607**	671,421**	16
1926	4,410,034**	740,530**	16.8
1927	4,896,061**	845,703**	17.3
1928	5,120,712**	913,522**	17.8
1929	5,385,616**	982,670**	18.2
1930	5,480,637**	1,016,883**	1.8,6
1931	5,924,215**	1,108,506**	18.7
1932	6,006,269**	1,162,923**	19.3
1933	5,718,505**	942,970**	16.5

For the years 1921, 1922 and 1929–33: 'General Budget of the League of Nations', in *Official Journal of the League of Nations* 1, no. 7, 453; 2, no. 9, 1034; 9, 1789; 10, no. 10, 1326; 11, no. 10, 1174; 12, no. 10, 1909; 13, 1602. For the years 1923–8: Budgets in LONA: C.713.M.425.1922.X; C.668.M.268.1923.X; C.618.M.217.1924.X; C.619.M.201.1925.X; C.581.M.220.1926.X. All numbers drawn from Schedule B: Salaries, Wages and Allowances of the Secretariat.

* represents gold francs; ** represents Swiss francs

primarily decided by the secretary general, who, together with the Secretariat's Treasury, distributed the funds given to the Secretariat as a whole.[28] Another powerful actor in budget-questions was the Supervisory Committee, a standing committee of the League's Assembly, which scrutinized the annual spending proposals of the secretary general and gave recommendations for changes.²⁹ Thus, the Information Section was subjected to two levels of control on its spending: the preemptive assertion by the secretary general as to what he felt could be spared for the section, and the more politically flavoured control by the Assembly (meaning the League's member states) through its Supervisory Committee.³⁰ This control unit would come down on the Information Section with severe cuts after the resignation of Comert in 1932, but during 1919–33 the Committee's power over the Information Section lay first of all in the pressure its existence exerted on Drummond in determining its allotment. Too many resources given to the Information Section risked stirring accusations by the member states that the League was spending its money on 'propaganda'.

Still, when comparing with the equivalent salary budgets from the second period (see Chapter 4) the 1920s stand out as a 'golden age' of the section. This reflected that public legitimization was given a high priority in the Secretariat, which in turn reflected an acceptance by League member states, during this early period, of the importance of these activities, and arguably, a successful shielding of them by the secretary general against their negative attention. The fact that the section grew steadily until 1932 tells us that League officials expected information to be expensive, because it involved building a large multinational staff to reflect international public opinion. Comert's section was given the muscle to populate the Secretariat with journalists and articulate a forceful vision for how information could legitimize the League. What did this mean in practice?

The politics of nationality in the Information Section

As we shall see, Pierre Comert did not always have complete freedom to decide whom to appoint to his staff. In fact, in the words of a later observer, he was obliged to 'maintain a quota system for various nations' something which reflected both an inherent ambition of diversity and the power-political realities in the League.³¹ Accordingly, he set out to gradually staff the section with a large number of different nationalities. There is little doubt that this resonated with his own ideas of how the section should connect with the public. As his officials would phrase it in 1928, 'Publicity in the League sense is international'.³² Comert asserted that he needed as broad a representation as possible in his section drawing on his internationalist persuasion that the League needed a powerful connection to public opinion, and at times he battled the secretary general, who was more cautious faced with a rapidly growing budget, on the necessity of individual appointments. At the same time, the Frenchman used his position to represent his government's views in the Secretariat, fusing them in his rhetoric with the demands of 'public opinion'. This illustrates the important point that national and international identities were not always perceived as mutually exclusive in the interwar period. In 1919 the section included nationals of only four countries – Britain, France, Switzerland and the United States – but this would soon change.[33] As early as 1920 officials came from more than ten different countries. In 1925, this number increased to twelve, and in 1932 the section employed twenty-six different nationalities (counting only people of the so-called First Division, the highest-ranking officials)[34] (Figure 2).

The importance of nationality in the Secretariat was by no means confined to the Information Section. As Gram-Skjoldager and Ikonomou have shown, the secretary general took care to maintain a hierarchy in the officially international Secretariat, particularly with respect to the first Council's Great Powers, Britain, France Italy and Japan. These countries were all strongly represented among the high officials. However, Drummond had to also make sure smaller member states were not ignored to an extent that it undermined the legitimacy of the League – its claim to be a progressive forum for the voices of all countries, great and small. This balancing act meant in practice that appointments in the Secretariat above a certain level were always politicized. Drummond's two 'lieutenants', his deputy secretaries general, for instance, whose function in the Secretariat was 'largely ambassadorial', routinely put pressure on Drummond to hire people from their countries. At other times, Drummond would use the appointment of certain people as a diplomatic instrument to gain the confidence of their

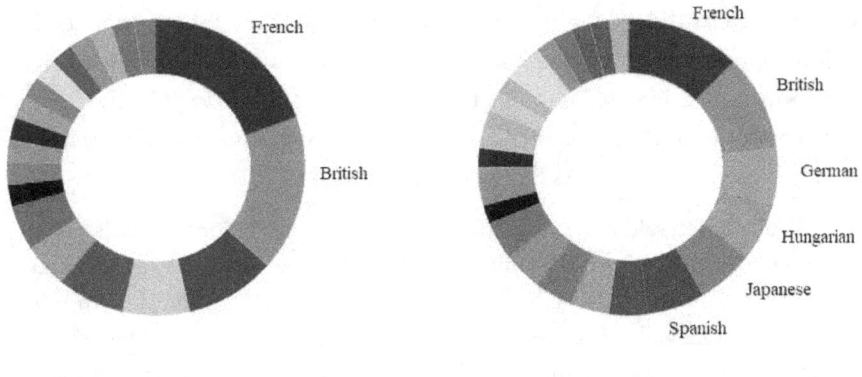

Figure 2 Citizenship of Information Section officials 1919–23 and 1928–32. Ikonomou, Chen, Hanteer, Tilsted 'Visualizing the League of Nations Secretariat' (25 May 2023).

Figure 3 Palais Wilson in the 1920s.
United Nations Archives, Geneva.

home countries.[35] In general, Drummond fought to preserve the right of section directors to decide on their own staff, but he would monitor the overall national composition in the Secretariat and retain the right to secure its balance.[36] For example, Drummond responded to Comert's 1919 staff list by requesting him to also hire 'a Spaniard as soon as possible'.[37]

However, when Comert built a very large and multinational Information Section, he also did so for reasons unique to the vision behind that section. Multinationalism was an integral part of the section's *raison d'être*, because of the connection it signalled not only to governments but also to publics. National representation was thus a key instrument in the construction of an *international* public opinion (Figure 3). As the section reported in 1921:

> It has often been said that the existence of the League of Nations depends solely upon the support of public opinion in the various countries. The Information Section is alone responsible, in the Secretariat, for keeping in touch with this public opinion; and the task is one of exceptional difficulty. It is for this reason that the Information Section includes a larger number of members than any other section.[38]

The first plans for the leadership of the section illustrated several things both universal to the ways in which Secretariat officials thought of nationality and things peculiar to the Information Section. They also tell us about the collision between ideas and practice among the progressive-minded officials who planned League information policy.

As hinted by Sweetser and Comert's planning-dinner in Paris, several people were involved in setting up the section, on a relatively equal footing. Drummond and his Organizing Committee had asked three men to submit draft proposals on how to organize an Information Section, Comert himself, Sweetser and a Brit named George H. Mair. Comert was given the position as its director, probably in part as a strategic friendly gesture to the French.[39] George H. Mair was a former official in the British Foreign Office, who had played a leading role in the British war propaganda effort 1914–18.[40] Mair's appointment in turn gave the third man, Sweetser, a strategic importance: Comert wanted Sweetser in the Secretariat to 'balance' the information policy of the section by keeping the British from exerting too much influence over what at the time was expected to be an instrumental part of the Secretariat. Years later, when these initial appointments were reevaluated during an internal conflict about increments, Comert assured Drummond that he had promised Mair 'a position as close to and equal to mine as possible [...] at the same time as I promised to benefit our American colleague'.[41]

Comert did so in late 1919 by assigning both Sweetser and Mair the title assistant director.[42] However, in 1929, after Germany's admission to the League, Sweetser discovered (to his fury and embarrassment) that the title did not formally exist. He made this discovery when, wanting to secure equal representation to the new German officials, the Secretariat asked him to stop using the title. Comert's granting of the title to his two colleagues rested on a discreet understanding with Drummond allowing them to consider themselves his equals, a reflection yet again of the de facto balancing necessary all the time in the Secretariat.[43] Nationality, one sees again, was always of great importance despite the formal international nature of the Secretariat. Both men's salaries did also reflect an elevated rank compared to other members of the section, so Sweetser was in the right in 1929 to point out that the title reflected more than just words.[44]

Despite these awkward developments, it is clear Arthur Sweetser's position in the Secretariat was predetermined to become special and highly prestigious, due to a combination of his merits and his nationality. During the fall of 1919 there was growing uncertainty about whether the United States could be part of the League due to the opposition of the US Congress, and when the Senate voted against ratifying the Versailles Treaty in November, the newly appointed American officials began handing in their resignations. For Sweetser, however, things would turn out differently. An unsent letter of his from the fall of 1919 reveals the earliest traces of this fact. In the letter, Sweetser recounted (flattered but exasperated) how he had been preparing to finally go home to the United States to oversee press relations at the International Labor Conference in Washington and then potentially leave the League, when things took an unexpected turn:

> It seems Comert became highly suspicious of what the British might try to do if there were no Americans in London [...] he went to Drummond and told him he did not think I would be particularly useful in Washington [...]. Drummond agreed that I had best stay. Then he went to Fosdick and told him he was [afraid] that if we left no one in London the British would run away with the League. Fosdick agreed that I best stay [...] so then Comert came to me, and I of course agreed with him, since I had originally felt the same way. There seemed no choice.[45]

Crudely put, Sweetser was used as a balancer and a buffer between the French and the British, but it was clear he would (paradoxically) become more important if the United States in fact opted out of the League. One of the reasons for this, which the men in Geneva may not yet have been realizing at the time, was that Sweetser had more of a free hand because no government was formally looking over his shoulder. Still, that did not mean he did not represent a link to that same government.

As we can see, information policy was riddled with power-political considerations. To build the best possible foundation on which to steer safely through these, Comert envisioned a section directed by a sort of French-British-American triumvirate which as far as possible would forge a 'balanced connection' to public opinion among the Great Powers. His vision did not materialize. The failure was partly due to chance – George Mair left the Secretariat due to illness in 1923 – and partly due to the unexpected withdrawal from the League project by the Americans which left Sweetser in a markedly new situation.[46] When Sweetser discovered that he had worn borrowed plumes for a decade he was initially humiliated but found other reasons to stay in the League whose cause he was passionately committed to – in particular to bring his own misled country into closer collaboration.[47] Later, from 1933, his honour would be restored when he became acting director for a year and was later promoted to a special kind of director affiliated to the Secretariat leadership.[48]

Between 1919 and 1930 the section gradually expanded its national composition to be able to liaise with the press and the public in still more member states, but Comert maintained a strong group of French members of section.

The section that Comert and Sweetser built together (they would remain on good terms despite their disagreement regarding Sweetser's false title) became a section which always fought to keep a strong and broad mandate – and which considered its obligation as going beyond press relations and information work in a superficial sense. There were instances when Comert challenged the secretary general to secure appointments he found important to keep the section connected to a given member state in a deeper sense than just its press. For example, on 27 December 1922 the Secretariat's Staff Committee discussed Comert's latest proposals for new staff to the section. Comert insisted that one Mr Popovich from Serbia was suited for the job, because he had been recommended by the Serbian government, he had good relations to both sides of his country's political spectrum, and because 'at the moment we have no direct connection to Belgrade'. Comert convinced the reluctant committee to hire Popovich, but not before Drummond had declared that he 'was not of the opinion that the Information Section should be a microcosm of the whole Secretariat. It was the duty of the members of the various sections to keep in touch with their own governments and not only the function of the Information Section'.[49]

The exchange illustrated the difference between the general principles of national representation in the Secretariat and the self-image of the Information Section, which Comert considered a hub not just of knowledge of public opinion but also sensitive political information or confidential lines of communication to national elites. The secretary general and the political bodies of the League accepted this view, an illustration of the extent to which they accepted the complex perception of the League's relation to the public held in the section.

Internationalism in the Information Section

Sweetser and Comert built the Information Section together. Understanding their two approaches helps us grasp the meaning of, and limits to, the internationalism disseminated and practised by the section and therefore by the League of Nations. Paradoxically, Comert and Sweetser were able to work well together because of the non-membership of the United States – the reversal of which was at the same time Sweetser's greatest ambition. It meant that Sweetser was never a threat to Comert's position because a position as important as director of the Information Section would always go to a national from a League member state. In terms of planning and directing the section Sweetser and Comert were almost equal. The first plan for the functions of the section was largely based on Sweetser's synthesis of Comert and Mair's proposals.[50] During the aforementioned title-disagreement in 1929 Sweetser also claimed in writing that it was him who had finally convinced Comert, in an emotional scene in front of the Hotel Crillon in Paris, to accept the position as director.[51]

Sweetser worked in the League throughout its existence and remained in the Information Section all through Comert's directorship. As we shall see, the two men entertained a similar species of internationalism, a practically minded, pragmatic kind that supported the League idea but was anchored in their devotion to their respective home countries and conviction that their interests could always be aligned with that of the League. They discussed continuously the activities of the section, and Sweetser acted as director when his French chief was not in Geneva.[52] Sweetser's daughter later recounted that their families became 'inseparably entwined' in the League expatriate community of Geneva. Comert's wife, Janet Comert, was a US citizen which added to the director's cultural compatibility with Sweetser.[53]

After the United States withdrawal, as we heard, Sweetser's outsider-role would go hand in hand with his commitment to the League's project. In 1919 he privately expressed frustration that Americans, in his view, failed to take the League seriously: 'Just as our whole army is going home so, and much more seriously so, our whole diplomacy is going home' he lamented.[54] In 1920 he privately published a book aimed at the American public in which he wrote on the League's relation to public opinion that 'beside that question all others are dwarfed' and that 'the future of the League of Nations' rested with it.[55] The book, based on series of opinion-articles, as discussed by Averbeck-Lietz, gave rise to a principal discussion in the Secretariat of the extent to which officials could express opinions about League matters ending when Comert interfered and clarified that no members could write opinion-pieces without his approval or take payment for it.[56]

As should be clear, Sweetser was a devoted believer in the League as a vision which should be implemented 'practically'. As early as 1918, on board the steamship to Europe, he had reflected on a special role of the United States in international society, closely aligned with the Wilsonianism of the day:

> On all sides it is a very real earnestness to be of some sort of service on the other side and to help restore the wounds wrought by war. It is a significant indication of America's transition from war to peace that as we pass troopships on the way back home, we are carrying with us so many people of real purpose.[57]

Sweetser thus connected his international outlook to his revulsion towards war, which he had witnessed himself on his bicycle, and his conviction of the

Figure 4 Pierre Comert, director of the Information Section 1919–32. United Nations Archives, Geneva.

prominent role of the United States in world affairs. This sparked a fruitful relationship with Comert, who was also a convinced internationalist (though perhaps a more cool-headed one) and who saw the advantage in keeping a close relationship to an American second-in-command who could provide a link to US public opinion (Figure 4).

Comert demonstrates the complexities of internationalism in the interwar period. He was close enough with his home government to return to serve the French Foreign Ministry as head of its press department after his resignation from the Secretariat in 1932. He was an admirer of Jean Monnet and close with the French officials of the Secretariat.[58] At the same time, he was a dedicated believer in international cooperation. In 1934, a nationalist French journal referred to him as a 'a pacific internationalist' and maliciously added that his long service in Geneva had 'killed the few remaining French fibers remaining in him'.[59] During his League years, he expressed commitment to the idea of a diplomacy that would be controlled by public opinion. In a confidential report on a conference, he had attended in Barcelona in 1921, he stated to his fellow directors:

> In future democracies, when public opinion, like a whimsical queen, will be the supreme mistress, and where no one will be able to do anything without her support, we might imagine a diplomacy whose main task will be to popularize, to explain to the public the technical matters around which the major conflicts revolve.[60]

The diplomacy of the future ought to open its doors as widely as possible to journalists. Comert believed in the League's promise of an open diplomacy and felt that a section like his own should promote the organization as forcefully as possible within the confines of an officially neutral bureaucracy. How he interpreted his mandate has been understood quite differently by observers. Pitman Potter, a contemporary professor at the League-associated Graduate Institute of Geneva, wrote in 1938 that 'especially the first Director of the Information Section, M. Pierre Comert' was in favour of 'reasonable publicity and even promotion'.[61] But he also wrote that his section had pursued its task using 'political maneuvering' rather than open promotion.[62] What remains clear is that Comert was cautious but ambitious on behalf of his section. In a 1928 report his officials stated that the section was 'not an annex of the Secretariat, nor [. . .] a Press bureau in the usually accepted sense of the term' but an 'organic part of the Secretariat closely bound up with the League work as a whole'.[63] This description sheds light on the fact that Comert believed, particularly in the early years of the League, that his authority transcended the formal boundaries of his own section. This could be seen too in the minutes of the director's meetings which were held once every week, usually in Drummond's office. Here, the directors discussed all things related to the work of the League, such as the agenda for upcoming Council meetings, or the settling of the lines of communication regarding some current political situation. Comert's statements at the meetings indicate to a twenty-first-century reader that the early Secretariat did not function in accordance with the stricter division of responsibility one expects today. He remarked at the very first meeting on 13 August 1919 that

> from a propaganda point of view there would be great difficulty in defending the admission of Germany as an act of the first assembly. [. . .] He saw the danger that Germany might be driven to make common cause with Russia, if she were denied admission to the League, but from the point of his Section,

he was bound to say his work would be made very difficult if her admission was allowed too soon.[64]

This meeting happened before clear procedures were settled in the Secretariat. In general, printed sources from the earliest months of the Secretariat are illuminating because professional codes and boundaries had not been laid down properly yet. It seemed clearly out of place that an information official should comment on the wisdom of admitting a member state to the League. Comert was obviously conveying the attitude of the French government, a government he was, according to James Barros, Drummond's 'main contact' with after Monnet's resignation in 1923.[65] However, the fact that Comert underscored that he was speaking 'from a propaganda point of view' might suggest that to him it seemed a justifiable point of view that the public included elite circles counting government officials and decision-makers; perhaps that these people constituted the most important part of it.

Indications are Comert was a popular and well-respected director. He held his position as long as Eric Drummond did.[66] In 1932, as we shall see, he was forced to resign for political reasons; Germany had been accepted into the League – and the League Council – in 1926 with the status of a Great Power, and when the Frenchman, Joseph Avenol, was set to succeed Eric Drummond as secretary general, the German delegation refused to approve two powerful Frenchmen in the Secretariat. They objected to the renewal of Comert's contract, which led to his resignation in December 1932.[67] The *Journal des Nations*, a Genevan pro-League newspaper, published a statement on behalf of the Geneva international press corps on the occasion crediting Comert with 'succeeding in putting the public conscience at the service of peace and bringing into the League a great power which does not figure on geographical maps', clearly referring to the power of public opinion.[68] The *New York Times* wrote that Comert's resignation was due to him having aroused the 'personal hostility' of 'the extreme German nationalists'.[69] It seems that when Comert's career in the Secretariat ended, it did so due to the combination of his two most visible characteristics: his close affiliation with the French government and his internationalism.

The propaganda spectre

The ways in which the Information Section used the word 'propaganda' suggest an ambiguity in the way the League saw itself at this point, and perhaps a lack of confidence. Towards the outside world, officials avoided using the discredited word to describe their work and rejected it outspokenly as well. However, in internal communication, they used it regularly and acknowledged the necessity of a forceful information policy and celebratory promotion of the League's work.[70] Ranshofen-Wertheimer remarked that the word was 'taboo' in the Secretariat, and he was clearly not wrong.[71] There was no formalized ban of making propaganda (probably because of the difficulty in defining such an activity) but was taken for granted given the neutral position of the Secretariat. The Staff Regulations, which were not instituted in the Secretariat until 1921, prohibited officials from engaging in any 'political controversy' concerning the League but did not specify further to what extent this covered speaking celebratory of the organization.[72] Propaganda was disavowed but its utility was articulated regularly. Particularly at the early meetings the feasibility of various actions of the League from a 'propaganda' point of view was regularly brought up by Comert or another member of his section. In the Secretariat's preparatory documents for the so-called Noblemaire Report in 1921, the Information Section regretted the lack of financing for League 'propaganda'.[73] On 15 July 1919, when plans for the Secretariat were still in the making, Fosdick forwarded a letter to Drummond from a Mr Pym who proposed an ambitious programme of

> propaganda. I am convinced that the League should concentrate here at once nine-tenths of its whole activities [...] There should be a League of Nations Flag, flown above the national flag; a League of Nations week for schools, superseding Empire Day, a League of Nations anthem sung after – and in a higher key – than the National Anthem. Daily Mail prizes ... but further detail is perhaps unnecessary.

Fosdick commented that while these suggestions were a bit excessive, he thought them 'somewhat in line with my thought' and felt that the Secretariat should 'consciously cultivate support for the League in the shape of public opinion'. He concluded 'I shall be very much interested to see what plans Commert [sic] and Sweetser have on the matter'.[74]

Fosdick may have been disappointed. In Sweetser's own first draft-proposal for the section he made a point of dividing League 'publicity' into two phases: publicity during the establishment phase of the League and publicity afterwards. During the first phase, its essence should be a flow of 'actual news' that should 'carry a continued suggestion to the public mind and should demonstrate beyond dispute that the League has a supreme part to play in human affairs'. But on the other hand, he warned, it should be 'very guarded, in order not to arouse the antipathy always attaching to propaganda'.⁷⁵ Here, Sweetser articulated a dilemma that came to be ever present during the League's existence: On the one hand, a propaganda department, like the ones attached to national governments in the interwar period (and during the war that had just ended), seemed vital in making the organization 'present' in the minds of the people of the world. On the other hand, since the League was not a national government but a diplomatic system entirely dependent upon often-disagreeing member governments, it had to avoid arousing their distrust by signalling independent international agency.

Sweetser, Comert, Mair and other high officials thus weighed the different options for promoting the League cautiously against the risk that the organization risked being accused of overstepping its mandate. In April 1920 the secretary general proposed cutting the 'review of the press' that the section produced for internal use because

> He did not wish to have to present to the Council a noticeably long list of personnel for the Information Section, since this might lead them [the Council] to think that we were using for propaganda purposes a part of the money paid by the Governments to the expenses of the League.⁷⁶

Eric Drummond was probably not personally troubled by spending resources on League-propaganda, but it was important to him that the member states of the League did not get that impression. That could result in increased political attention and budget cuts. Pitman Potter deemed that Drummond, like Comert, was optimistic about the potential of information and publicity but that the personal opinions of these officials were of secondary importance because they had decided on a high degree of caution and neutrality as their 'theory of publicity', which 'has been worked out by the Information Section [. . .] in the face of the suspicion and hostility of the Member States as a theory of what it may do *in view* of that hostility'.⁷⁷

Conclusion

The League attributed key importance to its Information Section in explaining the intricacies of the new diplomatic system to the world, in securing the feeling of an open diplomacy and in keeping internationalism alive. In the words of Ranshofen-Wertheimer publicity became an 'inseparable element of League action' permeating the Secretariat and giving Comert a high status among the directors.[78] It served many purposes (to which we shall return) but from its organization, staff and leadership alone can be seen that it was expected not only to tell the world about the League and why it mattered but also to be an 'honest broker' of information in the Secretariat, to offer its opinion on matters outside its own strict terms of reference, to channel talented officials into the Secretariat and to reflect and imbue with personal devotion the League's multinational composition.

However, the section had been dealt a tough hand. It was expected to fight the League's cause and find ways to legitimize it to the public. Still, it hesitated to use propaganda, because that could potentially discredit the whole Secretariat and complicate the League's work. The earliest plans for the organization of the Information Section reflected an attempt to create an organization that concentrated equally on public opinion in the three most powerful member states of the League. This prioritization combined with Comert's own rhetoric and actions suggested that while Comert was indeed a convinced internationalist who believed the League should popularize diplomacy and spoke of his work as a democratic effort, he was also cautious and pragmatic, prioritizing French interests, and promoting an identification of public opinion that remained rooted in nation states. Once the United States had withdrawn from the League this set the stage for a fruitful relationship and division of labour between Comert and Sweetser, because the latter was also a devout internationalist who simultaneously had a constant eye on the relation between his own country and the League. This fusing between the belief in the universal power of public opinion and the priority of connecting to member states and powerful stakeholders within them showed that it considered the securing of elite support as important as securing that of the 'man in the street'.

2

More than a press bureau
The Information Section at work, 1920–32

By the early 1920s, Europe and the world were settling into an uneasy peace. Aftershocks of the war, such as a Polish-Lithuanian conflict, a French occupation of the Ruhr district in Germany and a fascist coup in Italy served as reminders that a vast array of problems stood unsolved after the peace treaties, and that social unrest could easily lead to political upheaval. Still, the League enjoyed the solid mandate that came with the Great Powers having few other horses to bet on. As the years went by, positive signals in international politics started to appear. The Pact of Locarno in 1925 between Germany and the prime Western European powers allowed for more tolerable relations between Germany and its neighbours and paved the way for the large country's subsequent admittance into the League in 1926.

As we heard in the preceding chapter, Information Section meanwhile conscientiously pursued its mission of disseminating and practising League internationalism. Its leadership designed a section, supervised by the secretary general, which combined a vision of a link between the public and the League with a solid anchoring in separate national publics.

We shall see that the League, steered by the section, came to address the public through three channels: through the press, through information material and through liaison with activists, intellectuals and public figures sympathetic to the League. In this chapter we examine the evolution of two out of these three categories of activity, namely its press relations and its liaison activities. It also discusses the challenges the section encountered trying to make itself a guarantor of open diplomacy, and traces the section's conceptualization of the public through these activities. Later, Chapter 3 delves into its information material.

The section strove to facilitate a spirit of confidentiality and even comradeship between its officials and the international press corps that covered the League. However, the League's mission of creating an open diplomacy, and the

Information Section's investment in this, turned out to be easier said than done. Council deliberations never became fully public, because Great Powers insisted that diplomatic negotiations must to some degree be protected from the public eye. The section sought to compensate for such defeats and avoid accusations of making propaganda, by adopting a cautious, indirect set of public legitimization strategies. These involved placing a heavy emphasis on its so-called liaison efforts, of collaborating with public figures and private associations in favour of the League.

Who was the League's audience? Did the Information Section ever attempt to define its target and purpose? The closest we get to this in the 1920s was in the so-called Noblemaire Report in 1921. The report, ordered by the Assembly, represented what Gram-Skjoldager and Ikonomou have called a 'dual process of capacity-building and formalization' of the Secretariat to which the League Assembly contributed by requesting a report on the principles that governed various questions regarding staffing, terms of reference and so on. The officials were therefore required to lay down some principles for their work and balance these with the expectations of member states. Here, the Information Section stated its duty as 'fully appreciating the meaning of the work carried out by the League and [...] supplying public opinion in the various countries with the most telling account of that work'.[1] Eleven years later, in 1932 it had not specified it much further: It was by then simply 'responsible for contact between the League and public opinion'.[2] The closest one finds to an identification of what people it targeted came in 1926 when it formally worked to explain the League's work 'to people coming from very different countries and classes'.[3] This indicated an awareness that the League needed to appeal to different layers of society, but it never elaborated much on this.

The Information Section's philosophy on *how* to address the public was clearer (Figure 5). Officials expressed the liberal notion that opposition to international cooperation was simply a question of misunderstanding or lack of knowledge. Arthur Sweetser explained to his American readers in 1920 that 'once the public familiarizes itself with the League, understands its workings, and feels a direct relationship to its success, it will put all its strength behind it'.[4] Therefore, the League did not need to use aggressive communication but should strive to be a neutral informer. This idea was key to understanding the self-image of the section.[5] It should strive to inform the public in as 'neutral' a way as possible. The keyword was reason as a progressive force of humanity, a point that resonates with Tomoko Akami's observation that the language of the Enlightenment and the idea of an 'age of reason' permeated the League's information policies.[6] Some contemporary

Figure 5 A group photo of the Information Section in 1923 or 1924. United Nations Archives, Geneva.

observers criticized this dogma of neutrality. Pitman Potter was a professor at the Graduate Institute of International Studies, a Genevan university founded in close collaboration with the League by Secretariat high officials William Rappard and Paul Mantoux. In 1938, he analysed the development of the Information Section that although it was staffed with competent people, it lacked 'moral courage'.[7]

Potter felt that the League ought to promote itself more aggressively and expressed scepticism about what he saw as its neutrality-obsessed 'theory of publicity'. What he could not see as clearly, as if he had been an official himself, was that to Pierre Comert, Arthur Sweetser and their successors in the Information Section, remaining neutral came with other advantages than avoiding accusations of propaganda. Defining one's own activities as neutral information *constituted* good propaganda, as Linda Risso has observed about the efforts of the NATO a quarter of a century later.[8]

From the gallery down to the floor: Working with the press

The Information Section collaborated with journalists in a multitude of ways going from the basic services of accreditation of reporters to League meetings and preparing a daily 'review of the press' to publishing the proceedings of closed diplomatic meetings. Officials eventually gained the confidence to instrumentalize the press proactively in legitimizing the League, as would be seen at its International Conference of Press Experts in 1927. The section rhetorically articulated its press services as part of its grander vision, for example in 1928 in material it presented as part of the enormous press exhibition in Cologne the PRESSA.[9] Here the section stated that the League's relationship with journalists had resulted in 'a kind of multi-national or international public opinion whose influence is increasing'.[10]

The press took centre stage in the worldview of the section. The daily interactions of League officials and reporters concretized physically the League's connection to public opinion and fed the section's rhetoric of having the ear of the international public. The press remained the most important gatekeepers of League information, and the comings and goings of reporters and correspondents in the halls of the *Palais Wilson* (the seat of the Secretariat in Geneva 1920–36) was always mainly what officials referred to when they wrote or spoke of the international public. The press was paramount to Comert, wrote Egon Ranshofen-Wertheimer. To the French director, 'Publicity [. . .] meant the closest possible relationship to the daily newspapers, especially those of the capitals of the permanent members of the Council',[11] and the press service, through its size and the intimacy provided between journalists and former journalists in the service of the League, became a show horse of the section and indeed of the Secretariat. Comert, Sweetser and most other key section members of course were former correspondents themselves. This meant that they were liable to trust journalists but also that they considered them stakeholders in, rather than threats to, the League's project. This is part of what Erik Koenen, Arne Gellrich and Stefanie Averbeck-Lietz refer to with their analytical concept of a common 'epistemic project' in the Secretariat during these years.

The section regularly compared itself to the press service of a national foreign office, underlining the higher degree of complexity and variety of tasks involved when dealing with an international public and an international press. The growing Geneva press corps was an essential element in this idea. In the closing years of the 1920s, about one hundred permanent correspondents from all over the (primarily Western) world resided in Geneva. Gellrich and Koenen established that the three dominant national cohorts in the Geneva press corps, decreasing in size, were the French, British and Germans.[12] Between 350 and 400 reporters would attend the annual meetings of the Assembly, and high numbers joined their national delegations for Council meetings or important conferences.[13] These numbers had gradually increased since 1919, and accordingly the workload of the section had expanded. The press service provided journalists with facilities for League conferences and commission meetings as well as for Assemblies and those Council meetings, which were public. Comert's officials accredited League correspondents and procured equipment for dispatch of news to their home countries.[14] The annual Assemblies convened in the large Reformation Hall of Geneva, which included an elevated press gallery with a capacity for 700 journalists (Figure 6).

Council and various committee meetings took place in the Secretariat, which until the mid-1930s was seated in the *Hotel National* – renamed *Palais Wilson* after the death of former president Wilson in 1924.[15] The Council (after its first two meetings in Paris and London) convened in the central part of the ground floor of the building and later in another ground-floor room called the Glass room, which could accommodate about 150 journalists. Committee meetings convened in different parts of the Secretariat and making room for journalists was often difficult. In the Press Room of the Reformation Hall building lists of the speakers of the day could be found. Next door, the Information Section copied ('mimeographed' at the time) minutes of all meetings and distributed them to the press. Here were also telephones (operated by Swiss telephonists), a telegraph and wireless dispatch equipment. In the Press Room were working

Figure 6 The Salle de la Réformation during the 8th General Assembly of the League of Nations 1927.
United Nations Archives, Geneva.

desks for correspondents, and the Information Section posted communiqués here together with minutes from big conferences and deliberations.[16]

The section took pride in the resources put into these services: It emphasized its unique and close relationship with the press in reports and publications and described how officials assisted journalists off-the-record a service its officials saw as illustrative of the political sensibility expected of them.[17] Beginning in 1921 it could reach the Geneva press corps through an association of journalists accredited to the League of Nations, a useful channel, for example when the section organized a social event for journalists or warned them about accepting leaked confidential information.

As a 'centre of world information' the interactions of the Information Section with the press were not one-sided. It was expected to inform the secretary general and other high officials on trends in public opinion. Its officials collected information on the League's standing in public opinion through 'daily contact', and 'constant personal relations' with journalists as well as through officials visiting their home countries. As is common for press departments, they circulated a daily overview of notable stories in leading papers of the largest member states. In 1928, it contained cuttings and summaries of 200 newspapers on top of which came similar services for magazines and reviews.[18]

The publication efforts of the section will be the subject of other chapters, but a quick overview may be helpful: On a daily basis the Information Section released news communiqués (press releases), and slightly longer 'explanatory articles,' aimed at journalists, and later on also a news service for countries outside Europe (from 1929).[19] All such documents were available as a minimum in French and English, the organization's two official languages. The section proudly declared that its communiqués summarized 'the broad points of any question under discussion in the League as a basis for individual and independent journalistic work'. Beyond Geneva, the section dispatched communiqués directly to the leading news agencies of the Western world, such as Agence Havas (French), Reuters (British), Agenzia Stefani (Italian), Associated Press (US) and Wolffs (German).[20]

During the first half of the 1920s, 300–400 communiqués were issued annually, rising to between 400–500 during the second half of the decade. Added to this came communiqués issued during the Assembly, registered in a different system.[21]

The section did not systematically broadcast until the opening of *Radio Nations* in 1932 – which we shall revisit in a later chapter. For reasons of economy, and hostility from the printed press, it never broadcasted *news* during its existence.[22] At some point shortly before 1930, it began releasing bulletins to broadcasting associations containing suggestions for radio talks on the League.[23] It additionally did a few experiments of broadcasting news in collaboration with national governments starting in 1928.[24]

From this brief overview, we gather that the press played a leading part in the League's self-image during Comert's time as director of the Information Section. Paradoxically, since most of this work was encapsulated in services provided to members of the press, the section repeatedly described these services as making it 'more' than a press service. Comert and his colleagues considered what they were doing alliance building with friends and colleagues in the international press whom they saw as collaborators in legitimizing the League. However, solidifying this alliance would prove challenging as the shortcomings of the League's diplomacy became clear, and the conflicts it was expected to tackle more entrenched.

Secrecy and transparency

A key challenge to the Information Section was its tackling of the tension between its own invocation of an open diplomacy and the wish of the Great Powers to keep some diplomatic conversations 'private' (meaning closed to the public and the members of the press). Although Comert and his section had a limited say in these things, their working conditions were directly impacted by them, as was the credibility with which they could defend the tenets of League internationalism. In the beginning, many officials were excited and optimist about open diplomacy. Arthur Sweetser cited his wife Ruth in his diary in 1920:

> Arthur's work has been quite exciting. Such a degree of publicity for a 'secret meeting' had never been heard of. It is one of A's fundamental principles however, that careful, intelligent publicity brings the greatest degree of success to all concerned.[25]

'Careful, intelligent publicity'. The degree to which the League integrated open diplomacy at its meetings varied depending on the exact meeting context. The annual Assembly plenary debates were entirely open to the press from day one, and so were most meetings of the so-called Permanent Committees after 1921. However, Council sessions, at which the Great Powers met, remained private all through the League's life, although at times a ceremonial open session preceded or followed them. From the very beginning, decision-makers involved in planning the League raised serious doubts about the feasibility of allowing the press to cover Council meetings at all. Sir Maurice Hankey, secretary of the British cabinet (and the original favourite for Drummond's job as League secretary general), wrote to Drummond in July 1919 that he was 'very disturbed' to hear that the Secretariat considered allowing the press into Council meetings. Hankey felt it would destroy the prospect of League success to admit the press.[26] He argued that it would undermine the very framework for settling of international disputes the League was trying to foster, and force statesmen to make the important decisions elsewhere.

Drummond circulated the letter among the upper ranks of the Secretariat. Raymond Fosdick thought that the decision was a choice between 'a more efficient – at least in a more expeditious – conduct of business' and 'a policy which will make for more public confidence and trust'. He strongly pushed for the latter, arguing that the confidence of the public was more important given that the war was still so recent.[27]

Drummond was a pragmatic and aligned with a British view on diplomacy, contrasted with Fosdick's, which was evidently Wilsonian-inspired. He opted for keeping the Great Powers committed to the League machinery and decided the Council should meet in private. While this compromise was unpopular among the Secretariat's idealists, the Information Section was empowered by it. From that point, it became a gatekeeper of information about the most important political decisions made under the League's aegis – concretized in its dissemination of news communiqués following Council meetings.[28] This was no simple task. On 25 April 1923 for example, a closed Council meeting had been held on the Governing Commission of the Saar Valley – a sensitive subject since it pitted Germany and its sympathizers against those of France.[29] After the meeting, the German foreign ministry filed a complaint to Norwegian Erik Colban, director of the Minorities Section, who brought the issue to the attention of the directors' meeting. Colban explained that too little attention had been given to German viewpoints and too much to the French. It was underlined that this was most certainly unintentional, however 'it made him consider it desirable to draw attention to the great political importance of our communiqués in the present situation and to suggest that it was better to give only very brief communiqués on such a question than to risk dangerous results'.[30]

Comert defended his section, maintaining that both Sweetser and the secretary general had approved the communiqué. He deemed that the matter was simply a very sensitive one, and there was little his section could do about that. The discussion was concluded by Canadian Herbert Ames, director of the Financial Section, who remarked awkwardly that Comert was 'not guilty this time, but don't do it again' possibly attempting to bring humorous relief to the tense confrontation among the directors and the indirect clash between Great Powers 'backstage'.[31]

Possibly, this was an example of Comert favouring a French official attitude. However, on a more general level, the episode underlines what members of the Secretariat often remarked both then and later: Any communication by the Secretariat about political disputes was potentially dangerous and subject to criticism by the Great Powers whose goodwill underpinned the entire organization. This point is essential to keep in mind when studying the work of the Information Section, since it concerns the balance point between pragmatism and the ideal of an open diplomacy. Comert managed to clear his section of responsibility in this case, but the episode illustrates that the work of his section was based on an identification of the League as a weak agent – as no more than 'the sum of its parts'. Officials did not just let go of their internationalism, but they had to navigate constantly on dangerous seas of Great Power interests. The section often abstained from advising full transparency on an issue. For example, at another directors' meeting about two years earlier. The directors were debating the work of the Temporary Mixed Commission on Armaments. This was another topic that involved Great Power interests. In this instance, the French and the British were at odds, which was partly visible in the discussion at the director's meeting. Comert remarked that he 'doubted whether it was wise to give publicity to each meeting unless we are sure that it would produce some tangible results'. His compatriot Jean Monnet supported him. The secretary general (who was, of course, British) concluded that 'we must be confident that publicity for so well-organized an attempt to solve a great problem could produce nothing but good'.[32] Here, Comert spoke against the idea behind his own section, possibly to avoid publicity that could hurt the French government, which was stalling the disarmament talks at this time. Seen in the light of Comert's stated conviction (only two months earlier) that his mission was to make diplomacy as transparent to the public as possible this episode was a 'smoking gun' – it caught Comert between his national loyalty and the mandate of his section. Arguably, he did the only thing he could, namely tried to justify his view with a warning that *public opinion* would disapprove of publicity on an area in which nothing was happening. The concept of public opinion always had to take a commanding role – even when one was advising against publicity.

Moral disarmament and management of the press

It should be clear at this point that although the officials who built the Information Section during the 1920s saw the press as its most important instrument and collaborators in legitimizing the League they were severely inhibited in their efforts. The secretary general placed constraints on the section from above out of fear of accusations of propaganda. They furthermore came from within in the form of the expectation that high officials represented the attitudes of their home governments – no matter if these were aligned with the section's ambition of creating an open diplomacy.

The primacy of the press and the inherent constraints on information policy – combined with its prestige by the second half of the 1920 – combine to make its efforts within so-called moral disarmament a promising public legitimization strategy. In 1927, the section sought to consolidate its role in mobilizing public opinion to support the League's internationalism, when it initiated and organized an international conference on matters of the press. The conference was hosted by different member states but remained under League auspices in 1932 and 1933. The official instigation of the conference happened at the Assembly of 1925, when a Chilean delegate, Eliodoro Yanez, a prominent former journalist himself, proposed that the League should host an international conference to discuss agreements on faster and cheaper transmission of news 'with a view to reducing the risk of international misunderstanding'.[33]

Moral disarmament would later be associated with the Intellectual Cooperation organization of the League and with the great Disarmament Conference in 1933. But the Information Section had been invested in the same strand of thought since the emergence of the 'Resolution of the Collaboration of the Press in the Organization of Peace', spawned by Yanez' proposal.[34] The phrase 'moral disarmament' emerged in a League publication as early as 1922.[35] The concept expanded the disarmament concept beyond the reduction of physical armaments. The organization for Intellectual Cooperation associated it with international coordination of public education in League matters, educative broadcasting, film production, 'propaganda in favor of the international spirit' and academic cooperation such as student exchange and international scholarships.[36] In addition, and most relevant to Comert's Information Section, it meant the press should play an active role as a promoter of peace and understanding among the public.

At the 1925 Assembly, the Belgian delegate Paul Hymans had declared that a conference of the sort should not attempt to take ownership of questions of press freedom or news regulation. The League, he underlined, must under no circumstances 'create something resembling a semi-official Press or [. . .] make propaganda'.³⁷

The hesitancy to get too involved combined with the urgent wish to confront these questions and bring them under the League's aegis is clear in a private 1952 letter from Sweetser to Comert. It suggested that the Information Section officials had been deeply involved in making the conference happen, perhaps even that the idea originated with them rather than in the assembly. 'Dear Pierre', he wrote:

> Thoughts of you kept coming into my mind yesterday as I read the attached 'International Code of Ethics for Information Personnel' and recalled our famous Conference of Press Experts in Geneva. [. . .] Do you remember our starting out our tumultuous voyage by getting the Council to ask the Assembly . . . to consider the advisability . . . of asking some journalists . . . to consider the advisability . . . of asking the Council . . . to consider the advisability of calling a Conference of Journalists to discuss such questions?³⁸

Many factors at the time led Comert and Sweetser to be attracted to the thought of an international conference under the League's umbrella. As Heidi Tworek and also Frank Beyersdorf have shown, a kind of cartel of the powerful European news agencies at the time (the *Agences Alliées*, consisting of Agence Havas, Wolff Telegraphic Bureau and Reuters) were encouraging the League to assume a leading role in such cooperation.³⁹ Upon discussing the question with his deputies, Drummond had charged Comert with investigating the League's elbow-room for such a conference. The Agences Alliées kept forwarding their resolutions and discussions to the League each of the following years as well.⁴⁰ The conference was an excellent opportunity for the section to construct itself as an international authority on issues relating to the press. However, they had to work hard to maintain a discreet background-role. Preparing the conference Comert, Sweetser and the Dutch official Adrianus Pelt appointed, in the name of the secretary general, three preparatory committees with members from largely, but not exclusively, European countries and the United States. One consisted of news agencies, one of governmental press departments and one of foreign correspondents.⁴¹

The presence of governmental representatives at the conference illuminates the challenges that League officials encountered when organizing international talks on a sensitive matter such as state censorship of the press. In April 1926, Comert updated Sweetser on the preparations: 'Our only concern', he wrote, 'is the attitude of the "Newspaper Proprietors" Association', in which Lord Burnham, quite conceitedly, 'is making some absurd objections'.[42] In a letter to Pelt, Burnham had demanded that specific organizations should not be invited to attend and that delegations should be national rather than sectional.[43] Circumvention of governmental authority at such an event was unwelcome, as it sent a signal of the League interfering in state interests. The wish of the Information Section to engage with public opinion was countered by national interests. The Secretariat did invite private news agencies, and the Council appointed Lord Burnham president of the conference, and governmental press offices were invited – as well, 'in an advisory capacity'.[44] The section was once again obliged to format its interaction with public opinion to the demands of national interests, and Lord Burnham would later celebrate the conference as 'the first independent conference the League ever had'.[45]

The Conference of Press Experts convened in Geneva between 24 and 29 August 1927 and was attended by 113 people, including 63 delegates.[46] It dispatched ten resolutions via the Secretariat to League member states with a recommendation to integrate them into law.[47] One of them concerned the publication of 'tendentious news', linking the abolishing of misleading news to moral disarmament, recommending university courses for journalists and advocating for newspapers exclusively devoted to League news. The preamble communicated neatly the notion of moral disarmament as it spoke of the press' 'responsible mission accurately and conscientiously to inform world public opinion and hence to contribute directly to the preservation of peace and the advancement of civilization'.[48] As has been observed by Nordenstreng and others, the idea of moral disarmament can take on an ominous ring in retrospect. The word 'responsible' did not just signal a belief in the preservation of peace but could also serve as legitimization for governments that wanted to control and censor the press – and it did on some occasions.[49]

The succeeding conferences in Copenhagen in 1932 and Madrid in 1933 equally adopted resolutions on false news, and the preparation for the Madrid conference is telling as to the importance attributed to this problem. In 1931, the Assembly passed a resolution requesting member states and their press organizations to suggest means of countering false news.[50] The International Association of Journalists Accredited to the League of Nations answered expansively arguing for more transparency in diplomacy and for more resources to the League.[51] This signalled what has been underscored by scholarship, namely that the League constituted an important pillar in the infrastructure of the professionalization of journalism internationally as the League could lend legitimacy to newly forged organizations such as the *Fédération Internationale des Journalistes*.[52] Seen from Geneva's perspective, it was an example of the League – and probably the Information Section – boosting its own agency in international life by nurturing an international public without engaging in propaganda. The international press conferences exemplified the peak of the section's involvement in making the League and the international press work on the same side in the cause of internationalism.

Cooperative publicity

From these efforts of the Information Section to forge a strong position for itself as an international news centre, a friend of journalism and a flagship in the professionalization of journalism it may be seen that the section was constantly grappling with a fundamental challenge: How could it on the one hand commit to fight for the League on the international stage, while on the other hand it was not allowed to take on a voice of its own, because it feared accusations of propaganda and internal divisions along national lines.[53]

The answer was to let someone else fight that fight on its behalf. Comert's officials believed in the power of the press, and considered journalists the most eminent speakers of the League's cause. However, to the extent that journalists could not be persuaded to devote themselves fully to that cause, other channels to the public would have to be used. The section therefore attempted to institute a division of labour between the Secretariat and private individuals and associations, often referred to as 'collaborators', a popular phrasing at the time. The Secretariat could refer to its own neutral status, while encouraging its collaborators to engage in more overt propaganda activities on the League's behalf. Thomas Davies hinted at this system in his work of League interactions international associations and the roots of the 'consultative status' that such associations, what would today be called International Non-Governmental Organizations, INGOs, could later achieve in the UN.[54] Arthur Sweetser argued from the start in 1919 that 'private international associations' (they were also sometimes referred to as 'unions') were of immense value and that the League 'must cooperate and not compete with these organizations, for they represent the purest form of personal interest and initiative'.[55] He called it 'cooperative publicity'.[56]

The result was a philosophy that was developed in a push-and-pull process between the section and the secretary general. Pro-League individuals and associations came to be seen as intermediaries to the masses and sometimes as constituting the public themselves. Consequently elites, and this was not entirely a conscious manoeuvre by the section, came to fulfil a key role in the section's legitimization strategy. The crux of the matter was that discreet cooperation with enthusiastic League sympathizers was considered the safest way the section could promote the League without being accused of propaganda.

In the eyes of some contemporaries the section almost managed to turn the constraints put on its work into a strength. Bertram Pickard, a prominent internationalist writer (and pacifist and Quaker spokesperson), wrote in 1936 of the 'offensive-defensive alliance between the International Civil Service, debarred from open advocacy of policy, and the unofficial organizations, often insufficiently informed of facts without which policy cannot be accurately devised and pursued'.[57]

In 1934 section officials themselves would remark, more cautiously, that the League's cooperation with private associations 'has been based on the assumption that public opinion is in a large degree informed through these organizations' and estimated that up until that year the section had been in contact with about two hundred private organizations.[58]

The Information Section stood for the majority of this work, but not all. Some activities that involved academic life involved the Intellectual Cooperation Section (called the International Bureaux Section until 1928).[59] This section served the League's International Institute for Intellectual Cooperation (IICI) in Paris which has been examined by Jean-Jacques Renoliet. Renoliet observed, in the record of the IICI and its Commission for Intellectual Cooperation, two weaknesses that are strikingly parallel to what the present monograph argues about the Information Section, namely that it was threatened from the outside by Great Power rivalries and shaped from the inside by a species of elitism characteristic of the time.[60]

A 1934 list neatly presents and categorizes the many different collaborators the Information Section sought to operationalize during the 1920s. It included sixteen categories of associations. Examples included all notable 'press associations', such as the Fédération Internationale des Journalistes (FIJ), the Association of Journalists Accredited to the League of Nations and unions of editors and of the largest news agencies. It also mentioned major war veteran associations, all League of Nations associations, the Labor and Socialist International, Zionist associations, the YMCA, the Interparliamentary Union, women's rights associations, student organizations and the International Cinematographic institute in Rome, just to mention some notable examples.[61]

It is neither possible, nor within the scope of this book to go into details about the exact nature of each of these endeavours. Some, like the League of Nations associations, were closely monitored by the Information Section. Others mostly received information material and visits by observers from the section who then reported to the Secretariat. More central to our point than the nature of such liaison was the vision of the League's embeddedness in international public opinion it represented. Officials envisioned the development of a vast network of 'influential individuals' whom it would keep constantly committed to fight the League's cause. In 1926 the section reported to the Assembly that such contacts with 'parliamentarians, skilled journalists, politicians, public officials, people from the financial world, academics, technicians or experts within the fields of work pursued by the League' represented its most promising means to 'secure a more complete collaboration between public opinion and the League of Nations'. It reported that it had 'a few dozen' such connections for each member state represented by a member of the section.[62]

The idea of running such a 'cooperative publicity' scheme was planted, like so much else, during the initial formative months before the League's official coming into existence. In 1919, Sweetser proposed various ways of obtaining information about what organizations could be beneficial League collaborators, including systematically contacting ambassadors and retrieving intelligence from them about the League's standing in their countries.[63] However, the secretary general blocked all suggestions, remarking to his deputies, Fosdick and Monnet, that if word got around the Information Section was being that intrusive 'great harm might be done, especially in America'.[64] He added that the best solution would be if Comert and his colleagues could 'establish such relations by personal contact with League of Nations organizations in the various countries as they may find possible'.[65]

Accordingly, Comert decided that correspondence with private collaborators should be 'unofficial', to avoid causing political problems for the League.[66] Although he made clear that they would have to be made official at some point, the initial secrecy meant many of the earliest lines of communication of the section set-up remain invisible.

The 'division of labor' strategy tackled two of the central tensions of the section that we discussed in the book's introduction: The tension as to what authority the League could claim diminished when League agency shifted to private collaborators. The League simply provided information, officially not interfering in how it was used. Neither could the section be labelled a propagandist. The easing of these two tensions came, however, at the expense of the League's audience. 'International public opinion' shrunk to meaning simply national elites.

The most intimate example of 'cooperative publicity' was the one pursued through League of Nations Unions and their federation, the International Federation of League of Nations Societies. With large memberships in Western countries like Britain and France, the landscape of such pro-League groups reflected the distribution of power in the League itself. The British League of Nations Union, with 650,000 members in 1928, was the largest single organization in the British peace movement. Helen McCarthy described its first executive committee as 'an eclectic line-up of politicians, journalists and intellectuals', yet it developed into a 'mass membership pressure group campaigning on international affairs'.[67] The French umbrella organization Association Française pour la Société des Nations organized 750,000 French peace activists.[68] Such societies emerged in almost all European countries and the United States, notably the British and French unions, the League of Nations Non-Partisan Association (US), the Associazzione Italiana per la Societá delle Nazione (IT) and so on.[69] They published journals, hosted events and organized public demonstrations in support for the League and its work. Some were controlled more or less directly by governments, but most were independent associations organizing private internationalist-minded citizens.[70]

Although the League appreciated these groups, the relationship could turn complicated. On the one hand, officials of the Information Section considered them useful for their spreading of more forceful propaganda than what the League could sponsor. On the other hand, they were difficult to control, and their actions sometimes reflected poorly on the League or even directed public attention to issues the League was unable or unwilling to address. For example, in early 1920 a furious representative of an India-based religious organization, the Universal Khuddamul Ka'aba, complained to the Information Section that a film about the Armenian genocide was marketed by the British League of Nations Union as a 'League of Nations-film'. In a letter, George Mair of the Information Section urged the secretary general to find some 'informal way' of letting the LNU know that such events were not helpful to the League.[71]

Mostly, the advantages of having relations with League of Nations associations outweighed the disadvantages. In November 1919 Comert reported from Brussels to his colleagues in the Secretariat that a number of national associations had come together there and founded the International Federation for League of Nations Societies (IFLNS), an organization labelled by Thomas R. Davies: 'the leading non-governmental organization for the promotion of peace between the world wars'.[72] Comert persuaded the Secretariat to appoint Christian Lange, the Norwegian secretary general of the Interparliamentary Union to act as the federation's 'guiding spirit'.[73] This seemed to mean that Lange should help the League steer the federation along pragmatic lines so that it did not become a liability to the League. Two years later, the IFLNS boasted member associations from twenty-four countries and had elected the French Théodore Ruyssen as secretary general.[74] At about this time, Comert circulated a confidential memo to the high officials in which he proposed to centralize all the Secretariat's dealings with the federation 'in a single office'.[75] Comert appointed the Lithuanian princess Gabriele Radziwill for this job. Radziwill had been hired into the Information Section the year before because when, following meetings between Eric Drummond and the British Women's Council in April 1919, the secretary general wrote to Monnet that he was convinced 'it would be very wise to secure a good woman on the Publicity Section [sic] through whom we can get in touch, for purposes of propaganda, with various women's organizations'.[76] Comert therefore went on and hired Radziwill – the 'good woman' – five months later. The job required her to attend meetings and congresses of these associations and keep them 'informed about the work of the League'.[77]

Comert's 1926 evaluation of Radziwill's job performance gives interesting insights into the versatility of Information Section officials. The director noted that Radziwill was in charge of liaison with Lithuania, that she read the German, Russian, Estonian and Lithuanian press for the section's press review and liaised with forty different women's rights organizations as well as with the IFLNS.[78] In 1931, a Spanish official, José Plà, would later take over the liaison after her.[79]

The position required her to attend IFLNS congresses, so that the section could prevent 'tendencies too radical or extremist'.[80] For example, Radziwill attended the 1924 plenary assembly in Lyon, accompanied by Comert and 'several other members' of the section.[81] The section deemed that attending such meetings enabled it to get an impression of public opinion in the member states – a conviction that once again demonstrated an elite-oriented idea of public opinion and, certainly, a biased one towards members of the public who already supported the League. Radziwill reported on the quality of the national delegations, whether there were disagreements between them, and to what extent they put forth realistic proposals. For example in 1926, she wrote: 'the delegates did seem to have [. . .] a better sense of proportion than usual and showed more moderation.'[82]

Radziwill also brought the IFLNS to Geneva when she facilitated the federation's League-themed summer school in the city, and welcomed representatives of the federation at the League buildings starting from 1921 when a delegation visited the Secretariat.⁸³ Officials took great pains to spend time with their collaborators, push them in desirable directions and report on their activities to the Secretariat. Radziwill, by all indications a very competent official, would later, unusually for a female official, be elevated to the rank of 'member of section' in the Social Questions Section.⁸⁴ The IFLNS, in turn, eventually felt a special connection to the Secretariat.⁸⁵ The Information Section thus tried to embed itself in an international network of private pressure groups, whose oversight it partly took upon itself and utilized as a network providing information on what it considered an informative window to public opinion. Delegating propaganda activities to the IFLNS and its component associations enabled the section to protect its own neutrality while still working actively to create and maintain an international public opinion (Figure 7).

The section nurtured other private 'collaborators' besides the dedicated pro-League groups. Women's rights organizations, meaning national or international associations or interest groups promoting women' rights within various fields, often connected women's rights to internationalism by envisioning a key role for women in a new world order, characterized by peaceful cooperation.⁸⁶ The League's engagement with such groups ran along many avenues to promote political and social rights for women.⁸⁷ In the Information Section, plans for

Figure 7 A group of students at the League summer school, organized by the IFLS visiting the Secretariat in 1922.

United Nations Archives, Geneva.

collaboration with such organizations began very early. In fact, they were likely to have been the first such liaison endeavour asides from that with national League of Nations Unions, a fact that probably parallels many League officials' determination (only partly successful) to make the League a mainstay in equal gender representation.[88] Radziwill, who, as we have seen, was the section's main responsible for liaison with women's groups, was assisted by Mary McGeachy (appointed 1928), a Canadian who became increasingly involved in this work after 1930.[89] McGeachy would later serve as inspiration for the protagonist in the 'Edith-trilogy', a successful dramatic novel about life at the League headquarters by Frank Moorhouse.[90]

On top of these major endeavours, officials of the Information Section were charged with a diverse set of 'liaisons' with different organizations on top of their activities regarding their home audiences (the public in their own home countries) and with other sections or League auxiliary organizations. For example Adrianus Pelt, liaised with the International Union for Radio Broadcasting, attended its meetings and in 1929 was inspired to suggest to Comert the establishment of a radio service in the Information Section – a scheme which was realized in 1932, and which would lay the ground for Pelt's future emphasis on new technology as the mainstay of information work.[91] Konni Zilliacus (later a well-known British parliamentarian) took charge of liaison with the Labour and Socialist International (LSI) formed in 1923.[92] Comert, who was among the left-leaning members of the Secretariat, defended Zilliacus's work from other directors who criticized the League fraternizing with a socialist organization.[93]

The section spent considerable energy on veterans' associations, particularly the French and the British, whose irreproachable position as part of the postwar legacy made them excellent promoters of the League's ideals.[94] They were, wrote the section, 'extremely valuable instruments of propaganda'.[95] Other valued friends, although in a different way, were American philanthropic foundations such as the Rockefeller Foundation and the Carnegie Endowment of International Peace, which were supportive of the League. As we shall see, Arthur Sweetser secured substantial fundraising via such connections for the League's activities.[96]

However, the section's efforts did not exclusively go through associations but through individuals too. In 1925, the Information Section asked the Assembly's permission to invite a group of people to Geneva and stay for a few weeks in the Secretariat on a learning scholarship. The resulting annual programme was emblematic of its wish to become a kind of hub between the Secretariat and national pro-League elites. The so-called temporary collaborators were men, and a smaller number of women, whom the section wanted to educate about the workings of the League. The section acted as their employer and paid them a small monthly grant. Throughout the programme's existence, the Spanish official José Plà was in charge of asking his colleagues each year to assist him, using their respective national networks of liaison, in picking suitable candidates.[97]

The collaborators did not actually work in the section but observed the League in business. The Secretariat underscored that while 'all possible assistance is given to them they are left absolutely free to come to their own conclusions'.[98] However, the aim was clearly to have them return to their home countries and speak its cause.[99] They were initially invited twice a year – first to stay during a 'normal' period and then to return and attend the Assembly. Later, most were invited to stay just during the Assembly. During the first year, 1926, the budget was 20,000 Swiss francs for which Plà invited eight people, seven men and one woman, from eight different countries. They were exclusively journalists and writers and came from countries not already represented in the section.[100] These early invitations reflected Comert's preference for the press as the most important conveyors of the League's message, combined with the ambition to broaden the geographical scope of the interaction with public opinion. Starting from 1928 the selection came to include schoolteachers and university students in addition to professors and journalists.[101] This signified a broadening of the understanding of what was to include in public opinion. The inclusion of schoolteachers and students signalled investment in the future of the educated part of the population. The selection continued to grow until 1931, when its allowance peaked at 50,000 Swiss francs.[102] That year, at least forty-nine persons were invited from thirty-six different countries.[103] Two or three spots were reserved for women, who were invited from women's rights associations at the recommendation of Radziwill. In general, officials specialized in reaching out to various groups, so that for example Adrianus Pelt usually recommended people from broadcasting organizations, Konni Zilliacus from socialist groups and so on.

To the officials themselves, this relatively modest programme was a show horse of the section's struggle for an open diplomacy. They strived to grant the collaborators the necessary credentials to attend most meetings of the League, even some that were closed to the general public.[104] In 1926, officials reported that the arrangement had 'fostered great results' and that the knowledge the visitors brought home with them 'allows them to dispel prejudices or errors which often result from ignorance'.[105]

This implication that hostility to the League resulted from ignorance about it was symptomatic of the general attitude of many internationalists at the time. Education, it was assumed, was the cure for most ills. The paradox emerges when one reflects on the audience addressed. The public addressed through the temporary collaborators was not any public. Collaborators would take part in the public debate on the League in their home countries, or they would spread knowledge of the organization in clubs, associations, over dinner tables or in government circles. The Secretariat wrote in 1930 that the collaborators were 'usually people in key positions'.[106] Why would one assume that educated people were ignorant about the fundamental workings of the League?[107]

The use of the system of temporary collaborators was a pillar in the section's presentation of itself as a centre of world information whose liaisons with private associations, interest groups, educational institutions and governments spread far and wide. There was also an idea of equal national representation in it. Referring to countries that were least represented among the officials of the Secretariat, José Plà remarked that it enabled the League to 'arouse, or increase, the interest of public opinion in those countries in the work of the League'.[108] He concluded: 'it is a system which the Information Section should try to keep up and develop at all costs.'[109]

Would-be diplomats

With the idea of an intimate connection between the League and the public and fluid boundaries between the 'broad' public and a more exclusive one it was unsurprising that diplomacy crept into the *raison d'être* of the Information Section, often under the label 'political liaison'. At times, the Information Section became a competitor of the Political Section – the department that supported and informed diplomatic negotiations in the Council and the Assembly. For example, some information officials corresponded with members of governmental circles to provide more smooth relations with the Secretariat, to secure confidential information through informal channels or to coordinate public relations favourable to League programmes.

Such genuinely diplomatic tasks were not formalized as belonging to the Information Section, but they nonetheless occurred and arguably played an important role in the section's self-image. Liaison with one's own home government was encouraged (to some degree) from all officials of the Secretariat.[110] As Gram-Skjoldager and Ikonomou have argued, liaison between officials and their home governments was pursued 'not just to gain access and legitimacy but also in order to keep the Secretariat itself from becoming insular'.[111] The Information Section, together with the Political Section, was utilized to perform 'less spectacular missions' than those demanding the involvement of the secretary general.[112] The line between such diplomatic endeavours and the mission of the Information Section of legitimizing the League could be difficult to draw.

Political liaison was hinted at in the earliest drafts for the section in 1919. George Mair's planning memo-draft included an 'intelligence section' which should have an office of 'mainly a secret service-character' with the purpose of removing 'causes of friction within the League'.[113] Although this phrasing was unusual, it is clear Comert and Sweetser imagined the section as a supplementary diplomatic agency of the Secretariat in competition with its Political Section. Scholarship has shed light on some examples. For example, Adrianus Pelt went to coordinate propaganda directly with the Austrian government to bolster the League's scheme of financial reconstruction in Austria.[114] We have also heard of Comert acting as Drummond's main contact 'with Paris and the Quai d'Orsay' after Jean Monnet left the Secretariat early and since Drummond disliked his then-second-in-command, Joseph Avenol.[115]

Of special significance was Arthur Sweetser, and his activities in the United States. Sweetser built close relations to journalists, writers, public intellectuals, civil servants and politicians and to numerous associations such as the World Peace Foundation.[116] He was a close friend of Raymond Fosdick, the League's short-lived undersecretary-general, who was an enthusiastic proponent of American League membership long after his exit from the Secretariat in 1919. The two men worked together in enthusing the American public about the League. Fosdick founded a 'League of Nations News Bureau' (later the League of Nations Non-Partisan Association) an American pro-League group which took advantage of its relations to the Secretariat through Sweetser.[117] Fosdick introduced Sweetser to John D. Rockefeller Jr. who would go on to donate two million dollars to equip and furnish the League's library in 1927. A happy Comert wrote in a confidential evaluation in 1928 that that donation 'was largely due to [Sweetser's] efforts',[118] noting that Sweetser's relations to important Americans had a bearing on 'large American contributions to League funds'. He added (Figure 8):

> [Sweetser] has a special position in the Secretariat. As an American he is in close relation with the State Department in the United States, with the leading American organizations and personalities at home and abroad and is, in fact, the main personal connecting link, not only between the Secretariat and America, but with the League of Nations and America, both officially and unofficially.[119]

Figure 8 Arthur Sweetser, assistant director of the Information Section 1919–32, director 1933 and independent director of the Secretariat 1934–40.
United Nations Archives, Geneva.

Fosdick and Sweetser, together with members of the Information Section, launched a campaign in American media following the death of Woodrow Wilson in 1924. Fosdick had spoken to the president on his deathbed and reported that Wilson had had a religiously worded epiphany about the League's mission to humanity. The two men took it upon them to feed this endorsement systematically to the American press, not signed with their own names but in the form of news-quotes by anonymous 'friends' in the League Secretariat.[120]

Sweetser, in other words, was half diplomat half information official. His special role probably owed much to the fact that the United States was not a member of the League and therefore had no official diplomatic channels to it. His regular travels among American journalists, politicians and businesspeople made him a valuable link between the Secretariat and the State Department that was unresponsive to official League communications. Madeleine Herren and Isabella Löhr first theorized on Sweetser's unique role as a 'media diplomat'. They also demonstrated how he was involved in a scandal in 1933, when his talks with US secretary of state Cordell Hull about setting up an American permanent representation in Geneva were exposed in the press, and the plan had to be dropped.[121] His promotion in 1930 from member of the section to 'counsellor' (an honorary position and not a paid one), then acting director in 1933 and finally director without section goes to show that at some point there had to be a limit to what an information official could do.[122] As Sweetser stated himself in 1930: 'After all, it is a bit anomalous for a member of the Information Section to be negotiating the Library, seeing Mr. Stimson on the Court, being active in disarmament etc.'[123] Although Sweetser represented an anomaly, the character of the section as a semi-diplomatic agency was something Comert actively strived for.

Conclusion

The Information Section assumed its most proactive and empowered role during the second half of the 1920s, when it supplemented its ambitious press relations in Geneva with an attempt in 1927 to establish itself as an international mobilizer of the press in the cause of peace through its International Conference of Press Experts. Simultaneously, its officials worked to facilitate 'cooperative publicity', a division of labour between the neutral League Secretariat and pro-League groups and individuals, whom it encouraged to propagate the League on its behalf while it guarded its own neutral role. Although in some ways unfulfilled, these efforts point to the question (one this book does not attempt to systematically answer) of the impact of the League's information efforts. The League was not just disseminating information – it was attempting to make itself a stakeholder in the rising information infrastructure of the twentieth century. This meant its impact may be hard to measure in terms of the concrete diplomatic aims it achieved. The Information provided and received legitimacy through its liaison with international news agencies, journalist unions and private international interest groups. As Carolyn Biltof has put it: 'the realist critique [of the League's lack of achievements] had missed [. . .] that immaterial signs and material reality had become coconstitutive in new ways through the intermingling of media, markets, and power politics'.[124]

These indirect strategies fed into and helped to construct a highly elitist identification of the public, focusing as it did on people of political influence, cultural standing and educations, just as it identified public opinion as encompassing largely people who were from the outset sympathetic to the League.

The emergence of this strategy, or set of strategies, must be understood in light of the strict supervision and control that was imposed on the section from above. Pierre Comert and Arthur Sweetser, together with George Mair and creative lieutenants like Gabriele Radziwill, developed its strategies in response to the 'taboo of propaganda' in the section. They built a section that tried constantly to wipe out its footsteps and operate 'under the radar'. It strove to use unofficial communication, and at times even semi-diplomatic activities, to compensate for its lack of muscle in terms of propaganda and its dogma of neutrality. Presenting itself as something 'more than a press bureau', it sought to tackle its inherent tensions by emphasizing indirect discreet communication.

3

Confidence and cynicism

League public information material, 1919–32

Officials of the Information Section were the authors of the League's public narrative of the world and of its own role in it. Cautious on the one hand of a 'taboo' not to make propaganda and empowered on the other hand by a large staff and ambitious leadership, they spoke to the public through the news and information material they published. How did they propagate the League and its values, when they could not advertise political ideas that might divide governments?

In this chapter, we take a closer look at the legitimization strategies visible in the publications of the section. Tracing the tropes, arguments and suggestions of the League's publications, the chapter sketches the species of internationalism the League projected. Considering their composition, omissions and foci as 'speech acts' to legitimize the organization, it describes a discursive development throughout the League's first thirteen years. From an enthusiastic language of 'action' and 'moral authority' in 1921 to a more confident one at the end of the decade, when Germany's entry into the League and the Locarno agreements meant that the League could start to utilize what was being said about it by statesmen and admirers instead of writing these things itself. By the turn of the decade there started to emerge also the outlines of doubt among officials as to the exact nature of public opinion and the early outlines of what has been called the League's 'reinvention' of itself after the economic crises of 1929–32, when its 'technical' work started to take centre stage in its work.[1]

It should be kept in mind that the section did not explicitly have such things as strategies: The only strategy it admitted to was one of informing the public in a neutral language. Nonetheless, it published news and information material for the press and the public to supplement the official documents released daily by the Secretariat, and thus it may be assumed to have strategized on how to put that opportunity to the best use. Publishing news and information required the section to address its inherent tensions: Balancing neutrality and the promotion of internationalism became more challenging as member states came into conflict with one another. One way of circumventing this challenge and deflect accusations of propaganda was to make strict 'officialdom' a legitimization strategy in itself. The result was that its publications became characterized by constant observance of a dogma of neutrality.

Publications of the Information Section

The League disseminated information material and news in a wide variety of ways throughout the League's lifetime. Publications and documents of the Secretariat were for sale (a substantial source of income, although most revenue came from sales of official documents and reports not produced by the Information Section), facilitated by the League's Sales Department and sales agents in member states.[2] The section also distributed documents to journalists and as part of liaison activities like those discussed in the previous chapter.[3] The extent of this distribution is difficult to trace in detail, but we know that in 1922 more than 80 per cent of all sales took place in Great Britain and the United States.[4] In 1936 the publics that bought the most were from the United States, the UK, Switzerland, Germany, Japan, France and Italy.[5] All publications were published in the League's two official languages, English and French, while some of the more popular came out in Italian, Spanish, German and Czech.[6]

Data illustrating the sales and distribution numbers of individual publications are not available. Some isolated figures suggest a relatively limited distribution of even the more popular publications. For example, about 20,000 of the *Monthly Summary*, which was among the Information Section's most popular publications, were printed in 1928.[7] Table 2 is the share of the section in the League's overall publication activities between 1931 and 1939 – this is simply to provide some wider context in which to understand the period 1920–30 for which unfortunately no consistent data can be found:

As will be seen in the next chapter (in which we shall also take a brief look at films and broadcasting taken on by the section), the section was dramatically reduced after 1933. However, this development is remarkably invisible in the number of publications published by it, in actual numbers as well as in relative share. This remarkable stability suggests that publications constituted a sort of 'base line' among the functions of the section – an uncontroversial activity which could continue despite the ups and downs of the section's status. A comparison

Table 2 Share of the Information Section in the League's Overall Publication Activities between 1931 and 1939

Year	Copies printed, Inf. Section	Copies printed, L.O.N total	%	Cost (Swiss francs) Inf. Section	Cost (Swiss francs) L.O.N total	%
1931	223,860	1,673,464	**13.38**	9,200,755	133,210,040	**6.90**
1932	214,840	2,951,263	**7.28**	9,290,585	130,447,503	**7.12**
1933	221,813	1,507,443	**14.71**	749,082	90,361,926	**8.29**
1934	297,183	935,775	**22.14**	64,490,25	63,650,895	**10.13**
1935	207,770	1,058,031	**19.64**	75,622,25	71,592,210	**10.56**
1936	205,522	1,104,879	**18.60**	81,325,45	749,192	**10.86**
1937	380,151	139,5078	**27.25**	84,132,4	79,569,395	**10.57**
1938	380,241	1,307,954	**29.07**	87,757,85	80,604,655	**10.89**
1939	291,040	1,045,397	**27.84**	7,220,595	58,122,040	**12.42**

Reports by the Publications Committee to the Supervisory Commission 1932–9 (figures for 1931 included in the 1932 report and 1934 report mistakenly marked with 1935): Publications Committee (PC), 'Publications éditées et réimprimées par la Société des Nations', 1932, 3127, R5525; 1933, 10453, R5525; 1935 (1934), 16406, R5525; 1935, 23454, R5525; 1936, 27263, R5525; 1937, 32612, R5525; 1938, 36753, R5525; 1939, 40225, R5525.

to the general development in sales revenue of League publications which, as demonstrated by Hannah Tyler, decreased slightly after 1932, adds further to this interesting stability of the Information Section's activity.[8] Ranshofen-Wertheimer observed that it was 'remarkable that in spite of the decrease of interest in the activities of the League in the thirties, in many countries the sales receipts were maintained at a higher level than in the late twenties, thanks to the special efforts made by the Publications Department'.[9]

The Information Section, as mentioned previously, provided daily communiqués for journalists, and these are discussed in this chapter in conjunction with a selection of information material – detailed publications aimed at the public rather than the press. The category of information material included books, booklets, pamphlets, the *Summary* and photo collections.

Target audiences

The target of all this material was 'public opinion'.[10] What did this mean more specifically? As we know, the Information Section did not really discuss the identity of this public in depth. It distinguished between *news* and, *information*, separately as well as between material 'for official use' and material 'for information purposes', but the different types of material were developed in conjunction with each other, the longer types of communiqués '(explanatory articles)' constituting the raw material for the *Monthly Summary (Summary*, henceforth), sections of which would at times be reproduced in books and pamphlets. They were often almost indistinguishable in their formal, official language.

Although most publications give an impression of targeting specialized and educated readers the section underlined that as opposed to the official documents of the League, the material of the Information Section were for a 'wider public'. The *Summary* targeted 'those who are interested' and specified this to mean 'delegates of the Assembly, members of various commissions, publicists, teachers, students'.[11] The Secretariat sent the *Summary* to 'Foreign Ministries, League of Nations Societies as well as universities and libraries'.[12] This demonstrated once again a consistently elitist conception of the public. The audience was not limited to people directly associated with the League or already highly specialized in its work, but it was certainly limited to educated people. The vague nature of the audience is tied closely to the fact that there can be found little or no systematic attempts by Secretariat officials to measure the impact or reception of their information material, whether we talk of printed material, or later films or broadcasting. Working through the Secretariat archives one finds passing mentions, such as a late 1930s comment in an internal report that there were 'complaints' that the *Monthly Summary*'s style was 'somewhat severe'.[13] But opinion polls only came into use at the end of the League's existence, and the section seemed to have left the evaluation up their efforts to friends and 'collaborators', whose anecdotal analyses sometimes, but quite seldom, came to the surface in various internal dossiers.

This chapter and Chapter 5 recount an organic development of strategies that have been inferred from the material the League released for the public. These should not be considered a series of entirely separate strategies (neither of two entirely distinct periods) replacing each other. Instead, they cumulated, and when some faded out others stayed at the forefront throughout the League's lifetime. In short, few disappeared altogether after having once appeared, but the balance of emphasis shifted between them and taken together they convey a story of how the section navigated the changing political tides of international politics and the shifting conditions within the Secretariat to legitimize the League.

Four strategies, 1919–33

What did one see when opening a *Monthly Summary* or a League information pamphlet or glancing at a news communiqué? Nothing very exciting. Mostly, space was given to summaries of negotiations between states, declarations of trust in this or that conference or Assembly, of lists of contributors to the League and official communications by member states. Neutrality and the provision of 'factual information' were front and centre in the Information Section's sense of mission throughout its existence. The narrative was clear: Just like a national civil service, the League Secretariat was a guarantor of trustworthiness, for everyone who wanted to understand what went on at the international stage. The dogma was informed by the 'taboo' of propaganda. Thus, the style of cool, bureaucratic discourse was one of the means used by section to legitimize the novel international authority. A glance at one of the section's few longer reflections on the League's relation to public opinion, a ten-year anniversary book for the League released in 1930, is an example of its own expression of this dogma:

> There is much that the League Secretariat can do but at no times can it be a propagandist. [. . .] No one who wishes to be considered informed on international affairs can afford to be ignorant of the League, and no one who wants the information need fail to get it. But to propagate support of particular theories in the League [. . .] is not part of the organized duty of the League.[14]

With this language of duty, the section elevated itself above opinion and polemic. In the foreword of the same book, the secretary general, stated that the book was not 'history' but 'a statement of facts'. Indeed it was 'not even the raw material of history' since that, he underlined, could be found in the *official* publications of the League.[15] The book was nonetheless intended for 'the student' or 'the historian', and if at this point the reader surmised that it was a piece of opinion Drummond added to the confusion by calling it 'if not strictly an official document by any rate a document produced under the limitations by which the official is hedged'.[16]

He added that he did not regret these rigid constraints laid on himself and his staff because he felt greater historical distance to the League was needed before its significance could be judged. However, the book clearly showed that the Secretariat and the Information Section considered themselves the first communicators of the intricacies of diplomacy, as Comert had imagined in 1921 when he wrote about a future diplomacy whose main task it would be to inform the public.[17] The first thing the public must learn was the absolute importance of neutrality and the complete abstention from taking sides. The pages of the *Summary* served as an example. In a 1937 report on the Information Section (referred to earlier), the section defended its dry style and almost conceded that it was deliberate: 'It is difficult to remedy this; For a greater freedom in style or in the subjects treated would remove this review from its position as a succinct but rigorously correct account of the League's work.'[18]

The Secretariat took great care in making this dogma of neutrality work for it. It resulted in a body of publications that contain almost no normative language, or ideology. As Comert wrote to Sweetser when updating the latter during his health-related leave of absence in 1924, 'our communiqués are more boring than ever'.[19] But this did not prevent the Information Section from pursuing a set of clearly identifiable strategies in its communiqués, periodical publications, books, booklets, pamphlets and films. The four most prominent of the League's first thirteen years are discussed in the following.

Action and progress

In the spring of 1919 Sweetser reflected in a memo that during its first years the League would have to make sure to release a regular 'flow of actual news' which should 'carry a continued suggestion to the public mind and should demonstrate beyond dispute that the League has a supreme part to play in human affairs'.[20] The organization was in its infancy, and after the first weeks no longer automatically newsworthy. No substantial League outlets or periodical publications had been developed yet, and the focus of officials was therefore on communiqués and on the preparation of their first informative project, the *Monthly Summary*. What characterized these earliest publications was a tendency to be a bit more aggressive in promoting the organization than what would later be the case. The section dared to bet on the necessity of breaking into the news stream and assume a voice on behalf of the League. The point was to underscore that the League was not resting on its laurels in the immediate crisis-ridden postwar world, and that despite the initial setback of the United States not joining, this was not a stillborn institution.

The section released its first communiqués after the ratification of the Versailles Treaty in January 1920. New conflicts threatened to emerge in several parts of Europe due to unresolved issues produced by the war. The questions of the control over the city of Danzig (Germany or Poland), the Saar Valley (Germany or France), Fiume (Italy or Yugoslavia) and Vilna (Poland or Lithuania) were just some of the immediate issues facing the League. The public perception of the project was threatened from the very beginning because of its association with a treaty that was regarded by many British and American observers as excessively punitive towards the defeated German Empire. The United States withdrawal and the initial refusal of France to allow German membership exposed it to accusations of being a peacetime continuation of the victorious alliance, the Entente. The continued Allied economic blockade or what Nicholas Mulder recently described as a 'chokehold of deprivation' on the defeated Central Powers contributed to this feeling of ongoing war which led to a crisis of trust in the League.[21] In this political atmosphere the public utterances of the organization were assumed by the Secretariat to be of towering importance, and, as we know, the secretary general kept close watch on the Information Section. In its earliest communiqués one notices the section's keen awareness that they were the most immediate means the League had of defending itself, stating its presence in international life and clarifying mistakes. The very first one, released on 28 December 1920, said:

> Contrary to a telegram by the Wolf News Agency on December 27th, the Council of the League of Nations proceeds to execute its decision relative to the organization of a popular consultation in the contested territories of Vilna.[22]

The section was keenly aware not only of the stakes if its communiqués were unclear but also of their potential to counter false information in the press. In this situation, it needed to underline that the League was pursuing a clear policy (the decision made by the Council). It underscored the vitality and willingness to act of the League: that it did not hesitate to involve itself in a conflict between two governments. The configuration of the uncertainty as to whether the League was a 'super state' of some kind or a neutral framework for diplomacy was in play here. During this unstable period in European politics, the League must give the impression of action without alienating its members. In the earliest *Summaries* we find a similar message to that seen in communiqué. The section warned in April 1921 that it was 'hard to imagine a more difficult task than that of keeping public opinion, in 48 different States [...] in touch with the many lines of activity upon which the League has embarked'.[23] A strong focus on 'progress', 'advancement' and other nouns suggesting that the League was moving forward, that it was not idle, was seen during the first year when the *Summary* was organized into headings such as 'political questions', 'social questions' etc. This arguably contributed to a relocating of some areas of League activities as political and others as not, implicitly arguing that some of the League's work could be pursued entirely outside the dangerous waters of politics.[24] The October issue of 1921 stated: 'Practically every activity entered into by the League of Nations' in the month of September was 'appreciably advanced'.[25] In the final issue of 1921 it was noted on the area of minorities protection that 'action has been taken in several parts of Europe' and that 'a considerable number of decisions' had been made in regard to potential amendments to the Covenant. In the October issue which included a detailed list of numbers of repatriated prisoners of war and cited Fritiof Nansen, the League's High Commissioner for a number of humanitarian issues. Nansen stated: 'This is indeed international work [. . .] it demonstrates that the League is an international machine which can be used for the carrying out of complicated executive duties for which the cooperation of a large number of governments is essential.'[26]

Many of the tasks laid upon the League outside traditional diplomacy had initially not been considered important parts of its work. The League's slow-working and hierarchical setup was not predestined to spawn an organization that legitimized itself with references to 'questions of international concern' like economics and humanitarian problems. Nonetheless, the 1921 December summary did just that.[27] Perhaps, this was the first hint, as Patricia Clavin has argued, of the Secretariat 'reinventing itself' by making the case that it was outside the realm of strict peacekeeping the League would see its noticeable successes.[28] More than anything else, it was part of an effort to legitimize the League by pointing to the abundance of tasks the world was laying on it.

In the December issue, the secretary general's recent visit to Rome took up five pages out of the *Summary*'s twenty-one pages, largely taken up by Drummond's official statement to Italian journalists (notably at a time of political turmoil in Italy, only a small year before the partial fascist takeover of power in 1922). Drummond explained that the League was not the instrument of 'one Power or a Group of Powers' and that it did not require 'any surrender of national spirit or feeling'. He asserted the League might very well have prevented the Great War had it been in place, and he urged the journalists to 'explain the principles [. . .] and the work it has been doing. The League can certainly now afford to be judged by its accomplishments.'[29] He mentioned four cases of the League working to settle territorial disputes between states. His treatment of these exemplified the League's ambivalent stance when addressing these questions. He admitted several points on which the League had been able to do only little. He conceded that the League was not omnipotent but that it was *trying* with all its force to carry the burdens laid on it. To Drummond, the important thing was that the League was doing its best and so to indicate that accusations of inadequacy would have to be aimed elsewhere.

The focus on the League's eagerness to serve and broad range of tasks was not exclusive to its news material. *La Société des Nations – son activité par l'image* from

1921 was the Information Section's earliest piece of broadly aimed information material. This photo collection showed an idyllic coloured front page of Geneva and filled with pictures showing League buildings, prominent delegates, experts and officials, sites from Geneva, maps of various territories under its responsibility as well as important treaty-signing sessions and pictures of documents upon ratification. The book was officially authored by the Second Assembly of the League and commemorated this event, but the Information Section prepared it.[30] Its narrative was one of an organic process of world collaboration directed by responsible European men. Nowhere in the book was its audience specified, but its layout and its language and style were elegant but simple, indicating that this was an attempt at reaching what the section considered the 'general public'. It told the story of how the world, for the first time, was coming together and making problems from all over the world everyone's problem. A central theme was demonstrating the zeal with which the League worked to establish itself quickly for the inauguration of international life. It recounted how work had gone on 'day and night' to transform the old Genevan Hotel National to suitable Secretariat headquarters, and the accompanying image showed a construction site only two weeks before the opening of the First Assembly.[31]

Another related theme in the booklet was the degree to which the League engaged itself in issues outside the scope of traditional diplomacy. Establishing that the League worked with problems of a political, an economical and a social nature, the book provided many pictures depicting the mandated territories, whose exoticism from a Western perspective made them exciting illustrations, one for example, of the skyline in Baghdad, belonging to the British mandate over Iraq. A chapter explained how a 'genuinely efficient collaboration' between the League, the Red Cross and the Polish government had put a stop to an aggressive typhus epidemic in Poland.[32] It argued the necessity of the League in terms of combating problems beyond the reach of national agency. It consistently underlined that the League had a perfect judicial mandate for such work: 'under the terms of the Covenant, work of humanitarian interest falls under the domain of the League of Nations.'[33]

This 'continuous flow of news' served to prove that the League was not idle remained a strategy of the section during the League's first decade. After the first half of the 1920s language that openly celebrated 'action' or 'progress' became rarer increasingly, leaving the League's achievements to speak for themselves. In many ways, this could be said to be a predictable development, since the organization needed less introduction as its procedures became gradually more well-known. It was also in accordance with Sweetser's proposal that this kind of use of League news should be exceptional to its early life. The strategy assumed a League that, to some extent, could act separately from governments and reproduced an idea of an observant public which was holding the League accountable and whose support could not be taken for granted. This contrasted an idea that the public was 'already on the League's side' helping it control governments and the old diplomacy. In these earliest days, the public needed to be won over.

The moral force of public opinion

During the early 1920s, parallel to the narrative of action and progress, the Information Section presented the League as an institution which could not be ignored *morally* and that owed to the special mandate given it by public opinion. We return to the League's first communiqué which recounted official communications concerning the Polish-Lithuanian dispute about the city of Vilna. It explained that in its letter to Poland, the Council had demanded that the Poles guaranteed the integrity of the planned referendum by withdrawing its troops, because 'The League of Nations cannot sanction with its moral authority a referendum under conditions that do not give satisfying guarantees to all parties'.[34]

The Council's use of the word 'moral', and the section's vitiation of it, drew on the Wilsonian visions that had spawned the League. It reminded not only the Polish and Lithuanian governments but the public as well that the League was intended a universalist institution representing all humanity. Referring to a moral authority was an act of constitutive rhetoric. It forcefully constructed the League as something more than the sum of its parts, an independent institution, which spoke to governments as their moral conscience and guide. In the first issue of the April 1921 *Summary*, an indication was seen of how this authority connected to the public: 'The most general demand made upon the League of Nations by public opinion in all parts of the world has been for a clear, direct summary account of the various activities of the League as they progress from day to day'.[35]

This image of a public all over the world *demanding* information on everything the League had been doing worked to substantiate that the Secretariat was not imposing on the public and spending unnecessary funds to propagate the League. More importantly, it constituted an act of alliance building with the public, mobilized a language of democracy and representation and addressed the tension of the section concerning the League's audience. Suddenly, the

League was the voice of the public, and the governments its audience. The rhetorical construction of an alliance with the public was also seen in *La Société des Nations – son activité par l'image* from 1921. Here, the section made an effort of showing the degree to which people outside the realm of high politics engaged themselves in the work of the League as well as in its physical arrival in Geneva (the League moved from London to Geneva in 1921). One picture showed the iconic Mont Blanc Bridge in Geneva on the opening day of the Assembly. The bridge was densely crowded with people along the tracks of the tramline. The caption stated:

> This photography is a demonstration of the immense interest that the population of Geneva has taken in this great international event. [. . .] The public is amassed in front of the hotel that houses most of the important delegates. On the great Mont Blanc Bridge, which can be seen on the right, and all the way towards the Salle de la Réformation the crowd is also very dense.[36]

Below the paragraph 'Geneva in Celebration for the Assembly of the League of Nations' the League visualized the public in its most concrete shape: citizens in the streets of Geneva. The reader could see the masses cheering and welcoming the organization.[37] If this was an appeal to the support of common citizens another part of the book showed a different layer of the public – the private organizations in favour of the League. A photo depicted a large group of members of the British League of Nations Union in the garden of the ILO. The photo was taken on the occasion of the union meeting unofficially in Geneva in August 1921, during which a reception was held 'in their honor' in the headquarters of the ILO.[38] The photo left an impression that balanced the grave, solemn seriousness of statesmen in other parts of the book with the looser atmosphere on the image of 'Geneva in Celebration'. In the picture (on which there were six women out of about seventy people) some were crouching or lying on the grass, and a few were holding wine glasses or a cigarette. Here the League communicated its devotion to those members of the public who supported it actively. Little distinction seemed to be made between the masses celebrating the League in the streets and the more distinguished company in the garden of the ILO. Both constituted 'the public'. The LNU crowd in the garden resonated well with the importance Pierre Comert's Information Section attributed to members of private pro-League organizations as harbingers of League support, particularly in this earliest period.

After this, there was one group left to which the section could be expected to address itself: its closest collaborators, the press. A large group photo showed representatives of the foreign press in Geneva during the Second Assembly. The photo had been taken during an excursion outside Geneva arranged again 'in their honor'. The host was the Association of League of Nations journalists, with whom we know the section had close interactions.

The book made three rhetorical gestures of gratitude to the public that corresponded to its three basic channels of communication: One went directly to the 'man in the street', one went through the private organizations in favour of the League and one went through the press. Depicting exciting common citizens in celebration of the League and journalists and well-wishers sharing a toast on its premises, the point was made that the public was the organization's lifeblood and portrayed it as a visible thing: a community in which the League was engaged and which, conversely, it empowered.

To what extent did this explicit way of constructing public support for the League persist? The answer is complicated. Of course, public opinion was a powerful concept with real meaning to the most devoted supporters of the League right until the end of its existence. But what exactly was meant by the public, and what power the Information Section attributed to it changed. In the earliest years the appeal explicit and a good illustration can be seen in Sweetser's words in 'The League of Nations at Work' in 1920 that beside the question of the League's relation to the public all other questions were dwarfed. The 1928 publication *The League of Nations and the Press* stressed the importance of publicity and described a certain kind of 'common outlook' which could sometimes be discerned among the circles associated with the League's institutions, the result, supposedly, of the work of the Information Section.[39] But even here, as elsewhere when the public was invoked, an ambivalence could be observed. Around the end of the decade, there are some signs that League officials became more uncertain about the extent to which public opinion was an unequivocally good thing, or at least that they became more cynical. The abovementioned anniversary book, *Ten Years of World-Cooperation* (*Ten Years*, henceforth) from 1930, a lengthy analysis was devoted to public opinion, and here it was portrayed as less unequivocally benevolent than earlier. A few years having passed since the publication of Walter Lippman's seminal *Public Opinion* the realization expressed in that work as to the complex and fickle nature of public sentiment was suddenly visible in League material too.[40] The voice of the League, expressed by the Information Section in the book, described public opinion as expressing itself very much 'in black and white' and to remain largely compartmentalized in national spheres.[41] It even concluded that public opinion 'on an international scale must be conceived largely as a collection of national opinions reacting to some extent upon each other'.[42] That public opinion could thus reflect and enhance polarization was an extraordinary admission when compared to the Wilsonian point of departure that public opinion would rise up to demand solutions to international matters.

What relation to the public did that leave to the League? Addressing this problem in the book, the League faced its three foundational tensions: What was the League, who was its audience and how could it speak to it? The authors persisted consistently that the League was a neutral association of states and rejected that it could ever make propaganda – in one chapter, the latter was underlined no less than four times.[43] They conceded that although the prevention of war and the promotion of international cooperation were hardly controversial subjects the means of achieving such goals could be highly so, but they were adamant that they could never advocate League policy because, quite simply, there was no such thing.[44] The first and the second tension thus became interdependent because both concerned the purpose of the Information Section. A sequence in the chapter discussed the idea of a League news service. Here the authors explained, quite radically, that the League 'has not, and cannot have, a universal news service. It neither interprets news, nor, in the journalistic understanding of the term, transmits it'.[45] For a section that often referred to its own news service, this was surprising. But the officials probably did not see the inconsistency, since, as we see, they constantly emphasized that the League was not interpreting or analysing events – and thus was not making news in the newspaper sense of that word. What complicated the matter was that the section would furthermore insist in many of its publications that these were not *official* communications of the League. If they were not official, but not *unofficial* either their exact nature was unclear. Nonetheless, the new hesitance about attributing agency to international public opinion became cryptically epitomized in the book's conclusion that 'public opinion in all the nations of the League shares the responsibility for shortcomings and the credit for success. The League of Nations is the sum of public opinion'.[46]

The authors confronted the reader with a dilemma: If the League's authority was to be strengthened there were two not altogether compatible alternatives: public opinion must 'either be a driving force towards accomplishment or it must be persuaded of the equity of particular measures or accomplishments submitted to its judgment'.[47] The immediate point of this was that the public must either back the League as a whole or be convinced of its utility on a case-by-case basis. Yet, it also exposed the conundrum that the officials could hardly have been unaware of: Was the League mobilizing international public opinion, or was it communicating with an already existing international public opinion – and using it to legitimize the League towards governments?

It is clear that a change in the way the League imagined the public occurred between 1920 and 1930. From being a mysterious energy source fuelling the League, doubt was now cast on its exact nature and capabilities. Public opinion was still occasionally invoked, but it was compartmentalized into national spheres, and its internationalist leaning no longer taken for granted. The initial representation of the public as cheering crowds in the streets of Geneva reminded League statesmen that expectations were high, and the world was watching. Thus, while the appeal continued to exist by the end of the 1920s and early 1930s the coherency of the public and the degree to which it stood by the League was increasingly doubted by the section. The League's belief in the loyalty of the public had changed. Initially, the public was not actually a target of legitimization but a collaborator in the League project, but at the end of the decade the section began to doubt the power of the appeal, and became inclined to let others legitimize it on its behalf through an indirect appeal that may be called 'legitimization by proxy'. The growing realization by information officials that speaking assertively on behalf of the League was an awkward business happened, paradoxically, at a time when the League had been going through some of its most confident years. In the second half of the 1920s the changing political landscape of the League increased the section's room of manoeuvring. The League was approaching general acknowledgement among its members, and the discourse became subtly focused on showcasing this general acknowledgement: By the second half of the 1920s political stability seemed suddenly within reach in Europe. Following the Locarno agreements in late 1925 between Germany, France, Great Britain, Belgium and Italy; Germany joined the League in the fall of 1926 and was granted permanent membership of the Council. The organization expanded the stage for its international 'technical' agency by hosting a large International Economic Conference, the Secretariat grew steadily, and the Information Section grew with it.

The Information Section realized that at this point constantly articulating the League's vitality and willingness to act would appear overly defensive. The League and the section was gaining confidence and 'faded out' the subtle praise. Instead, it began systematically letting others praise it.

For example, in May 1927 the section paraphrased a speech by Georges Theunis, the Belgian president of the League's International Economic Conference that year. The gist of the quotation was a celebration of the League's hosting of such a conference and of its success, since, he declared, economic divergences between nations were among the gravest threats to peace.[48] In this way the section borrowed legitimacy from others when it could not express too strong ideological discourse itself. The section not only capitalized on political decision-makers: The September *Summary* of the same year reported the two million dollars donation that the League had accepted from John D. Rockefeller Jr. for a new League library. A telegram from Rockefeller was printed in the *Summary*:

> Happy to have opportunity to co-operate in so good a cause with a group un-selfishly devoted to the promotion of better understanding among nations. Appreciate profoundly the actions of Council, Assembly and Secretariat.[49]

The section was operationalizing the legitimacy of agents outside the Secretariat – often statesmen from national governments, to praise the League system. Still in 1927, the December *Summary* stated that an 'outstanding feature of the past year was the presence at Assembly and Council Meetings of a considerable number of Foreign Ministers'.[50] The participation of a high number of important politicians bolstered the League's authority. It was furthermore seen in the detailed recounting of the speeches of Theunis and Villegas at the Economic Conference praising the League's work and in the advertising of a film showing the historic German entrance into the League. In July, the deputy secretary general communicated to the Queen of Romania:

> the respectful sympathy which we feel for Rumania in her loss. The friendly feelings which His Majesty King Ferdinand showed with regard to the Secretariat at the time of his visit to Geneva have left an effaceable memory and enable us to appreciate the extent to which his lofty personality strengthened the cause of world peace.[51]

Here, the Secretariat conveyed sympathy, not simply on behalf of the populations of the League's member states, but on behalf of the League 'itself' – the Secretariat. Arguably, the Information Section was doing in a new way what it had been doing by invoking the public back in 1921 – it was constructing the Secretariat as a public institution on equal footing with national ones.

Sometimes the borrowed voices from national figures of authority merged completely with the narrative of publications. For example, the last *Summary* of the year, as well as the pamphlet *The League from Year to Year* quoted directly from Theunis' speech, making it appear as if there was no distinction between his words and the voice of the Secretariat.[52]

The use of rhetoric from statesmen to support the League may look like a tame strategy. But this depended very much on what was said. The credibility of the Information Section was at stake when the section pursued this legitimization by proxy: If a powerful speech by a Great Power politician was deemed to align the

League with that power, its neutrality would be compromised, and the idea that the League represented 'world public opinion' as well as the easy coexistence of national and international identity would be challenged. On Theunis' much-quoted speech at the close of the Economic Conference the section paraphrased that

> In the President's opinion, [. . .] one important and extremely encouraging fact had emerged and [. . .] had become increasingly manifest as the work had advanced. This was the unanimous desire of the members of the Conference to make sure that this Conference should in some way mark the beginning of a new era, during which international commerce should successively overcome all obstacles in its path that unduly hampered it.[53]

Although clearly liberal, this appeal was a vague one that concerned *unity* as a goal in itself. The good news was that so many had participated and that hopes had been high. As we shall see, legitimization by proxy became a lasting strategy of the section, though in changing shapes and guises. It grew out of the same inclination that could be seen in the early years of the decade when the League's vitality and intimacy with public opinion had been articulated time and again: the Information Section's desire to borrow legitimacy for the League from the nation states that underpinned it (Figure 9).

Figure 9 Gustav Stresemann, addressing the League General Assembly in 1929. Stresemann died one month later.
Erich Salomon/Getty Images.

Confident indirect legitimization

By the mid-1920s, the procedures and annual political schedule of the League was becoming settled, and as the League was borrowing legitimacy from national decision-makers, the foundation could be laid for educating the public into achieving a more reasonable idea of the distribution of responsibility for world peace between League institutions and member states. The Information Section began working to establish the League through sheer abundance of facts, information and procedural nitty-gritty. This was legitimization through boredom. In line with the League's dogma of neutrality, several of the mid-1920s publications began to resemble thicker, denser versions of the *Summary* listing meetings, communications, statements and resolutions. A visible tendency was an increasingly dull, meticulous recounting of events. Publications appeared, which were hardly discernible from unedited official documents of the League, but which were nonetheless intended to target a wider public. For example, the first of a series of smaller books titled *The League from Year to Year* of 1927 recounted events between the Assemblies of 1926 and 1927. Compared to more colourful publications, like the photo collection from 1921, the book looked like an enlarged *Summary*, simply recounting facts and events. A pamphlet called *The League of Nations: Its Constitution and Organization*, appeared already in 1923 and was republished in 1926. It explained, quite detailed, the building bricks of the League organization. While the first chapter was a kind of 'reader' to the Covenant, the second discussed the differences and characteristics of the League 'mother organization' as compared to its auxiliary organizations. In the first and the third chapters, it laid out the procedures for handling disputes between states, some existing and some that were threatening to break out. I was conveyed that perceiving the League as a separate entity from governments was a mistake. Now was the time to get things right in the public mind. What the League provided was merely an 'adaptable' system of definite obligations with a certain level of flexibility or 'elasticity'.[54] One sensed a certain fatigue with criticism in the voice of the section:

> [The League] has no magic power to dispel rapidly and easily all the necessary complicated issues of the world. States, on entering the League, do not by this step relinquish their national aims and interests, and these aims, and interests may just as easily clash with those of other states when problems are dealt with through the League as when they are dealt with outside it.[55]

The section was cutting loose some illusions about the incongruence between states and their publics – governments were not simply the bad guys and the public the good. Indirectly, the League asked the readers to look inward before criticizing the organization.

The Secretariat always officially rejected that the League was comparable to a government which made it even more striking when, even as it was making that point, it categorized it as one. The League, it stated in 1930, 'is not an institution with an existence separate from the Governments; it is organically nothing but the totality of states which are its members. The League is not at Geneva any more than the British Constitution is at Westminster or the Weimar Constitution at Berlin'.[56]

Nevertheless, the message during the late 1920s was clear: The League was not a separate entity but simply the sum of its parts. The strategy was in line with its dogma of neutrality; honest information could be the only response to scepticism or hostility. No one could accuse the Information Section of propaganda, neither in favour of any specific Great Powers or for the League institution itself, since the narrative made clear there was no such thing as 'the League'. There was a system, promising the public stability, flexibility and the empowering of countries, if *they* were willing to cooperate rather than fight. In exchange, the League asked for patience. The strategy seemed to reflect a growing realization that it was among educated members of the public that the League should be promoted. The material was not exciting to read, but it was rigorously correct, and toning down the League's ability to change the world was hardly expected to raise support for it among the general population of any member country. Rather, it refuted the claims of opponents that the League was interfering in national sovereignty and asked for *patience* from its impatient liberal internationalist devotees.

Although peacekeeping by means of collective security was still the *raison d'être* of the League, at the close of its first decade there were signs that some of its other activities were of almost equal importance. What League publications referred to as 'technical work' now became connected to the organization's original purpose of securing an orderly diplomatic conduct. This made sense in the context of the international situation at the very end of the 1920s, which was now undergoing drastic developments from what has been called the 'Locarno equilibrium'.[57] A world economic crisis was breaking out, tariff walls between European states were coming up. In the words of Patricia Clavin, by this time, the League Secretariat, was still 'staffed almost entirely by proponents of classical liberalism'[58] who believed confidently, in 1927, 'in the power of experts to generate unanimity among the states'.⁵⁹ The focus of the section on the League's responsibilities in terms of transnational technical cooperation in a certain respect reflected an attempt by the League to shield itself against the negative consequences of its own confidence, against accusations of arrogance, by not actually taking its solid mandate for granted but continuing to rhetorically expand even further its range of responsibilities. This supports what would later be observed in League historiography, namely the League's 'reinvention' of itself during the 1930s as a forum for expertise in various 'technical' fields as demonstrated by Clavin.⁶⁰

The anniversary book made clear that 'Many wars have arisen through the failure of civilisation to devise means of close and continuous cooperation between States on subjects where their interests and needs overlap'. It added that its chapters about economic cooperation, public health or intellectual cooperation would show 'how the common life of States has been organized and developed under the stress of immediate necessities'.⁶¹ 'International co-operation' referred here to cooperation within economic questions, communications, public health, intellectual relations and social and humanitarian questions. Back in 1918, the authors claimed, it had not been realized that the 'negative functions' established to prevent war were not sufficient, and that 'positive international cooperation' was necessary too.⁶² They added that the incentive to economic integration did not just rise out of the realization that protectionism led to hostile competition. They rose equally out of paradoxical wartime experiences of cross border cooperation: 'Both the belligerent alliances had been forced to pool their resources and devise methods of international co-operation and administration that represented an almost revolutionary departure from the traditions of diplomatic intercourse.'⁶³ This links to Wolfram Kaiser and Johan Schot's idea of 'technocratic internationalism' – an expert-focused internationalism, promoted by men who shared experiences of transnational wartime cooperation in bodies like the Allied Shipping Control and thus came to prefer the circumvention of traditional diplomacy by having experts from different countries work together directly.⁶⁴ The section was arguing that 'the decision to concentrate the activity of the League in its early years upon the development of international co-operation appears as perhaps the most important single act of policy during the first decade of its existence'.⁶⁵

Ideas of the significance of international cooperation could be instrumentalized in vastly different political visions. Marco Moraes has argued that the League's second secretary general Joseph Avenol pushed (unsuccessfully) for a corporatist internationalism as part of appeasing the Axis powers in the predominantly liberal internationalist Secretariat.⁶⁶ Yet there are no clear suggestions the League's public legitimization strategies of the 1920s on technical cooperation were systematically imbued with such alternative economics thinking or, conversely with liberalist ideas about the ideological combating of customs, ideas whose presence in Geneva were recently discussed by Quinn Slobodian.⁶⁷ The Information Section was simply not ideological in its news or publications. Instead it insisted in its catch-all way that such work was about 'reconstruction and re-knitting the bonds between nations severed by the war'.⁶⁸ Its dogma of neutrality stood fast, as did its taboo of propaganda.

More than the legacy of war

At the turn of the decade the Information Section began to universalize or de-historicize the League by narrating it as the natural conclusion to mankind's struggle for peace and cooperation. In this narrative, the world war of 1914–18 had escalated pre-existing developments and illustrated the need for the realization of ideas much older than the war. This strategy separated the origins of the organization from the specific historical circumstances of the war. The narrative was not invented by the Information Section. The 1918 report of the so-called Phillimore Committee, which produced one of the earliest schemes for a League, drew a line backwards from the Covenant to ideas of the French seventeenth-century thinker Abbé de Saint-Pierre and further back to the Roman concept of the *Pax Romana*.⁶⁹ In a way, this development in the foundational narrative of the League fitted well together with other strategies that have been observed: the world had passed out of the postwar crisis, and the section's internationalism in practice now became about affirming to the world that the League held the promise of a permanent system. 'The idea of a League of Nations', said the introductory chapter of *Ten Years*, 'is very old. But it was first brought into the realm of practical politics by the war of 1914-1918. The way the war broke out and developed [. . .] gave convincing proof of the need for an international organization to preserve peace and to save civilization from the recurrence of such a catastrophe'.⁷⁰

This rhetorical manoeuvre felt valid at this point because Germany was now a member of the League – with the status of Council member and the historical healing process had begun.

Of course, the idea of a system to secure peace and understanding among the peoples of the earth *was* older than the League. Nonetheless, the narrative worked as a historical recontextualization of the organization hinting as it did at an old intellectual heritage without going into too much detail.[71] The League was presented as a product of political thought stretching far back in time, and other concepts were pushed back with it. The suggestion that a League of Nations was an old idea pushed the relatively new political concept of the nation back in time as well, reinforcing the League's legitimacy since the concept of the national was inextricably linked together with that of the international.[72] It was understood that the eternal march of nations towards self-determination was simply so mature at this point that a League of Nations had to come into existence to organize their interactions and commit them to peace.

However, although the League sought to rewrite its heritage as a guardian of the peace treaties, it was clear from the wording that the war was still significant even though the treaties that had concluded it were not. The point was that the war was a trauma that had demonstrated the League's necessity. Thus, the narrative was in fact linked to the concrete experience of the war. It was embedded in the progression of chapters and the tone of the conclusions that the war was a turning point of great importance if one wished to understand the League. The book mentioned six 'recent disputes' between states which exemplified the various articles of the Covenant under which the League could address a dispute. Its example of a case that had presented an 'imminent threat of war' was the so-called Greek-Bulgarian dispute, in which Greek troops briefly entered Bulgaria following the assassination of a Greek officer in the border town Petrich. The book made a schematic 'Comparison with 1914' going through the procedure followed by the Council in this case and comparing it to what options for settling the dispute had existed in 1914. The fact that there had been no organization to which such disputes were automatically referred along with several other conclusions in the League system's favour all pointed to the overall conclusion that 'Once the danger of hostilities had been removed, the Greco-Bulgarian question became simply a political dispute of the type ordinarily submitted to the Council'.[73]

Supposedly, the Council's handling of the Greek-Bulgarian dispute demonstrated that success in mediating could be achieved once a separation of war from politics had been accomplished. War should no longer be perceived as an escalated type of politics but as something *different* from politics. The Greek-Bulgarian dispute was called 'the classic example of the League's method of acting in an emergency'.[74]

The League, it would be seen, was 'bigger than the war', but that it had been finally brought to life because of it. Significantly, examples of what exact earlier projects or ideas had inspired international cooperation were never mentioned, keeping the League unassociated with any troubling earlier experiences of organizing the world. In the international calm following the Locarno agreements the League's foundation could be disentangled from the painful memories of the peace treaties without arousing French suspicions that the League was clearing Germany of responsibility. The historical re-contextualization of the League was a 'safe' type of promotion because it did not assume more power for the League than it possessed or align it with any Great Powers – quite the opposite. It certainly did not compromise the idea of an international public.

Conclusion

The Information Section's case for supporting the League of Nations during its first thirteen years operated on a 'base line' of neutrality, of sticking to 'the facts', and even performing a kind of deliberate boredom in order to imitate the dull workings of state power. This was always the most important underlying public legitimization strategy that could be seen in the material released from Geneva. However, other strategies run as undercurrents below this implicit argument during 1919–32, as do a subtle shift in how one may think about the League's relation to public opinion.

Up until 1925, the Information Section sought to underscore the multiplicity of League tasks and the energy with which it pursued them, striving to live up to the expectations of the impatient international public. In addition, it articulated a special bond to the public and the 'moral force' that emanated from this bond. Its early public communication thus took on an urgent, sometimes moralist voice.

In the second half of the 1920s, and in the early 1930s, the League could present itself as a more confident entity with an acknowledged international legitimacy. Hesitating to give the appearance of having a voice of its own, it leaned on internationally renowned decision-makers to speak its praise. It systematically quoted such League sympathizers in its publications. At the same time, one observes an increasing cynicism in its printed material as to the nature of public opinion, which was now no longer presented as a unified force empowering the League but as more fragmented, unpredictable and reflective of different national attitudes. Finally, information officials clearly felt that after half a decade of portraying the League as the emergency response to the disaster of war and subsequent humanitarian catastrophes, it was time to separate the League of Nations from the concrete historical experience of the world war of 1914–18. The section began to narrate the League as rising out of an ancient project, much older than the war; the high point of humanity's struggle towards unity and peace. This did not mean the memory of war was 'silenced', but rather that it was commemorated as the decisive event that had finally sparked this project's necessary realization.

These strategies that have been discussed reflected international events. They were never simply rhetoric, planned long in advance and separated from social reality. For example, it was no coincidence that economic cooperation took centre stage in publications after the rehabilitation scheme for Austria and the League's big Economic and Financial Conference in 1927. In addition, it is worth noting that they emerged cumulatively; once they had emerged none of them ever disappeared entirely again but were redeployed in changing settings throughout the lifespan of the organization. Taken together they represent the body of rhetorical manoeuvres League promoters used to bolster and nurture the League's cause from the League's tumultuous birth after the war to its years of relative success and acknowledgement up until 1933. Parallel to what we saw in the last chapter, about how the section discreetly built up relations to elites, the development of these rhetorical strategies shows how the Information Section gradually came to dismiss their original Wilsonian idea of public opinion as a unifying force, which could bolster the League's authority. Instead, the section realized that public opinion was compartmentalized into unpredictable national spheres, and that appealing to elites and sympathizers of the League was a safer strategy.

Part II

4

Downscaling ambitions

Reorganization of the Information Section, 1933–40

On 10 January 1934, all the members of the Information Section were gathered for a special section meeting. Adrianus Pelt was to address his colleagues for the first time as their director.[1] The section had lost Pierre Comert due to a clash of Great Power interests, and to avoid further territorialism about the position it made sense for the newly elected secretary general, Joseph Avenol, to appoint a national of a small country as his successor. Pelt was born in the Netherlands, in Koog aan de Zaan in 1892. He had worked as a foreign correspondent at various Dutch newspapers in London and Paris until 1919.[2] During the Peace Conference he edited foreign news at three different Dutch newspapers, until Comert appointed him to the Information Section in April 1920.[3] Thus, having been present in Paris during the planning of the League, his route into the Secretariat was similar to those of Sweetser, Comert and short-termed George Mair.

There was probably more to the choice of Pelt than his nationality. The new director needed to be an efficient and discreet official, capable of executing radical changes. To understand fully the conditions under which Pelt took over the League's information apparatus, this chapter examines the organizational changes to which the Information Section was subjected starting in the fall of 1933 and what these reflected about the changes in conditions faced by the League's internationalists during these critical years.

At the beginning of the 1930s, the Secretariat and the League in general were entering a new political climate. A growing share of member states challenged the League's principles and key assumptions, something that would have dramatic consequences for the Information Section. That 1933 would mark the beginning of a disintegration of international trust and cooperation building up to the Second World War was obviously not clear to League officials or anyone else. Still, the chapter shows how the instability of the international situation and the weakening of the League's legitimacy among its members states directly impacted the working conditions of the Information Section, and thereby the premise for how the League could disseminate its internationalism. Pressured by the Assembly's Supervisory Commission, the secretary general cut the section to about half its original size and distributed some of its functions (specifically some of those that shaped its self-image as 'more than a press bureau') to other sections.

During the early 1930s, the League's claim at the centre of international politics was weakening. Zara Steiner labelled the period from 1929 to 1933 the 'hinge years' of the interwar period signifying a tipping point between the two decades at which a number of political crises ended up resulting in catastrophic outcomes for the proponents of liberal internationalism. The Great Depression originated in the United States but catalysed a series of economic and political upheavals in Europe and cast doubt on the League project, because its setup was historically associated with the war reparations schemes. This resulted in a European economic crisis that hit the internally embattled Weimar Republic in Germany hard.[4] The subsequent political developments in Germany are only too well-known. However, Adolf Hitler's Reich was not alone in openly defying the League. The years following the so-called Manchuria Crisis in the fall of 1931 and the withdrawals of Japan and Germany in 1933 marked the beginning of the decline of the League's prestige and authority. The decade saw a long line of dents made in the principles of the Covenant, the Council could not act effectively against its own members, and when the League's authoritarian challengers withdrew from the organization (Italy followed Germany and Japan in 1937) and launched aggressive wars of expansion, Western nations reacted with what has been called appeasement and non-intervention.[5] The League's Great Disarmament Conference of 1932–4 more or less fizzled out with no concrete results, and the second World Economic Conference of 1933 did not result in a concerted tackling of the consequences of the Depression.[6] All these developments reverberated not only in the Secretariat in Geneva but also in the atmosphere among its international staff, by limiting the resources member states were ready to grant it and tightening the political control it was subjected to.

The Secretariat in the shadow of crisis

What we now know to be the closing decade of the Secretariat's peacetime existence tells a story of the emergence of a complex set of overlapping crises, some in international politics and some of an internal, institutional character. In 1930 and 1931 the so-called Committee of Thirteen, a committee appointed by the Assembly, produced several reports giving recommendations for the future organization of the Secretariat. Delegates of Germany and Italy opposed some of this report's conclusions and challenged it in a so-called Minority Report. The gist of the conflict was that the majority reports retained the fundamental principle of an international civil service, in which officials were loyal only to the League of Nations. The minority, on the other hand, argued that high officials in the Secretariat should represent 'public opinion in their countries', which interestingly in this case meant they should be loyal to their home governments rather than to the international Secretariat. Even the majority reports, however, conceded the need for an increased focus on the double nature of international civil servants as being loyal both to their national governments and the international institution.[7]

This confrontation over the role of an international civil service reflected mounting tensions between the so-called *status-quo* powers and revisionist powers of the interwar period. The use in the Minority Report of the phrase 'public opinion' pointed, again, to the ambiguity of that concept. Clearly, 'public opinion' could describe the attitude of a government as much as of members of the public – the distinction was not clear.[8] This supported an impression that the concept of public opinion as used in the interwar period sometimes fused a later understanding of public opinion as describing the sentiments of common citizens with an idea of public opinion as the attitudes of elites.

The emergence of these reports catalysed a series of changes, opened the doors for strife and suspicion in the Geneva halls and justified tighter control by the Assembly of the Secretariat, and not least of the Information Section. Eric Drummond resigned as secretary general and left the Secretariat in June 1933. His resignation happened at his own initiative – he wanted out of the Secretariat after thirteen years, and was positioned to be appointed British ambassador to Rome.[9] However, despite Drummond's exit not being a direct consequence of the crisis in the Secretariat, Arthur Sweetser's reaction to the news signalled a profound despair, widespread among his like-minded officials, which clearly reflected a deeper concern than that resulting from losing a respected chief. He wrote to Drummond:

> I just cannot imagine the Secretariat without you – cannot see the future at all. This is the first major wrench; I am truly alarmed for the consequences. [. . .] I am not sure I myself would not have left long ago except for your help and

friendship. You will always have my loyalty and affection, for whatever they may be worth.[10]

As we know, that was not the last farewell-letter Sweetser would write in 1933. In December 1932, Comert had resigned as director of the Information Section after thirteen years. Despite regretting Comert's forced decision, there was little Sweetser, Drummond or others could have done for him, his resignation being the German price for allowing the French Joseph Avenol to succeed Drummond as secretary general. The 'squabble over succession' among high officials, notes Patricia Clavin, 'was not unusual in the League as national rivalries surfaced at every senior appointment'.[11] However, the ousting of a sitting director reflected an escalation of political tension in the Secretariat. James Barros, in his scathing portrait of Joseph Avenol, has illuminated the confidential political considerations that ended in his appointment to secretary general. That a Frenchman was to succeed Drummond had been arranged between the Great Powers back in 1919 without Drummond's knowledge, and German objections were ignored in that process. This back story set the scene for Germany to push back by taking what it could get and getting rid of a 'smaller fish', namely Comert. The entrance of a new European power, and that power's subsequent turn to the extreme political right, was uprooting old understandings.[12]

'Smashed under pretext of economy'

The Information Section would come to feel the rumbles of the changing world order in more substantial ways than the resignation of its director and the secretary general. After Comert's exit, Sweetser took over as acting director during 1933. In the fall of that year, after an uneasy period of awaiting the consequences of the new conditions, the section was presented with a reorganization scheme, which would fundamentally alter its position in the Secretariat. It fell on Adrianus Pelt, the new director from 1934, to organize the section's work in accordance with this plan.

The origins of this plan can be found in the summer of 1933. Following the abovementioned Minority Report's call for the League to reduce the Secretariat's spending, the Assembly's powerful Supervisory Commission stated in a report that it saw as its goal 'to distribute between several sections the work that has hitherto been exclusive, or almost exclusively, to the Information Section'.[13] The Supervisory Commission for the Assembly of 1933 consisted of chairman Štefan Osuský of Czechoslovakia, a British vice-chairman, a Frenchman, a Venezuelan and a Norwegian.[14] The report recommended, first, the sacking of officials of the Information Section and the transfer of others to other sections. Second, the discontinuing of some its work areas that the Commission felt did not belong to a 'press service'.[15] Third, the report sharply underscored that the section should not make propaganda, hinting a conviction that this had been the case before.[16]

The report pointed to something bigger than just questions of departmental responsibility. It fundamentally challenged the idea behind the Information Section. It cited the section's most recent terms of reference from 1932 recognizing 'that the Covenant imposes on the League special obligations in relation to public opinion' but asked rhetorically, did this necessitate that one section be charged with all this work? A reinterpretation of the meaning of public opinion was taking place, the Supervisory Commission obviously seeing it as a narrower, exclusive group of stakeholders and government elites, liaison with whom could easily be dealt with by the specialists who worked in other sections of the Secretariat. Additionally, the commission contested the idea that the Information Section should appoint officials from as many member states as possible, objecting that this ambition would mean eternal growth. Its report concluded by recommending 'limiting the strength' of the section.[17]

Five years later, in 1938, Potter interpreted this event in the following way:

> The Information Section was smashed by the [Member States] in 1933, under pretext of economy [. . .] and converted into a mere press bureau of half its previous size.[18]

He elaborated, explaining that the League's member states

> hold back the Secretariat in its publicity work. This is especially true of the Great Powers [. . .] who are jealous of this new super-national organization. [. . .] The States feel compelled to permit dissemination of factual information but do not desire promotion or propaganda even for League principles. Although they cannot avoid this respecting the main League ideas – peace and cooperation – they hamper it respecting details of League action (minority protection, revision) where the effects may displease them individually.[19]

Potter argued that the section was predestined from its birth to be targeted in this way, and that it therefore might as well have pursued more aggressive kinds of propaganda from the start.[20] To say that economy was a cover for a purely political witch-hunt against the section was probably a dramatization. It was a fact that the Secretariat was going through a general phase of retrenchment, and that the section was the largest in the Secretariat making it an obvious target for the general trend of budget cuts. A combination of factors contributed to its downfall.

We recall that since its inception in 1919 Comert had struggled to maintain as a principle that the section should be directed by one or more officials from the Great Powers and be gradually expanded to include as many nationalities as possible to reflect public opinion in the League's member states. We saw in Chapter 2 how the setup was used to secure lines of liaison to private groups in favour of the League as well as to news agencies, journalists and politically influential figures. This was what the section referred to in 1928, when it insisted that it was not 'a Press Bureau in the usually accepted sense of the term' but an 'organic part of the Secretariat closely bound up with the League work as a whole'.[21] This, according to Potter, was what changed in 1933, when the section was reduced to 'a mere Press Bureau'. On the level of organization, it will be seen that the change took place most forcefully in terms of the resources granted to it, and a narrower mandate given to Pelt in terms of what functions were given to the section.

At the first meeting of the new section, Pelt told its officials 'in fact, there would be little change in the functions of the section, except that it would in future be a technical press section and would no longer undertake any political liaison work'.[22] This was clearly Pelt attempting to cushion the blow, and it may also be an illustration of Pelt's overall temperament as a League official. In contrast to his more idealist colleagues, Pelt was keen on the importance of discretion and the ability to set aside one's personal convictions and follow directives. Stefanie Averbeck-Lietz exemplified this when discussing Pelt's annoyance with Konni Zilliacus, a left-wing official who disobeyed Secretariat regulations by writing anonymously for the *Manchester Guardian*.[23]

Proportionally, the section continued to be among the largest of the Secretariat, and its officials were still overwhelmingly journalists by profession. However, the section's *raison d'être* was contested from 1933 and onwards. The secretary general and the Assembly put it under scrutiny, and its activities became subject to returning criticism on suspicion of propaganda activities. It never regained the same prominence in the Secretariat as it had enjoyed during the 1920s.

All this made it simpler for information officials to tackle the tensions inherent in their work, the tensions regarding what they were promoting, how far they could go and towards what audience, because they now had a much smaller room of manoeuvre. Following the reorganization, the Supervisory Commission and the secretary general explicitly reinstated the taboo of propaganda. As we shall explore in more detail, their tolerance when it came to liaison activities with agents outside the Secretariat decreased (and in the case of some activities, disappeared). The audience seemed now to have been limited to simply the Geneva press corps.

The section resisted these changes to some degree and sought to compensate for its loss of territory by beefing up the things it could do. Under Adrianus Pelt it supplemented its traditional publications by experimenting with new technologies. This hardly represented a technological revolution (there was too little money for that), but they planted the vision among leading officials of a future information department that would be more focused on genuine, global mass communication and less on liaison with educated elites. We shall return to this point in the last chapter.

Looking back a decade later in 1944, Pelt would assert that the way that Pierre Comert had thought about the section was outdated; it had 'corresponded to the then existing state of public opinion in the world',[24] a public opinion which the section had sought to address largely through the printed press and through liaison with private 'collaborators' in the various countries. We do not know if Pelt envisioned such a fundamental change as early as 1934, but he must have acknowledged that the section was no longer positioned 'at the point of contact between the League and public opinion'. Arthur Sweetser, whose extensive networking activities had encapsulated what the old section had been about, was removed from the section after his one year as director during 1933. His modus operandi no longer belonged there, because the section was discouraged from liaising with private associations, and its mandate for pursuing 'political liaison' was taken away from it. It would henceforth focus on its role as a press service, on releasing purely 'factual' publications and on disseminating information through its nascent radio service.

The dominant conceptualization of public opinion in the Secretariat was suggested by the rhetorical question of the Supervisory Commission on justifying the 'smashing': Why did all relations to public opinion have to belong to one section? If one considered public opinion as the sentiments of common citizens, the 'masses', this was a weird question. It seemed obvious that duty should lie with an Information Section. On the other hand, if public opinion was simply another word for 'official opinion', that of decision-makers, diplomats and other powerful stakeholders, it made good sense to ask whether such relations could not be run as part of the general national liaison activities of Secretariat officials. Table 3 shows the share of salaries and allowances of the Secretariat taken up by the Information Section after 1933, including the last two years of the preceding period for comparison. Table 4 shows the development of its size in terms of high-ranking staff.

Table 3 Share of Salaries and Allowances of the Secretariat Taken up by the Information Section 1931–40

Year	Salary budget (Secretariat)	Salaries (Information Section)	Share (%)
1931	5,924,215	1,108,506	18.7
1932	6,006,269	1,162,923	19.3
1933	5,718,505	942,970	16.5
1934	9,296,383	935,963	10
1935	9,003,707	537,068	6
1936	8,955,107	560,954	6
1937	9,451,335	572,268	6
1938	9,704,633	592,383	6
1939	9,667,822	N/A	N/A
1940	N/A	N/A	N/A

Budgets in *O.J*: for 1934, (1933), 1188; for 1935, (1934), 1263; for 1936 (1935), 1011; for 1937, (1936), 1017; for 1938, (1937), 704; for 1939 (1938), 703; All figures from 'Schedule B: Salaries, Wages and Allowances of the Secretariat'.

All salaries provided in Swiss francs.

Table 4 Development of size of Information Section

Year	Members (director)	Staff incl. branch offices and correspondents
1931	21	74
1932	21	81
1933	19	51
1934	14	31
1935	13	32
1936	13	31
1937	12	31
1938	12	33
1939	4	18
1940	N/A	N/A

Staff lists of the Secretariat in *O.J.*: (1934), 1339; (1935), 1090; (1936), 1098; (1936), 1098; (1937), 789; (1938), 789; (1939): 461.

These numbers reflect a section reduced to half its original size with a slight majority of dismissals having taken place among the lower ranking officials. Some were transferred to other sections, the reasons for which are examined in Chapter 5.

A critical moment

What did all these organizational reforms mean for the League's way of practising its now contested internationalism? The Information Section's position in the Secretariat during its last years of existence was summarized neatly by Avenol in a report to the Assembly in 1937. Citing the Supervisory Commission's 1933 report, Avenol explained in 1937:

> 'If the example of the propaganda organisations set up by many States were to be followed, the budget of the Section would have to be as large as that of an important Ministry of Press and Propaganda. But that was evidently not the intention of the Assembly in the first place because there is no question of transforming the Information Section into an international Ministry of Propaganda and secondly because the Section is necessarily obliged to remain within the budgetary and administrative limits laid down for the whole Secretariat'.[25]

Avenol was trying to level down the radicalism of the original idea behind the Information Section. The withdrawn position of the Secretariat as an administrative service to the political bodies of the League had been contradicted by the size and scope of the Information Section resulting in a tension as to whether the Secretariat should promote itself as a kind of government towards the public. Avenol tried to correct this misconception.

This levelling of the ambitions of the new Information Section seem to have planted a conviction among its veterans – Adrianus Pelt prime among them – that future international organizations ought to legitimize themselves to the public through genuine mass communication helped by new technologies, rather than partly through elite channels or what Sweetser had called 'cooperative publicity'.

The Supervisory Commission's report was only supervisory – it proposed some (rather concrete) principles for what to do but left the practical implementation of them to the Secretariat itself. Thus, in the fall of 1933, the Secretariat entered a phase of planning and sectional competition. A new division of responsibilities between sections in terms of information work was to be organized. Avenol appointed his deputy Pablo de Azcarate, along with Pelt, Sweetser, Henry Cummings and Julian Nogueira of the Information Section as well as Valentin Stencek of the Central Section to study the Information Section and make recommendations for the reorganization. At the end of September 1933 these six officials submitted their report to the secretary general. Although, as can be seen, the section was strongly represented in this committee the presence of two of the highest officials of the Secretariat indicated that its deliberations were closely supervised, and that the committee was expected to draw the consequences of the Supervisory Commission's report and plan for something entirely new. Avenol asked them to work on the assumption that 'the essential function of the Information Section [. . .] is to maintain relations with news agencies and newspaper correspondents who feed the Press of the whole world with their reports from Geneva'.²⁶ Thus, to the veterans of section, it was not a happy occasion.

This was a quite substantial redefinition. Although the commission refrained from labelling press relations the only remaining task of the section, Sweetser, Pelt and the others clearly felt an existential threat to the section they had built. The report objected to many of the services that went beyond press relations as well as the idea of the staff being recruited based on nationality. None of this went down easy with the long-time officials. In a written objection to the process, Pelt, Sweetser, Cummings and the rest of the committee responded in a tone usually not seen in official documents. They stated that the task given to them had clarified the problem of drawing 'a definite line of demarcation between relations with the press and relations with public opinion'.²⁷ They objected to being asked to build a section whose functions, 'speaking in technical sense', would 'not essentially different from those carried out by the old section'. This was especially problematic, they thought, because it would have to be done with half the staff and since 'nine months ago the official who had been the organizer and inspirer of the Section during its first thirteen years, and who had a truly extraordinary knowledge of world press matters, left the Section'.²⁸

Were they right that the future section would have almost the same functions as the old? Judging from what the Supervisory Commission said, not really. The statement by the information officials was probably a piece of defensive constitutive rhetoric – or wishful thinking.

The Commission's four 'principles' for reorganizing the section were that (1) The Information Section should supply information to the public and remain responsible for relations with the press. (2) The Political Section should be in charge of all collection of information in the future. (3) The Secretariat as a whole should maintain contact with member states. (4) The Intellectual Cooperation Section should maintain contact with private organizations interested in the League.²⁹

This meant that two former functions of the Information Section were under attack; namely its 'political liaison' and its liaison with private associations. The commission added some specific points; it recommended examining whether branch offices were economically efficient enough and making sure that they refrained from 'propaganda'. Interestingly, the commission also criticized some of the section's publications, warning that, at this point when the League 'has long since taken its place as one of the essential parts of the machinery of international life' there was no need for pamphlets designed 'exclusively for the purposes of propaganda'. Finally, it requested that the production of films and photographs should be cut to an absolute minimum.³⁰

Pelt, Sweetser and the others seem to have realized that some functions had to go, but they resisted, producing, among other things, a list of functions they felt were indispensable for an Information Section. They pleaded not to reduce their section any further since 'such sweeping changes seem [. . .] already to approach the point of danger'.[31] In terms of press relations, they protested that excluding relations to newspapers and news agencies outside of Geneva would mean that distribution of League news outside Europe would be monopolized by a few agencies who could afford sending people to Geneva: 'The richer and less numerous thus profit at the expense of the many poorer countries and newspapers. This is dangerous and contrary to the general interests.' They invoked a resolution of the Assembly of 1932 which had called for the Secretariat to develop 'by all the means at its disposal' the supply of information about the League to the press of the world.[32] These arguments bore witness to an enduring idealism among the key officials of the section. Despite the fact that Comert had built a section which prioritized the press and League sympathizers, the obvious amputation of the section's span in terms of reaching less important national publics as well as less important newspapers and news agencies bothered its old guard.

They also defended liaison with private organizations, writing that it 'seems desirable that this relation should be maintained, as other sections do not have the press equipment to render the services required'.[33] However, as mentioned, this task was to be taken over by the Intellectual Cooperation Section (at this time, 'the International Bureaux and Intellectual Cooperation Section'), a section which would supposedly neglect much of the work that did not relate to its own area of science and education.[34] This was an early foreboding of the competition in international organization between a department facilitating cultural and intellectual exchange and the information and publicity work performed by the Information Section. In the future United Nations, the power balance would shift definitively so that the United Nations Educational, Scientific and Cultural Organization (UNESCO) became much better funded than the successor to the Information Section.[35]

Yet the objection of the internal committee reflected more than a turf war between sections. Pelt, Sweetser, Cummings and their colleagues felt that other sections were not capable of carrying the League's obligations within information work, and that assigning this liaison work to those sections was a deliberate attempt of crippling the Secretariat in terms of its information policies. They reminded the Supervisory Commission that the Assembly had previously declared the press to be an important collaborator of the League in the struggle for world peace. This was an appeal to Wilsonian ideals of open diplomacy in the face of what they deemed was short-sighted retrenchment. The six officials even invoked world public opinion. 'The changes already effected in the personnel of the Section', they warned, 'come at the most critical moment in world public opinion that the League has yet had to face. Never before has there been a greater need for the wide dissemination of complete and accurate news'.[36]

They clearly saw the reorganization as a *nadir* of the League's muscles for public legitimization: one that coincided with a similar low point for liberal internationalism and European unity. Hitler's withdrawal of Germany from the League came just weeks later. Arguably, the officials were referring not just to their reduced manpower when they wrote of a change in the League's 'approach to world opinion' but also about the section's broader mission of making the League a central hub for internationalism being under attack as part of a deliberate attempt at centralization of the Secretariat. Information work, according to these veteran information officials, was about building a network of personal contacts of private citizens and private organizations as well as semi-official and even official circles, a strategy which could only be pursued with a big section spanning many nationalities.

Despite these objections, the secretary general set the reduction and reorganization of the section in motion. Avenol approved a gradual reduction of the section's working budget from 1934 and onwards based on the 'suggestions and recommendations' grudgingly accepted by the internal committee.

What this meant in practice for the functions of the section going forward was in fact left to decide for yet another internal committee. In December 1933, two months after the first committee had submitted its report, the Liaison Committee, a new permanent committee of the Secretariat to oversee liaison activities on a general level, gave its recommendations. Avenol chaired it himself and included one representative from each of the sections which were henceforth to maintain liaison with bodies outside the Secretariat, the Information Section, the Political Section and the Intellectual Cooperation Section. The old guard of the Information Section was once again represented in Pelt and Sweetser, although the latter acted as 'rapporteur' since he was no longer employed in the section. Looking at the recommendations of that committee, it is clear that the protests made by the old information officials had partly worked.[37] Rather than stripping the Information Section of its old tasks they had become subject to oversight by other sections.

This reflected a move towards centralization and internal surveillance which emerged during Avenol's term as secretary general. The new regime was illustrated by the change to the so-called French system of secretariat correspondence, in which such correspondence seeped 'downwards' from the new Central Section rather than being received directly by officials from many different sections and then forwarded if needed.[38] An example was a so-called Standing Instruction circulated in the Secretariat in 1934 asking all sections to hand in a monthly report of their activities. In the Information Section, Pelt asked each of his officials to provide a monthly summary of their work that he would then synthesize for Avenol. He often had to remind his officials that they could not just copy last month's report.[39] Such developments, although they look like details, speak to the atmosphere of the Secretariat in the 1930s and the way in which a new cautiousness in the League about its mandate and legitimacy resulted in more strict and hierarchical work procedures which probably stunted creativity and a feeling of independence. The Information Section was an example of a section which was vulnerable to such change because, as we have seen, much of its work had been based on the independent spirit of its officials, their internationalist zeal and their willingness to work 'unofficially' below the radar. This could no longer be tolerated.

Exit diplomacy?

The reorganization and trimming down of the Information Section meant that its special position in terms of political liaison – liaison with governmental or semi-governmental circles – was eliminated. To be sure, such relations had never belonged exclusively to the Information Section in the first place, and it is thus difficult to pinpoint exactly what changed. Ranshofen-Wertheimer insisted that political liaison activities of the Secretariat as a whole 'remained casual and were never standardized', and that in the case of 'less spectacular missions', members of 'the Political or Information Sections were particularly favored'. The Supervisory Commission had specified that only the Political Section could from now on 'gather information', but it also mentioned that it remained the responsibility of the Secretariat in general to 'maintain liaison with state members'. Upon hearing that an 'information department' had been set up inside the Political Section the Polish member of the Information Section, Stanislas Neyman, protested at a section meeting in 1935. He felt the establishment of such a unit proved that the Press Review of the Information Section was 'not what it should be' and that he had always argued that this review ought to provide 'other items of importance' such as confidential political intelligence. Neyman, perhaps not fully understanding (or accepting) the more limited role recently given to his section, felt that it was due to this failure of the section that it had lost its relevance. He was supported by the Belgian Frédéric Blondeel who recalled that in earlier days members of the Section had often 'been asked individually to supply information of importance to the Secretary General'.[40] Pelt shut down that debate, saying that it was not due to any failures of the Information Section that this task now lay with the Political Section but a decision that had come from above.[41]

Arthur Sweetser continued his activities as a key link of liaison with the United States in this period and thus did pursue political liaison, but he did so outside the auspices of the Information Section. Thus, with its dramatically reduced size, the oversight it was being subjected to and the new political climate in the Secretariat it seems unlikely the section was a key player anymore in terms of gathering intelligence and information for the Secretariat.

Continuities or breaks?

Despite the crisis in international cooperation spurred by the deadlocked Disarmament Conference and the withdrawals of key member states, by the middle of the 1930s the technical arrangements and the physical setting for the Geneva press corps were expanding. The prestigious new League headquarters, the Palais des Nations, stood finished after many years of delay and architectural disputes. What some newspapers cynically termed the League's 'mausoleum' offered new opportunities for public legitimization.[42] On 22 May 1936 Pelt informed his section of the upcoming inauguration of the Press Room of the new building. Invitations to a festive dinner were sent to all press associations in Geneva and Secretariat officials who dealt with the press.[43] On the day following the dinner, members of the section were encouraged to make sure to spend some time in the Press Room to make the journalists feel at home.[44] The section thus exploited the new physical grandeur of the League in the interest of continuing to portray Geneva as a centre for the world press.

It is thus important not to get the impression that League press relations faltered completely after the 1933 crippling of the Information Section. The League did not lose its 'voice' simply because its many of its resources for addressing the public were taken from it. In a way, communicating international cooperation became more urgent as the pillars of the organization – the staunch support given by Great Powers – which had been taken for granted, gave way. In 1934 the highest press-attendance at any League conference was still just two years past. This was at the start of the infamous Disarmament Conference in 1932 at which the Information Section had issued press cards to over six hundred journalists. Still, in 1934 over one hundred permanently residing correspondents from twenty-five news agencies covered the League in Geneva.[45] After 1933, the attention of the international press for the League began to wane, probably a consequence of the rise of totalitarianism in several European states, which brought an abrupt end to the liberty of many journalists to cover League business. From 1933 the number of resident correspondents started to slowly decline, however, it remained on levels comparable to the second half of the 1920s for several years.[46] The expansive machinery of the League thus did not disappear from one day to the next simply because of unfavourable political developments, and while the organization was increasingly criticized it still provided a forum for diplomatic deliberations worthy of intense news coverage. Only as European tensions mounted and the prospect of war loomed larger towards the late 1930, the mood started taking its toll on the League as a news centre. Although information is scarce, we know that in 1938 the section distributed 348 regular news communiqués.[47] This number reflected a drop: it was on the level of 1922–4 and significantly lower than the second half of the 1920s and the early 1930s when between 600 and 700 hundred communiqués were released annually.[48] The news service had peaked between 1932 and 1933 and was by the second half of the decade definitively declining, reflecting the general drift of the attention of the press from Geneva.

As for the section's liaison activities, the Supervisory Commission's report did not mean the section completely ceased to regard such liaison among its tasks. At a section meeting in October 1934 Hungarian official Elemér de Radisics asked Pelt whether the fact that 'liaison with international organizations were in the future to be centralized under the International Bureaux Office' meant that the Information Section should cut its relations with these organizations completely. Pelt said that was not the case at all and referred Radisics to the Standing Instructions of the Secretariat.[49] These stated that the International Bureaux Section was to be a general agent of liaison with all international organizations, 'official and unofficial', but it also stated that while that section should be informed about all correspondence with such bodies, other sections could continue to deal with 'those aspects of liaison with international organizations that are exclusively within their technical competence'.[50] Publicity and information being the competence of the Information Section, it could continue its activities, but correspondence would from now on go through the International Bureaux Section.

Thus, many of the lines of communication between the Information Section and private organizations which had developed in 1919–33 still existed but were nurtured in a whole new climate of centralization and surveillance. In 1935 Pelt circulated a list to his officials which showed what associations the section would continue to correspond with after the reorganization, and assigning officials to each. The list included thirty-three different organizations and looked quite similar to the earlier lists – only now the work was divided between half the staff that had been available earlier and according to a scheme that need everything to be cleared by another section.[51] Yet the section held on to the task. By the end of the 1930s the information officials sketched an emergency plan for how to keep the section running during the mounting European crisis. At this point officials were already leaving the Secretariat for their home countries and plans for what should be done in the event of the outbreak of war were underway.[52] In one of the planning memos, we find the section leadership stating in an almost defiant note that 'The Information Section has always been in charge of the liaison with international organisations as for instance the International Parliamentary Union, the Federation for League of Nations Associations, Rotary International, Federations of ex-servicemen and various Women's Associations'.[53]

As can be seen, the section still used national League of Nations Unions and their umbrella, the IFLNS, to some extent, although we shall see, that after 1933 this liaison met less enthusiasm from above. When Gabriele Radziwill left the Information Section in 1931, the Spanish José Plà (whom we know to also have been responsible for 'temporary collaborators' since 1926) was put in charge of liaison with the ILFNS. It made sense for the two tasks to be entrusted to the same official, as they partly overlapped. There is evidence the IFLNS used temporary collaborators as intermediaries with the Secretariat and sources of information on its activities. For example, in connection to an upcoming International Youth Conference, an advisory committee of the IFLNS on education stated in 1934 that their draft proposals were based on 'consultation between the Federation Secretariat and the temporary collaborators at the League Assembly'.[54] Plà said at a section meeting in 1936 that 'as usual' two spots as temporary collaborators would be reserved for members of 'student federations'.[55]

So, the section kept its temporary collaborator scheme going and integrated it into its liaison idea of connecting the League to public opinion through liaison with influential members of the public in the member states. The collaborators constituted a channel going both ways: On the one hand, they spread information about the League – to newspapers, through personal contacts, and in organizations like the IFLNS. On the other hand, they provided the Information

Section with analysis on the trend of opinion in these organizations and among the public. The system itself was altered in connection to the reorganization of the section. Pelt announced in early 1934 that collaborators would be invited for a longer period that just during the Assembly, but fewer would be invited.[56] A progressive analysis of the number and diversity of temporary collaborators in 1934-40 shows that the system was maintained in a comparable fashion with the period 1919-33 but with a slightly smaller number of people invited. Thirty-four collaborators came in 1935, thirty-seven in 1937 and thirty-six in 1938. In 1936 only seventeen came, but this was mainly because as a special 'happening' the section exclusively invited people from outside Europe that year – Argentina, Brazil, Mexico, Peru, Guatemala, South Africa, Australia and New Zealand, resulting in higher travelling expenses. The scheme thus stayed intact and seems to have been considered as lying at the heart of what the section offered besides its press services. With fewer officials working in the section it could be utilized to ensure a broader representation of different national 'publics' in accordance with the principles of Comert's old section.

As for the IFLNS, it seems the section was committed to working closely together with the federation before 1933, but then this started to change. Before the plenary meeting of the federation in Montreux in 1933 Plà wrote to Sweetser (acting director at the time) that he had circulated the agenda and other relevant documents for the meeting in the Secretariat, as he did every year.[57] However, as noted by Davies, the period when Plà took over was one of increased scepticism as to the wisdom of such closeness with the federation and other pro-League groups like it.[58] Prior to the Montreux-meeting, Drummond, the departing secretary general, and Avenol, the incoming one, both made excuses to avoid attending even though Montreux is very close to Geneva. After that year, Plà's reports from the plenary congresses became increasingly distanced and less analytical compared to those of Radziwill up until 1931. One gets the impression he was merely fulfilling a duty whereas Radziwill had felt she were doing valuable fieldwork for her section. The suggestions Plà brought home for the Information Section, more often than not, were shot down or postponed indefinitely by the secretary general. This happened after the plenary congress in Brussels in 1935, when he relayed the idea that the section should distribute its publications at international exhibitions, and that it should vastly expand its radio-efforts to include a larger European public than was the case with the *Radio Nations*. Both suggestions were killed in their infancy.[59] Interestingly, the Publications Department commented to Pelt about the former suggestion that 'there are [...] certain political reasons these exhibitions are not a good idea, reasons that you know better than me'.⁶⁰ Implying that the director of the Information Section was well aware of what he was talking about suggested these political reasons were identical with the problems pointed out by Pitman Potter – that the work of the section was always under potential fire whenever it went too far beyond its duties as a neutral, Geneva-based press section. These institutional uncertainties and hesitations were a reflection of the international political climate and meant that the League's legitimization strategies during the second half of the 1930s often became more about avoiding losing legitimacy in the eyes of member states than about legitimizing it to the public.

The collapse

By the closing years of the 1930s, the Secretariat operated in a large-scale international crisis visible everywhere in what observers called a concerted effort to destroy the League by Germany, Japan and Italy. The institution lost credibility by events like Italy's invasion of Ethiopia (Abyssinia) in 1935, the ongoing illegitimate rearmament by Hitler's Germany, the Spanish Civil War in 1936 and the covert interference in it by Italy, Germany and the Soviet Union. In addition came a Japanese war of expansion in China, the withdrawal of most South American countries from the League and the German annexation of Austria.⁶¹ There was little or nothing the League of Nations could do to stop these developments as even its loyal supporters increasingly were realizing.

Then, on the opening page of the 1939 September issue of the *Monthly Summary*, the Information Section could announce the outbreak of what would soon be the Second World War:

> The work of the League in the latter part of August and in September was overshadowed and partially interrupted by the outbreak of war in Europe.⁶²

Upon hearing the news and making a short statement, the *Summary* reported that Joseph Avenol had 'received those officials who might be mobilized'.⁶³ International civil servants, until then devoted to operating a neutral international forum for the peaceful settlement of disputes, could now start getting ready to go home and fight each other on the battlefield.

By this point, Avenol had, for months, been reacting to the League's crisis of legitimacy in a way historians have considered further destructive to the liberal internationalist ideas on which it was founded.⁶⁴ He attempted to align the League with the policies of the Third Reich and fascist Italy by making a bid to bring those powers back into a reshaped organization. This led him to engage in virtual purges in the Secretariat, dismissing officials that were disliked by these powers. When war became a reality and the European dictatorships still showed little interest in the League, he opted for surprising career move. In the summer of 1940, immediately after the fall of France, he suddenly left Geneva in a bid to secure a position for himself in the Vichy regime and, rejected entry on the border, was obliged to return in disgrace to Switzerland. The Irishman Seán Lester took over stewardship of the disintegrating League as its last secretary general.

In this new situation, the Assembly's Supervisory Commission moved again and instructed the Secretariat to economize drastically across all sections. The ensuing plans for the 1940 reorganization of the Information Section included lists of officials to be transferred to other sections and lists of officials to be dismissed immediately. It also included a scheme for 'voluntary' reductions of salaries on all levels.[65] The last staff list available from the section shows which officials were to be retained in Geneva during 1940. It mentions ten people altogether, including Adrianus Pelt and Elemér de Radisics, the latter in charge of publications since 1931. The Canadian Mary McGeachy also held out and would report to a British newspaper in November 1940 that she had been appointed the 'Acting Head of Section' in the Information Section, providing possibly a rare example of a female official in charge of a section.[66] Arthur Sweetser left for the United States in April 1940 and officially quit the Secretariat in 1942.[67]

Of course, officials had no way of knowing exactly what would happen during the runoff towards world war. The League's final legitimization efforts therefore are worth studying in detail, no matter the feeling of impending doom so often associated with the late 1930s. Two such endeavours, both discussed in previous scholarship, stood out from the regular activities of the Information Section. Both aimed largely at Americans and involved Arthur Sweetser to a high degree, but both were also officially efforts of the Information Section. One was the promotion of the League's new buildings, the Palais des Nations, which stood more or less finished in the Parc Ariana in Geneva in 1936, and the other was the League's exhibition pavilion at the New York World's Fair in 1939. In both these efforts, Sweetser was positioned to promote the League towards his countrymen in the United States, a country considered to be the League's great hope by many internationalists during this period and towards whose citizens less restraint was shown in terms of promotion, because there was little to be lost with a country already not a member of the League. Timo Holste has shown how Sweetser, now less constrained by the formal limitations of the Information Section, worked together with the American Committee of the League of Nations Association to facilitate visits to Geneva by a flow of educated Americans. They came to see the way the architecture of the buildings epitomized 'l'Esprit de Genève'.[68] David Allen has unfolded the story of the League's ambitious pavilion at the World's Fair, which he asserted reflected the League's shift in focus from 'political' to 'technical' fields of work as well as a return to the use of high-minded liberal internationalism.[69] The two cases seem to convey that during the final years of the League's existence, when political despair was settling over much of the world, the promoters of the League made a final bid to use the aesthetical features of the organization and the emotional appeal it still held to legitimize it towards the United States. In each their own way the tourism effort at the Palais des Nations and the promotion at the New York Pavilion demonstrated a continuous conviction close to the heart of at least Arthur Sweetser that elites were still what mattered. Tourism at the Palais targeted educated Americans, and Sweetser is cited by Allen to have conceded that the installation was difficult for 'the masses'. Instead, Sweetser wanted the League to focus on catching the attention of 'the really effective and important people who in the end decide the policy of this country'.[70]

Conclusion

The story of the Information Section after 1933 was one of a decline in resources and freedom of action even if the section resisted these developments somewhat. Pressured by a new climate in the Assembly of financial restraint and suspicion towards too much independence among the international bureaucrats, the Secretariat leadership subjected the section to tighter control. The result was a significant limiting of the section's strength. It became clear that the key role imagined for the Information Section by its own officials was very much determined by the resources granted to it and that these could fluctuate because information policy was sensible to political conflict. The section was still multinational after 1933, and it still pursued press relations and liaison activities, but the idea that it not only informed the press but also collaborated with members of the public and was its voice inside the Secretariat was diminished. The section would no longer collect confidential information for the secretary general, and the input it transferred from the IFLNS to the Secretariat was largely ignored. 'Political liaison' no longer served any prominent purpose in its work, and Arthur Sweetser was made to pursue his extraordinary lobbying activities on the organization's behalf outside the section. These developments all pointed to a League on the defensive, which refrained more and more from risk-taking and thus dramatically scaled down its ambitions in terms of spreading its internationalist message.

The diminishing of its staff and resources left it with its publications and its new channels of communications, broadcasting and films. Since these functions never became richly funded, the experience of being left with them is likely to have strengthened the last director Adrianus Pelt's lasting conviction that concentrating resources on these emerging media of mass communication, rather than nurturing an exclusive network of educated collaborators, was the future of public legitimization by international organizations.

5

Crisis and retreat to aesthetics
League public information, 1933–40

This chapter revisits the League's 'voice', as observed in its public information material and studies the development this underwent across the dramatic 1930s. Again, it is important to keep in mind that the League of Nations did not formulate very explicit legitimization strategies nor would its officials have cared to acknowledge the existence of such strategies. The fundamental assumption of its officials was that the League needed to justify itself through calm, neutral, 'factual information' delivered in the language of unbiased diplomacy. Nonetheless, as we saw in Chapter 3, a set of subtle strategies could be inferred. Rather than marking a dramatic shift, the chapter should be seen as adding to Chapter 3 a further set of strategies that emerged during the League's more challenging years, and in response to the narrowing of the Information Section's mandate.

Before we get to those, some words ought to be spared on the new technologies that entered the arsenal of the Information Section during this period. On top of printed publications, it now began to address the public through broadcasting, photographs and films, and, as described previously, it made use of the League's radio station, operational from 1932, the *Radio Nations*. Ranshofen-Wertheimer lamented in 1945 that experimental types of publicity, such as films and the radio, encountered numerous obstacles and resistance because 'European traditions were averse to treating film or the radio as equals of the press', or to providing for the broadcast of parliamentary procedures over national networks.[1] There were financial reasons for this as well, as seen in a directive to the section in 1933 only to produce films in exceptional circumstances.[2] As a result the section always pursued these activities with a tight budget and mostly had to make do with more antiquated means, such as its extensive photograph collection (showcased in several illustrated albums on League history and activities), educative posters and lantern slides available to private individuals on request.[3]

Detailed information on the *Radio Nations* is quite scarce in the archives, but it is clear the Information Section broadcasted weekly radio lectures on various topics from the fall of 1932.[4] Its short-wave transmitter enabled it to transmit news for the press in 'New York, Shanghai, Nagoya, Buenos Aires and Rio de Janeiro'.[5] In addition came four more comprehensive radio talks each week: One in English for North America, one in English for Australia and New Zealand, one in Spanish for Latin America and one in French for French-speaking Canada and 'certain French colonies'. On the broadcasts Information Section officials broadcasted on Saturday nights, and shows included a speech by the president of the Council, a paper by an official on the registration of treaties, or a talk on the eight-hour workday by a representative of the International Labor Office.[6] Long-wave transmission equipment for covering European countries was only entering the planning of the Information Section in 1937 thanks to external funding by the Carnegie Endowment for International Peace, but seemingly it was never realized. Countries far from the League that received fewer of its printed publications were given priority.[7]

This slow development made sense, because broadcasting attracted the suspicion of governments as well as print media.[8] *Radio Nations* only transmitted 'information bulletins and lectures' for the public while it was only allowed to transmit news in telegrams in Morse code to news agencies.[9]

A small collection of films remains today as evidence of embryonic attempts by the League to embrace this new medium.[10] In 1937 the Information Section complained that its resources for film production were inadequate and pointed out that the films it had released until that point were the work of 'private cinematograph companies who from time to time asked permission to film various League activities'.[11] These would include Realist Film Unit and the Italian Luce Films (Instituto Luce) associated with the International Educational Cinematographic Institute in Rome. This institute, financed by the Italian government, operated under the auspices of the League, specifically its International Committee on Intellectual Cooperation.[12] Documents regarding audiovisual material transferred to New York from Geneva in 1948 suggest the Information Section edited about ninety-three homemade 'cinematographic films' in total of great variation in length and quality.[13] Many such clips were short silent recordings of delegates entering a building, the secretary general at his desk or the like, but there were some examples of more ambitious films. Towards the end of the 1930s the Information Section seemingly sought to expand its cinematographic activities through confidential agreements of co-sponsorship with private production companies who would produce pro-League film material. A correspondence from 1936 recounted a meeting between Pelt and a representative of Gaumont-British Film Corporation. The latter agreed to produce 'a number of short, educational films' the distribution of which should be financed by the Carnegie Endowment for International Peace (CEIP) and be disseminated 'throughout the British Empire and the USA'. The section reserved a seat in the film's production committee and the arrangement should be 'of the closest possible nature but unofficial'.[14] Pelle van Dijk has recently delved into the section's endeavours when it came to producing film material and has shown that this, along with other attempts, never came to pass. The reason, as so often, was the fear among Secretariat officials of being accused of making propaganda.[15] In 1930 the section had only just begun to plan the making of a 'talking film'.[16] One of the results was the 1937 picture *The League at Work*, produced by Realist Film Unit, a film we shall return to later in this chapter.[17]

Overall, in its information material the Information Section in the early and mid-1930s pushed the purpose of the League news and information material in three directions: First, it sought to rhetorically extend the League's line of defence by emphasizing its many other 'technical' purposes besides the politically sensitive ones of peacekeeping and disarmament. Second, it underscored the gravity of the mounting international crisis it faced and reproduced gloomy declarations by pro-League political leaders who explained how the League could not be expected to act efficiently against a concerted effort to destroy it: peace needed to be actively sought by member states, or the League would mean nothing. Third, it attempted a partial 'retreat to aesthetics' by focusing more on League symbolism and regalia, like its new headquarters which stood finished by 1936, and such as commemorating life and deeds of its most loyal state representatives.

Even before the change of secretary general and the subsequent reorganizations of the Secretariat studied in previous chapters, the international situation and its consequences for the prestige of the League took its toll on the atmosphere among the 'bureaucrats with visions' in the Secretariat. Back in 1931 in Arthur Sweetser's sixty-page Manchuria Crisis diary one sensed already a dark shift in the atmosphere in Geneva, as Sweetser did his best to convince his American network to pressure the United States to putting pressure on Japan. The diary reflected a growing sense of dismay that the Council stood powerless in the face of dissenting members.[18] However, as such tensions mounted after the year 1933 the assumption underpinning the rhetorical strategies in the section's publications did not change. Its mainstay continued to be neutrality and a calm, routinely recounting of facts. Its news and information material did not give the impression of a total state of emergency. News emerged daily and monthly reporting on every aspect of League action, whether related to the crises that challenged the Covenant and the League's authority or not. Even after being 'smashed' the Information Section maintained a steady production of news and of information. Its printed material accounted for about 10 per cent of Secretariat spending before 1932, when Comert resigned, during 1933, when Sweetser was in charge, and continued to do so after 1934, when Adrianus Pelt had taken over. Publications were not untouched by the cuts and the reorganization. As mentioned, the Supervisory Committee's report had questioned the section's production of pamphlets that it regarded were 'exclusively for the purposes of propaganda' and made a request that some publications 'should be discontinued' without specifying.[19] The section seemingly reacted by discontinuing its publication of photo collections and the thematical pamphlets it had categorized 'regular pamphlets'. Yet, the emergence of new types of pamphlets suggests a resistance from the section towards the intervention.[20] Also, Pelt, the official formerly in charge of liaison with broadcasting associations, was now the director of the section. This indicated that the weekly broadcasts of the Information Section through the *Radio Nations* constituted a hope to the section. Although 'Films and photographs should be strictly limited to those of exceptional interest'[21] hopes for a future with more resources were placed in new technologies.[22]

Despite such signs of continuing normality, and despite the fact that Pierre Comert's ousting had taken place before the political takeover of national socialism in Germany in 1933 the section became increasingly aware of the tense political landscape it operated in and wary of whether its publications made the League vulnerable towards attacks from the press or political circles. The presence of Italian fascists in the Secretariat (a fact since the 1920s) became gradually more serious as Germany and Italy became more aligned. Elisabetta Tollardo has shown how the consequences of this presence were ambiguous. While a fascist deputy secretary general embarked on a 'fascistification' of 'his' people in Geneva, some Italian officials fought for their autonomy as international officials and stayed in Geneva after Italy's withdrawal in 1937.[23] A small handful worked in the Information Section during the 1930s. The highest-ranking, Guiseppe Bruccoleri, oversaw liaison with Italian press and with the International Educational Cinematographic Institute (IECI) in Rome.[24] He died in 1937 while working in Geneva, the same year Italy withdrew.[25] Although the effect of such presence is difficult to assess from the section's 'base line' of strict neutrality it is worth remembering among its constraints. In its selection of news and publications, the section thus attempted to uphold business as usual throughout the dramatic years after 1933.

From reading League publications, one did not immediately get the impression that the League was in deep trouble. Its membership, its publications impressed upon readers, was still high, it was expanding its efforts within several of its 'technical' programmes, the Soviet Union assumed membership in 1934, and there were small signs that the United States wished to develop closer ties with Geneva. Even during the last years of the 1930s, which saw an escalating existential crisis for the League (F. P Walters, in his chronicle of the League's history, called them 'the years of defeat'), the public legitimization efforts of the Information Section continued to operate on the fundamental assumption that the League's neutral stance should not be compromised and that it could not 'speak its own cause'.[26] As we shall see, a common feature of the strategies it employed to supplement this neutrality was an 'inwards turn' in focus towards the League itself: its aesthetics and procedures. The Information Section strove to subtly disavow responsibility on behalf of the League for the international conflicts looming still larger and maintained the message that should the dissenting Great Powers one day decide to return to the League it would stand ready.

Enter the technical

Building on what it had begun during the second half of the 1920s, the section increasingly depicted the League's technical efforts, which included a wide range of tasks, as equally important to peacekeeping by traditional measures and increasingly fused it with the latter. Areas such as technical assistance to non-Western countries, public health and intellectual cooperation were increasingly portrayed as working directly to prevent a new world conflict.

This trend is likely to have had had several explanations. Secretary general Joseph Avenol took a special interest in European economic cooperation. Additionally, the report of the Supervisory Commission which forbade 'propaganda' countered the idealism of the Information Section and pushed it towards preferring the coverage of the 'safe' ground of technical cooperation.

The increased focus on technical cooperation could be sensed in what material the section published as much as in the content of each individual publication. So-called regular information pamphlets were replaced by a series called 'League of Nations Questions'. Out of these twelve books only one treated a topic which the League had at times termed political – *The Saar Plebiscite* (1935). The remaining eleven books treated what it would typically refer to as technical and humanitarian topics. Several of the titles suggested a connection between such work and the struggle for peace between nations, such as *The Settlement of Assyrians – A Work of Humanity and Appeasement*, or *The Economic Interdependence of States* both from 1935.[27] Similarly, communiqués and the *Summary* increasingly linked technical cooperation to peacekeeping and thus wove the former into the fabric of the League's *raison d'être*. This was a way not only of making sense of the League's many technical efforts but also of demonstrating that the cause of peace could still be fought along many avenues, despite the exposed weaknesses of the League's peacekeeping apparatus. The important end-of-the-year *Monthly Summary* of 1934 reported that 'The efforts of the Intellectual Co-operation Organization for intellectual *rapprochement* and mutual understanding went forward alongside of the great political and technical problems of the League'.[28] Connecting intellectual cooperation directly to the maintenance of peace in this way was new. Back in 1921, intellectual cooperation had only been mentioned in passing in the *Summary* alongside economic activities, and in 1927, it featured as an effort to facilitate academic cooperation as important in its own right – not to the purpose of 'rapprochement'. Of course, we know that the link was not completely new; intellectual cooperation had related to 'moral disarmament', since the mid-1920s. But it was moving up in the world – from a specialized activity with positive side effects, to a genuine source of League legitimacy in the struggle for peace. The same was happening with specifically technical efforts as signalled first in 1930. Several communiqués concerned the technical cooperation programme between the League and China, a programme that had begun in the late 1920s particularly involving the League's Health Organization and later developed along other venues.[29] They were remarkable in length and level of detail indicating again an impression of the League's efforts within areas beside peacekeeping. While a communiqué from September 1934 included a lengthy annex of statements and reports, one from November contextualized the scheme historically, offering background on the effort since its inception in 1931.[30]

In October, a communiqué concerned a convention on the limitation of possession of dangerous drugs in member states. The section highlighted a statement by the Assembly in which the world was reminded that the League's supervisory arrangement for the limitation of dangerous narcotics was 'the only piece of machinery as yet set up by the League, which is truly universal, applying as it does to every state and every separate administrative unit in the world'.³¹ This statement served (it said so itself) to impress on governments that they had to stick to the League's deadlines for providing their estimates.³² Publicizing such deals was at the core of League public diplomacy. The public was hoped to be of service in pressuring governments into adhering to their own promises. The section also took the opportunity to remind the public of the intended universality of the organization, which, after 1933 when several Council Members had left, was important to impress.

In 1937, technical work played a leading role in a film released by the section. The section commissioned *The League at Work* from the production company Realist Film.³³ The result was a so-called infomercial: a short, informative sound-film designed to run before the main show in movie theatres or at special events. The infomercial was the most ambitious longer sound-film released by the section and was the culmination of an effort it had begun pursuing particularly during the second decade of its existence.³⁴ It took its point of departure at the Secretariat, with the secretary general at his desk. Avenol himself introduced each of the five thematic chapters of the film after which point a professional voiceover-narrator took over. The film opened with an introduction-bit telling the story of how the war constituted the background for the League and showing President Woodrow Wilson speaking at the Paris Peace Conference. Then followed three separate chapters each covering a field of League work: First, a chapter on the General Services of the Secretariat, including the Treasury – and the Information Section. Second came a chapter on the League's political work, including disputes between states, minority protection, the mandates system and disarmament. Third, the 'equally important' technical efforts of economics, health, the fight against dangerous drugs and the traffic of women and children. As an epilogue, the British foreign secretary Anthony Eden offered some general reflections on the state of the League from behind his desk. Keeping in mind that this book does not claim to delve into the reception (or 'impact') of the League's information strategies, recent scholarship on the League's film production gives a rare glimpse into the popular reception of League material. Pelle van Dijk takes us into some of the reviews in Dutch newspaper of the film, which were mixed. A liberal newspaper found the film vague and lacking in passion and persuasiveness.³⁵

The chapter on technical work led the viewer away from Geneva in several scenes, showing smuggler-boats and equipment for drug-use during a bit about opium-trade. It showed suspicious figures walking the streets, illustrating the work of the Social Section with regards to transnational prostitution and the protection of 'neglected and delinquent children'. For this section only, the narrator voice was female, perhaps reflecting the notion of social work as female work – the Secretariat's Social Questions Section had been directed by Dame Rachel Crowdy between 1922 and 1931.[36] The chapter recounted what kind of concrete action had been taken. Viewers were told of conventions regarding the outlawing of brothels, the prosecution of traffickers, the technical cooperation between the League and Chinese health authorities in fighting epidemics, how much the world's gross production of cocaine had decreased since the advent of the League, and so on. Contrasted with the political work, the technical work looked more important than simply 'equally' important. It was the longest chapter of the film. The emphasis on technical work was not only a 'safe' appeal but also a conservative one. It never compromised the League's promise that it was nothing more than an intergovernmental framework working to ensure cooperation wherever it was in everyone's interest. Accounts of economic cooperation and measures to counter human trafficking ('white slave trade' at the time) could not be labelled propagandistic. However, the appeal to some extent happened at the expense of celebrating the democratic link imagined to bind the League and the public together in a common strive for peace. As was underlined in a publication from 1933: 'The members of these organizations are not delegates representing governments. Designated with the titles of experts by the Council for their technical skills, they are experts of the League of Nations.'[37] When emphasizing the importance of technical cooperation, the League was addressing a closed club of educated people, letting go of its representative vision and its appeal to the masses.

Crisis rhetoric

Another key trait of news and publications after 1933 was the open admission of a looming international crisis, not as defeatism, but as a way of challenging the public to reflect on the safety provided by a stable and standardized diplomatic system like the League. For all its weak spots, the League was what was available, it was *there*. And it was still backed by some Great Powers. This appeal was made consistently but was crippled by the unwillingness of the Information Section to attribute guilt on specific states or 'name the elephants in the room' when recounting the most pressing political crises in Europe. The *Summaries* of 1934 and 1927 may illustrate the contrast between the mood in the mid-1930 and that of the League's 'Golden Age', a short decade before. Back then, the end-of-the-year issue had stated: 'The year 1927 was a period of intense activity and continuous work, affording striking evidence of the League's vitality.'[38] In December of 1934, the equivalent issue stated: 'the League passed through another difficult year in 1934. The work of the Disarmament Conference was held up and, from the economic point of view, the decline in international trade and financial relations has persisted.'[39]

The League admitted crisis, arguably not simply as a stating of the facts, neither as defeatism but in order to reinstate to the public that the League provided hope as the last barrier against international chaos. Edvard Beneš, whose eloquence the section often drew on in the *Monthly Summary*, came in as a voice of comfort:

> On striking a balance between the whole of the debt and the whole of the credit items in the present general situation, I thus find that the result is not discouraging for the League. There are doubtless many destructive forces at present at work in the public, and they are acting with extraordinary violence and energy. They are, however, being opposed and neutralised [sic] by positive and beneficent forces and tendencies which are no less energetic and effective. The first and most important of these forces is the League of Nations itself.[40]

In an earlier version of the same statement by Beneš, he said that despite the League not always being strong enough to prevent 'misfortunes' it was nonetheless an 'insurmountable barrier to the powers of darkness'. On the growing fear of another war, he added that although such fears were partly justified war was in no way 'ineluctable'.

As has been seen before, the section spoke through eloquent personalities and thus spared the Secretariat from assuming a voice itself. The solemn statesmen through which it spoke now openly conceded the risk of a new war as well as the League's failures within peacekeeping. Yet their real purpose was to convey the positive story of the signs pointing in the opposite direction.

Although one should be wary of retrospective readings of these critical years in European history, it is clear that end of the 1930s was overwhelmingly characterized, in League publications, by fear and uncertainty about future international peace and security. This mood permeated news recounted about Europe as well as other parts of the world. By 1938 the *Monthly Summaries* recounted the withdrawals from the League of Nations of Chile, Guatemala, Honduras and Venezuela. Then came the German annexation (*Anschluss*) of Austria, Fascist Italy's violent subjugation of Ethiopia, Europe's scramble to tackle a tidal wave of Jewish refugees fleeing Hitler's Germany, and a mounting desperation from the Spanish delegates in their appeals to the League for support in the Civil War. In short, crisis was visible in news about most areas of League work, political as well as 'technical'. For example, a communiqué from March of 1937 described the first meeting of the Committee for the Study of the Problem of Raw Materials, a committee instituted by the Assembly of 1936 to study 'The equal commercial access of all nations to certain raw materials'. The text was made considerably longer by a statement from secretary general Avenol. Underlining that the question of equal access to raw materials had been on the League's agenda since 1921, Avenol commented that 'the enquiry that you begin today [...] coincides with a rise in the prices of raw materials, a rise which is perhaps accentuated by the failure of the Disarmament Conference and the consequences of this failure. Finally, the problem of raw materials is addressed in a political atmosphere of which you are all aware'.[41] The characteristic abstention of Avenol or the Information Section from further elaboration of this 'atmosphere' leads us to comment on the strategy of confronting crisis. The open discussion of crisis was often combined with a reluctance to *name* the responsible member states. This clearly owed to prudence – the League was a diplomatic, multilateral forum. The logic of diplomacy was (and is) to never be direct and to always keep a door open. Also, as we know by now, the section did not want to place itself in a position where it could be blamed for stirring up unnecessary ill-feeling, and this was still the case if the powerful countries involved were no longer members of the League. The reluctance to naming the elephant(s) in the room additionally had to do with the reluctance of bureaucrats to keeping within the confines of the bureaucratic language, thus sustaining an institutional legitimacy. A note in the September issue of 1938 was simply headed 'The European Situation' and reported that 'the general anxiety caused by the situation in Europe in the second half of September was echoed in the Assembly' and that the Assembly aligned itself with the encouragement of US president Roosevelt to find a solution 'by peaceful means'.[42] The situation referred to was the general one; a Europe divided between Germany and Italy on the one side, France and Great Britain leading the other side. It specifically concerned the Munich talks in the last days of September resulting in the German annexation of Czechoslovakian Sudetenland. Bleakly concluding upon this episode, the *Summary* of December the same year opened thus:

> The international tension, which constantly increased, narrowly missed giving rise to a European conflict in September. The League declared that recourse to war, whatever might be the outcome, was no guarantee of a just settlement and would imperil the structure of European civilization.[43]

Again, there was to be no naming and blaming. Two somewhat earlier examples show this point, the coverage of the Spanish Civil War and that of the Mandates System, specifically the British mandate of Palestine. The Spanish Civil War regularly emerged in the pages of the *Summary* and illustrated forcefully the League's problems. While officially labelled an internal conflict between the democratically elected Republican government and rebelling conservatives allied to parts of the Spanish military, it was widely known and reported that the rebels received extensive military support from Hitler's Germany and Mussolini's Italy, and Spain was a member of the League. The conflict, which had begun the previous summer, appeared in almost every *Summary* under 'Political Questions'. Spain repeatedly appealed to the Council for its acknowledgement that the Axis powers (as they were now known) were militarily present in the country. The fact that the League aligned itself with the British–French initiated policy of non-intervention (which Germany and Italy did not respect) is less significant than the discrepancy between the *Summary*'s description of the matter and that of the Spanish government. While Spain was allowed time and again to protest in the pages of the *Summary* that 'Germany and Italy' were waging war on Spanish soil against the democratically elected government the *Summary*'s own voice stated cautiously, in May for example, that 'The Council considered once more the situation created by the intervention of certain Powers in Spain'.[44]

The reluctance to name these powers was an act of keeping the League neutral and outside the nexus of events. Ultimately, it was an extreme example of the constant navigation performed by the Information Section between neutrality and advocacy of the League's system, since Italy waging war against the elected government of another member state was a crystal-clear violation of the League's Covenant. The *Summary* not being an official document of the League, and Italy almost not a member state anymore (at the beginning of the war at least), the section might have gotten away with mentioning the elephants in the room. But it did not.

A spectacular example of how the League operationalized well-known figures to give credence to its crisis rhetoric occurred in the *Summary* in December 1937. It included a special note which featured printed versions of two special New Year addresses that had been transmitted by the Information Section through the *Radio Nations* to English, French and Spanish audiences. One was from the secretary general. The other was from Jan Smuts, the South African politician who had played an important role in the earliest drafts for the League.[45] Both men conceded that the League had not been able to solve or prevent the crises it now faced, and both reaffirmed nonetheless their support for it. However, the differences in the position of the two statements in relation to each other are telling as to what use they were put to by the Information Section. Smuts' statement drew on a dramatic literary reference and invoked the ethos of the speaker:

> I venture to plead the cause of the League of Nations as one of its original conceivers and begetters still sees it. Well might the League exclaim in the words of Hamlet: 'The world is out of joint. O, cursed spite, that ever I was born to set it right'.[46]

'The Covenant', Smuts explained, 'is the truest, most realist vision yet seen in the affairs of the world, and simply carries into world affairs that outlook of a liberal, democratic society which is one of the great achievements of our human advance. Perhaps that is why the new dictators object to it'.[47]

Smuts' association of the organization with a liberal outlook and his near-open naming of 'the enemy' – the dictatorships in Italy and Germany – made for unusually powerful pro-League rhetoric compared to the prudence normally seen in publications. His address injected a dose of enthusiasm and unfiltered idealism into the mostly neutral *Summary*.[48] He even compared the League's peacekeeping scheme to a national government's crime-prevention efforts, regretting that the world was 'not yet ripe for a super-State'. The former soldier paradoxically used allusions to battle and chivalry in his case against militarism, conceding that 'there have been defections, failures, losses. Let us admit all that. But in membership the League still remains a formidable army, able to do battle against militarism and reaction. When these have run their course and done their worst, many will return in chastened mood to their vacant places at the Round Table of the League'.[49]

It was certainly Smuts' association with the foundation of the League that had made him attractive to the Information Section as a New Year speaker. The secretary general did not speak of liberalism, neither did he regret the absence of a more powerful League. His statement was an assertion that the League was necessary, and that there was no credible alternative to it. He concluded that the world quite simply had to choose: 'not between the League of Nations and some other system of international relations, but between the League and a state of almost total anarchy, combined with the use of force'. He did not outrightly support the arguments of the South African statesman. Instead, he simply stated: 'It is an honour for me to be associated on this occasion with General Smuts, who has been speaking to you all as one of the authors of the Covenant'.[50]

This mythologizing of Smuts forebodes another 1930s strategy to which we shall return later: one of constructing League symbols and regalia.

During the League's final and most difficult years, the crisis rhetoric evolved into more emotional appeals which did not stick completely to the dogma of neutrality. An example was a topical pamphlet released in 1938, *The Refugees*. The booklet was part of a *League of Nations Questions* series published by the section and gave a general overview of the machinery that had been in place since 1919 for settlement and aid to the streams of refugees in Europe. Its main purpose, however, was discussing the issue of Jewish and political refugees fleeing Hitler's Germany. In 1938, the handling of refugees had once again become pertinent in Europe. Under the heading 'The new problem', the pamphlet explained: 'Early in the year 1933, a new refugee problem was created by the coming into power of the National Socialists Party in Germany' and went on to describe the racist doctrine of this ideology.

Seen in its totality, the booklet reflected an Information Section which was giving way to more value judgement than earlier. It historicized the phenomenon of refugees and explained how history was full of tales of people made homeless by 'invasion, war, civil conflict, religious dissension, famine and pestilence, fire and flood', and that 'It would be difficult to exaggerate the privation, loneliness and insecurity that have ever been the lot of the refugee'. It added that the problem had turned increasingly critical in modern society since the loss of citizenship was 'an immeasurable calamity'.[51] Particularly the latter phrase categorized the phenomenon as one made more acute in the age of nation states and thus very much the business of the League of Nations. In this way, the Information Section articulated the specific problem of refugees as a clear mission of the League. It also demonstrated a ripple of the old strategy observed in 1920–21 of constructing a moral legitimacy for the League through its connection to the public. Here, it was subtler than the depictions of cheering crowds in the 1920s, but the manoeuvre was similar – the unafraid reporting in public of this dangerous tendency of stateless people fleeing Germany gave legitimacy to the League as a humanitarian endeavour. It fused the League dogma of transparency with its technical, efforts. The text presented the history of the League's efforts of engaging with refugees whether Russian, Greek, Bulgarian, Armenian or German and described in detail the bureaucratic backs and forth of establishing a system directed almost singled handedly by Fritiof Nansen. Its wording demonstrated a (re)claiming of a moral standpoint by the League. This was fused with one of its core features – its endeavours to secure transparency:

Above all, the League's organization, with the opportunities it provides for the public discussion of questions of international well-being, has kept the problem of refugees before the conscience of the world.[52]

In its report on this 'new problem' the pamphlet reflected this harmonization of humanitarianism and open diplomacy as well. It recounted meticulously the process that had led to the difficult situation faced by the League's High Commissioner. Germany had protested the fact that such a commissioner would report directly to the League itself and thus pressured the League to institute a separate 'High Commission for Refugees coming from Germany'. This, the publication reminded its readers, had been unacceptable to Sir James McDonald, the first High Commissioner, who had consequently resigned from the post in protest.[53] The text recounted drily the Council's observation that since the number of refugees in 1938 was about 600,000 the problem 'could not therefore be regarded as solved'.[54]

The booklet offered an extraordinary look into the European crisis during the last years of the 1930s. It conveyed highly disturbing information on a problem that the League, so it admitted itself, was not equipped to handle. At the same time, it demonstrated the advantage in admitting crisis: If the League could not actually solve problems, it could publicize its own impotency thus keeping the problem 'before the conscience of the world'. This positioned the universal public, a united 'humanity', recognizing the anguish of refugees, as an existing force that supported the League. The organization became the embodiment of the international conscience.

It was clear that the section in late 1937 still used impassioned League proponent for 'legitimization by proxy' as a cautious way of attributing importance to the League. Yet Smuts' statement went, perhaps, a little further than what was common when he openly attacked 'the dictators' and spoke in favour of liberal democracy, thus partly aligning the League with one group of powers. Or perhaps the gulf between the power blocs was simply becoming too wide to bridge. As the atmosphere heated up, such breaches of the League's neutrality occurred from time to time. The film *The League at Work*, which came out the same year, included a similar manoeuvre at its ending: an address by Anthony Eden. The message of the British foreign minister was clear: the British Empire would continue to support the League. The organization, Eden conceded, was 'not perfect', but if only nations would adhere to its principles, it pointed the way forward for a world of peace and prosperity. With this finale, the League openly opted for the Great Britain as its guarantor, a rhetorical necessity that underscored the gravity of the situation. Eden's statement was a solemn, composed appeal to the support of sensible educated people of liberal persuasion, similar to the statements of Joseph Avenol and Jan Smuts.

The Information Section, it is seen, addressed the resulting uneasiness and the threat of war it gave rise to by using emotional appeals, at times resulting in inconsistent arguments, like Smuts' militarist rhetoric in favour of an anti-militarist vision. Most prominently, however, the public was reminded that the League had a strong card on its hand, which separated it from any proposed alternative; it existed. And it still had strong friends.

This crisis rhetoric was pragmatic before anything else. The section rhetorically asked readers to think of a viable alternative to the League, and portrayed its work as a long, dark struggle which only the bravest could take up: 'O cursed Spite, that ever I was born to set it right', said Smuts, quoting Shakespeare and regretting that the world was not ready for a super state. The tension of the Information Section regarding the League's agency was cast aside for a moment when it made these appeals, since it would not have endorsed Smuts' message under normal circumstances, usually using 'super state' as an example of what it was *not*.[55] Most of the time, it held on to its dogma of neutrality and ensuing taboo of propaganda as it was rarely outright hostile towards Germany and Italy, the states openly rebelling against the League system. Now, however, the pretext of crisis was used as an opportunity to return to the foundational ideas of the League and legitimize it through a combination of pragmatic and idealist appeals, which aimed at sustaining the League's continued anchoring in an undivided public.

Retreat to aesthetics

By the early 1930s, the League had existed for a long enough time that it could be said to have built up a 'mythology' which could work as a supporting pillar in its public narrative. The section was starting to nurture a mythology and institute rituals of the League organization to the effect of having the League mimic the authority of a state with Geneva as its (international) capital. It was seen, for example, when news and publications recounted official acts of the League that one would normally associate with state ceremonies, and through a systematic coverage of the planned new League headquarters in Ariana Park in Geneva, the compound that would come to be known as the Palais des Nations. Also, the Information Section used commemorations of deceased statesmen who had supported the League to ritualize the institution. In the *Summary* of January 1934 the Council honoured recently passed Vittorio Scialoja, a prominent Italian politician and one of the original drafters of the Covenant.[56] The Council president commemorated the Italian senator with kind words, and Italy's delegation added that Scialoja had always been able to successfully 'reconcile his position as representing the interests of his country with a co-operation in the work of harmonizing the interests of all members of the international community'.[57] This, it is seen, served both as a commemoration of a person and as an underscoring of the virtue of reconciling national and international interests, which, quite remarkably, was cited from fascist Italy's delegation. The *Summary* stated that Scialoja's qualities had made him an asset to the League in its early years, and thus the Council looked ceremonially back more than a decade into its own existence. In the May issue the president of the Council was reported to have paid tribute to the memory of a representative of Panama, who had been involved in the League since its early days. M. R. Amador was praised for his 'loyal' cooperation with the organization.[58]

Loyalty had different levels of meaning in the League world (Amador's loyalty had not been that of a civil servant but rather that of a politician to an idea). In September 1934 the *Summary* reported that the secretary general and his high officials had made declarations of loyalty before the Council in accordance with new provisions in the Staff Regulations.[59] The official swore to be loyal to the League and not to 'seek or receive instructions from any Government or other authority external to the Secretariat of the League of Nations' (the secretary general himself simply said 'to the League of Nations'). This should be understood in conjunction with the political development in the League at the time. The oath had been taken since 1932 but did not appear in *Summaries* until 1934. Its inclusion by then suggested the section saw a value in underlining the existence of an international level of loyalty to the public, a paradoxical adherence to an ideal which was being contested at exactly that time in the minority protest to the Committee of Thirteen report, discussed in Chapter 4.

The section thus demonstrated the League's celebration of its loyalists through commemorations and through reporting on the emergence of physical League symbols and regalia. During the fall of 1934 three statesmen, including Scialoja again, were honoured for their services to the League, and in addition two bronze busts, one of Scialoja, presented by his family and one of Arthur Henderson for his presidency of the Disarmament Conference (he received the Nobel Peace Prize the same year) were mentioned in the *Summary*. Finally, the finishing of a portrait of Eric Drummond, the former secretary general, was covered conscientiously.[60]

The qualities brought up and quoted in the *Summary* about these men were illustrative. Scialoja was said to have mastered the reconciling of national aims with international ones, Amador had been loyal to the League, Henderson had presided over the largely failed attempt to disarm the Great Powers. Drummond needed no introduction – he had held office back in an era when the *Summary* would use words like 'intense activity' and 'vitality' to report on the League's work.

This flow of ceremonial memory may be understood as working in three ways: First, it attributed a certain authority to the League by pointing towards all the important people who had invested their careers and oratory in it – an ethos-appeal to the effect that such people could not be wrong in their judgement that the organization was worth fighting for. The strategy was an open celebration of the League, which attributed to itself the authority to commemorate its loyalists. Second, the strategy signified an 'inwards turn' of the League towards its own aesthetics, a movement which could be observed in other strategies of the time as well. Rather than celebrating its achievements (there were fewer than there had been), the League was celebrating itself and its endurance against all odds, focusing on its machinery, its symbolism and its physical settings. Finally, the commemorations mimicked the official voice of a state (in an obituary of Japanese International Court-judge Mineichirō Adachi the secretary general extended the Secretariat's grief to Adachi's wife and expressed to the court that his death was a great loss to 'the international community')[61] and created symbols of power – like busts and portraits. The Secretariat constructed an officialdom for itself that resembled the officialdom of state ceremonies. Rather than persuading people who were uneducated about, or new to, the League, commemorations and rituals constructed public opinion, which was imagined as remembering the 'golden age' of the League back when these men had been invested in it. Thus, it aimed the League's public legitimization towards an educated public already associated with the League or at least strongly in favour of it. It was telling of the mood of the *Summary* that so many of the great League figures were dying or retiring in the early 1930s.

Arguably, when the Information Section emphasized such commemorations of League figures, it navigated the tension inherent in its work between the potential for public support and the presumption of one that already existed of an 'international society'. Arguably, it celebrated the League's 'constituency' – a network of internationalists who supported the organization through thick and thin. These people were those who primarily received the publications, the same who were the targets of the section's liaison efforts: those engaged in League of Nations associations and other organizations such as veterans' associations, women's organization or students' unions. The creation of League rituals and regalia constituted the League's interaction with the people whose lives crisscrossed the emerging 'international society' illuminated by scholars such as Daniel Gorman, Daniel Laqua and Glenda Sluga.[62] This group was most often what the section referred to when it spoke and wrote of 'public opinion'.

Commemorations became an increasingly common type of content in the *Summary* towards the end of the 1930s. *Summaries* throughout 1937 commemorated League personalities who had passed, like Austen Chamberlain (British), Åke Hammarskjöld (Swedish)[63] and Manuel Vicuna (Chilean).[64] A melancholic note about the international situation permeated them; a tribute paid by the Assembly to the memory of Austen Chamberlain, its president, stated that the historic example set by Chamberlain, together with Gustav Stresemann and Aristide Briand, had ever since been an inspiration to the Council and 'never more so than today'. Anthony Eden added that the Locarno talks had been the closest thing to realizing the League's true objectives that had happened at any time 'before or since'.[65]

Commemorations were just one aspect of the mimicking of statehood on behalf of the League by the Information Section. It additionally employed a focus on its physical settings, its architecture and the aesthetics of Geneva. Architecture David Allen has remarked on the League's exhibition at the New York World's Fair in 1939: 'can communicate national and international power'. Marco Ninno has observed that the Palais des Nations was given the semantically loaded label of a 'palace' already by the international jury instituted to judge in the competition for its design, suggesting the early awareness in the League of its potential as a political symbol.[66] The *Summaries* reported on the advancement of the construction of new headquarters of the League in the Ariana Park in Geneva which had begun in 1929. In May 1934, a richly detailed article described the aim of the soon-to-be finished buildings, the construction process, the materials used and its financial aspects. The text promised a concrete (literally) physical imprint of the organization on the world and underscored the nature of the League as a place as much as an organization or a concept – it even compared the new compound to the Palace of Versailles which had been standing for centuries through revolutions and wars and still was.[67] The occasion for the coverage was the fact that the Council had formally inspected the building site, however, the text was a mixture of celebration and a service to public accountability – after all it was indirectly the money of the 'international public' being spent. However, it did not fail to address the paradox of the ambitious project going on during an international financial crisis, mentioning that the project was being pursued 'despite the difficulties of the present time'.[68] Nonetheless, it stated proudly that 'All the foundations, the framework of the building and the floors and roofs are constructed of reinforced concrete'[69] (Figure 10).

It would be quite difficult to literally get rid of the League. Descriptions of the multinational constitution of the workforce employed at the site reflected the international site on which they were working and dutifully recounted the instalment of electric wiring, window frames, staircases 'in beautiful freestone', lifts, central heating and skylights. It added that 'no strikes, no stoppage has disturbed the work. No serious accident has occurred'.[70] The Information Section was determined to exploit the symbolic potential of the project and not let the buildings speak for themselves.[71] Arthur Sweetser remarked internally about the tourist-potential in the Palais: 'This is of course very useful propaganda. The mere visualization of the League's new home creates a lasting memory. Such memories will be carried home to every country in the world.'[72] Timo Holste has demonstrated how the focus on the physical characteristics of the buildings, the material, the architectural style, the cost and size were used to distract

Figure 10 A meeting of the League Council in the brand-new Palais des Nations, April 1936.

United Nations Archives, Geneva.

tourists and visitors at Geneva from the political realities facing the League. He recounted how the Information Section during the 1930s received complaints that guides exclusively talked about the buildings and did not spare one word on the work or accomplishments of the League.[73]

The creation of League symbols and regalia mimicking national power was fused with a related emphasis on the League's presence in international society through a focus on its materiality and the city of Geneva as a symbol of international life. In 1938 the section published *The League of Nations – A Vital Necessity in the Modern World* at the occasion of the one hundredth session of the Council (January 1937). The book celebrated the League's continued survival, and it consisted entirely of legitimization by proxy; statements made by delegates on the occasion, affirming their devotion to the League. Its opening page was illustrative of the section's use of Geneva: it showed the whole world illuminated by beams coming from its 'centre' – Switzerland, conveying the message that the League lit up the world with information from Geneva.[74]

Back in 1934, a new type of pamphlet released by the section had foreboded this focus. The series *Essential Facts of the League of Nations* exemplified another aspect of it. It came in different colours (blue, yellow, red, grey) and was filled with illustrations. The series supplemented the *Summary*'s legitimization through rituals and symbols by anchoring the organization geographically in the minds of its readers. The focus represented a movement which had been ongoing since the mid-1920s – away from the accomplishments of the organization and increasingly towards the organization itself and its procedures. The *Essential Facts* was richly illustrated with visualizations of various League institutions, maps of mandated territories or of disputed border areas, and visualizations of new rules and regulations, some of them affecting peoples' everyday lives. An illustration depicted street sign designs agreed upon through the League's Communication and Transit Organization in 1931. 'Geneva' was printed on the example of a sign showing a city name.[75] Geneva was thus portrayed as a centre from which waves of useful progress emanated, some of which was useful in everyday life. There was a small chapter on new League of Nations stamps issued in Switzerland and Spain.[76] The first page of the book featured a map of northeastern Geneva on which the League's 'old' Secretariat (still in use in 1934) in the Palais Wilson was marked as well as the site of the new Palais des Nations in the Ariana Park.[77]

Such illustrations familiarized the reader with the League and downplayed its character as an abstract place of intrigue between statesmen and dictators. With the little map neatly marking the League's placement in Geneva the section situated the League as a physical thing in a real city and nurtured an idea of a symbiosis between the League and the public. In this narrative, it seemed to be a core message that Geneva was not a distant, powerful place or a place of incomprehensible power politics but at the centre of 'public opinion'. The section addressed here their tension between formal and informal communication – the distinction became redundant as Geneva as the hub of diplomacy was identical with Geneva as a hub of public opinion. While this constructed a specifically elitist notion of public opinion, the authors clearly felt they were addressing a public outside the Secretariat. They compensated for the dull style of the manual with accessible visualizations that blew life into the League.

In one 1935 publication on the League's buildings and Secretariat, the entire preface consisted of six quotations by prominent League-affiliated figures. Several praised the League, some equating nationalism with 'egoism'.[78] Among them were Woodrow Wilson, Aristide Briand, Anthony Eden and Hungarian politician and League proponent Count Albert Apponyi. It is worth noting that these grand leaders were cited in a book about the League's architecture. Establishing rituals and symbolism that portrayed the League as a world community and a system of communication with Geneva at its centre as a kind of international capital mimicked official language of statehood and so hinted at a tendency to utilize what has been pointed to by some scholars – that internationalism sometimes functioned as a twinned concept to nationalism.[79]

Glenda Sluga has argued the application of Benedict Anderson's theoretical framework of nationalism as imagined communities on the case of early-twentieth-century internationalism.[80] The application of this argument to our study would require us to ask if League publications played a role in nurturing a cultural community across borders, paralleling the processes that brought about national communities. However, League publications did not have what one could call a mass-readership or a systematic use in education systems that would make the comparison relevant. Furthermore, a state did not (and does not) equal a nation. No matter the degree to which the League mimicked the language of a state bureaucracy it could not pretend to represent any nation, as it existed, in accordance with its Wilsonian heritage, to maintain a community of sovereign, separate nations. Being that as it was, the section suggested a parallelism between the idea of the national and that of the international and thus in a superficial sense pushed the, at this point already near-discredited, notion of the latter as an extension of the former. This, to a great extent, was what its internationalism in practice looked like or, put differently, how far it could go. The strategy pushed the tension in the Information Section about the nature of the organization towards making it appear as a separate political agent. Its identification of the public moved closer to a 'world public' looking for a higher identity than respective national ones, whether to supplement or to replace them. The section was constructing symbols subtly associating the power of the League with the kind of power exerted by states.

Conclusion

Although one should be wary of drawing a simplistic trajectory of rise and decline, the story of the League's public voice after 1933 is a story of the League trying to maintain a consistent narrative throughout a growing complex of crises. As Zara Steiner put it, this was 'not a happy time in Europe'.[81] What League communicators faced following the organization's apparent inability to confront the Japanese invasion of Manchuria, the failure of the Disarmament Conference, the withdrawal of Germany from the League and the economic repercussions of the Great Depression makes a 2023 observer think of the World Economic Forum's recent warning of 'polycrises' – multiple crises interacting to make the overall impact exceed the sum of each part.[82] The League sought to communicate its way through this using a toolkit of changing and overlapping strategies.

First, it highlighted the League's 'technical work', including efforts not specifically labelled technical but unrelated to peacekeeping such as intellectual cooperation. The Information Section consistently made the case that such efforts fostered world peace and therefore belonged to the League's overall task of peacekeeping.

Second, it articulated the acute political crisis in world affairs, particularly during the second half of the 1930s in a kind of 'final plea' massively exploiting the pro-League politicians it could muster, to rally support for League internationalism.

Third, it systematically constructed League symbolism and constructed Geneva as a physical manifestation of the League idea which mimicked a 'stateness' for the organization. This was seen through commemorations of League personalities and institutions and the highlighting of the new League buildings and their grandeur.

Overall, we may think of the League's voice in this period as a more experienced voice with more cynical sense of what the League could hope to achieve than had been the case during the more optimistic 1920s. The fact that the section had fewer successes with which to legitimize the League through its *activities*, and that its taboo of propaganda had been sharpened (as we saw in the previous chapter), made it strive to legitimize it through its *existence*. The result was an increased use of the presence and distanced bureaucratic cool-headedness of the League itself rather than what it had accomplished. In the early and mid-1920s the institution had capitalized on the confidence that came with broad political support and subtly ascribed itself a higher degree of agency. Now, it was disavowing agency while underscoring that if member states chose to empower it, it would stand ready to serve. What had not changed was the fact that its strategies still aimed at a relatively narrow audience. The imagined public were already leaning towards supporting the League's project, educated on international affairs and associated with the landscape of private associations that backed it. The League was preaching to the choir or, put more sympathetically, building a defensive alliance with its 'base'.

6

Exit Geneva

League legacies in UN publicity planning, 1942–46

When the Second World War broke out in 1939, the League of Nations, now widely discredited if not outright ignored, went into hibernation. The core of the Secretariat remained in Geneva where, from August 1940, it would be overseen by its new secretary general Seán Lester, but as officials fled continental Europe many scrambled to salvage archives and institutional memory of key branches and auxiliary organizations.[1] What then happened to its Information Section? How did its officials fare in the war, and did they take part in the planning of future information policy in the UN?

This final chapter sketches the legacy of the section in the UN using as an analytical lens the wartime trajectories of its former officials. The reader is invited to trace the footsteps of officials as they went into exile. As the war began in earnest, they mulled over the League's communicative achievements and shortcomings, and when the preparatory work for a United Nations Department of Public Information began, the imprint of former League officials can be identified in the drafts they produced. The advice of League veterans differed slightly. While Arthur Sweetser would underscore the value of unofficial cooperation with elite stakeholders, Adrianus Pelt made the case for a transparent department employing fewer journalists and not trying to compete with the League's diplomatic service. Most agreed that the new department should be better funded and utilize a broad variety of new technology in its work.

As was expected by many but not fully realized at the time, the Second World War catalysed a shift in the global political power centres from 'old Europe' towards the United States. After the United States entered the war in 1941, the British worked to convince their great ally of the utility of a new permanent peacetime organization to take up its mantle – one with a British-American partnership fulfilling a key role.[2] Formally, as we heard, the League was still in operation and would not close until 1946. However, as we shall see, many of its former high officials gathered in the Allied countries to plan for the future, and several of its institutions moved across the Atlantic. Mark Mazower has illuminated the move of the Economic and Financial Organization of the Secretariat to Princeton University, New Jersey, a process in which Arthur Sweetser was instrumental.[3] The International Labour Organization set up an exile seat in Montréal, Canada. A substantial group of former officials settled in London. The centres of planning for a postwar intergovernmental organization became Great Britain and the United States.

The Information Section was on the move too. The three leading officials we have come to know all spent the war years in one of these two power centres, now serving their respective countries within information and propaganda activities.[4] In their spare time they took part in the evaluation of the League experience. Adrianus Pelt and Pierre Comert both became associated with the so-called London Group, a gathering of prominent ex-League officials led by Eric Drummond (the 7th Earl of Perth since 1937).[5] Arthur Sweetser, along with a few other former officials of the Information Section, was in the United States, where, in New York City, they took part in a similar evaluation of the Secretariat, to which we shall return. Thus, all three leading figures of League public information were consulted, but among them Sweetser and Pelt would be most directly involved in the planning of the future information policy of the UN; a policy which, compared to the League's, would reflect a bigger, more professionalized and globalized vision for the public diplomacy of international bureaucracies, employing a less elitist conceptualization of 'world public opinion'.

Crossing the Atlantic or the channel

By 1940, no leading officials of the Information Section remained in Switzerland. Pelt had resigned and left for London joining the Dutch exile community there, and Sweetser had gone on a final mission to the United States from which he would not return to Geneva as a League employee.

Pierre Comert had been out of the Secretariat for eight years. After his resignation in 1932 the French government had charged him with the press department of the French Foreign Ministry – the Quai d'Orsay. Then, in 1938 he was demoted, partly due to his outspoken opposition towards appeasement of Germany, and he worked during the last two years before the war in a department for liaison with the United States. When France was overrun by the German army, he fled to London, and here his League career suddenly showed its relevance again. Comert met his compatriots in the French exile community but soon deemed them too loyal to general de Gaulle whose authoritarian style Comert cared little for. He approached his old friend Eric Drummond, now a leading official in the British Ministry of Information.[6] Through Drummond, Comert was quickly able to secure British financial support for the establishment of a news bulletin for the French exile community, *FRANCE*.[7] Comert insisted on the magazine's independence from de Gaulle and his Free French movement to the general's open annoyance, and consequentially Comert remained a peripheral figure in the London of exiles, compared to many of his former colleagues who worked closer together with their respective governments or decision-makers.[8]

As we can see, Comert was not the type to make easy choices. The same applied to his family, who did not pass through the war unscathed. His son was arrested by the Gestapo on suspicion of affiliation with the French resistance but was later released. Comert's wife spent the last two years of the war a prisoner in the concentration camp Ravensbrück. She survived but died shortly after the war.[9] Warren Kuehl's observation that Comert's friends 'noted, in his later life a sense of disillusionment in contrast to his earlier League years of selfless idealism' is unsurprising in light of these events.[10] Although fighting an uphill battle among his own countrymen, Comert also spent the London years connecting with his former Geneva colleagues. He corresponded warmly with Sweetser during the war and took part in the social gatherings of the London Group.[11]

Leaving Geneva after the German invasion of the Netherlands in May 1940 Pelt had not tried to return to his occupied home country but had managed to reach Britain. Here, he directed the information office of the Dutch exile government in London. In recent years, new scholarship has emerged on the 'London of exiles'. The British capital, during the five years of the war, became the seat of eight governments-in-exile plus a greater number of exile movements. Journalists and other writers significantly contributed to running the public relations of such exile movements.[12]

Despite Comert's foundational role and fourteen years of service in the League, it was Pelt who joined the group of six men who, under the auspices of the Royal Institute of International Affairs, published the so-called *London Report* in 1944. The report was a small but significant book on the administrative experience of the League, which included recommendations for the future. Historian Benjamin Auberer has suggested that antipathy felt towards Joseph Avenol's administration disinclined the group from wishing the project to be associated with a Frenchman.[13] However, Comert had been close to Drummond exactly because of the secretary general's distrust of Avenol. A more acute explanation of

Comert's alienation is probably Comert's having been out of the League system for a decade combined with his lack of intimacy with the Free French.

The utilization of League experience in deliberations about future international organization took place across the Atlantic as well. In early 1942, after the US entrance into the war, the Carnegie Endowment for International Peace (CEIP) hosted two intimate conference sessions to evaluate the organizational lessons of the League of Nations Secretariat. The conferences aimed at serving decision-makers who would initiate a future global organization expected to emerge after the war and, certainly, consolidate the CEIP's role as a key stakeholder in such questions. The secretary of the first conference in 1942 was the former Information Section official and later Secretariat-historian Egon Ranshofen-Wertheimer. The list of invited participants (thirteen) included two Americans who had been members of the Information Section, Benjamin Gerig and Arthur Sweetser.[14]

In a 1947 letter to Comert, Sweetser summarized his movements immediately before and after the outbreak of war, remarking that in comparison to the former, 'life has gone on relatively uneventfully'. He had left Geneva with his family in May 1940, 'just as the Germans passed Compiegne', then travelled to the United States via Italy before this country's declaration of war on the Allies in June. He had then 'had a part in getting the League's Economic and Financial unit to Princeton, and ourselves settled there till 1942', before finally, after the United States entered the war, he returned to national service as deputy director of the Office of War Information in Washington.[15]

That Sweetser, who had entered the League via his service at the press section of the US delegation in Paris in 1918–19, was now in the Office of War Information (OWI) counted as a full circle. His new job was war propaganda, and Comert did not fail to compliment his former colleague in 1942: 'The little I know of your propaganda in France strikes me as satisfactory. Roosevelt, and the United States in general, are very popular in France.'[16]

Sweetser, unsurprisingly, oversaw the OWI's information regarding the UN. At the time, that name referred to the wartime alliance and not a peace organization, but behind the scenes there unfolded a British-American standoff over the control of the organization to come. Giles Scott-Smith has demonstrated how Sweetser was the senior American involved in the process of bringing the British-led Inter-Allied Information Committee (IAIC) under the auspices of the United Nations Information Organization (UNIO), an institutional vehicle for future planning of UN information programmes.[17] Later, Sweetser was a delegate at the founding of the United Nations Relief and Rehabilitation

Administration-organization (UNRRA) in 1943 as well as at the important Bretton Woods conference the same year before finally attending the 1945 San Francisco Conference that founded the UN we know today.[18]

Herren and Löhr have discussed Arthur Sweetser's unique interwar experience of League 'network diplomacy'. He bridged the League and UN experiences through his constant 'in-between presence' and multi-affiliations in institutions, think tanks and international organizations on both sides of the Atlantic.[19] In 1946, when Sweetser was appointed special advisor to Trygve Lie, the first UN secretary general, this made him a colleague of Pelt who had then become Lie's assistant secretary general.[20] Fifteen years after that, in a letter to a spokesperson of the World Federation for United Nations Organizations (the successor to the IFLNS) Sweetser summarized his relation to Pelt: 'not only a life-long colleague but a very dear friend'.[21] Of the relations between Pelt and Comert we know that they socialized in the London Group and that Pelt would later tell Sweetser he was consulting Comert on the planning for future information policies. Thus, relatively close wartime relations could be seen between all three of the significant personalities of the old Information Section.

The Carnegie project in the United States and the London Group in Britain mirrored each other. Both were the results of connections between former League officials and influential policy think tanks: The London Group began meeting in early 1941 and the Carnegie group in mid-1942 after the Japanese attack on the naval base at Pearl Harbor in late 1941. The Carnegie project only produced its proceedings, but Ranshofen-Wertheimer's book *The International Secretariat* was spawned by the project and published by the CEIP.

The two networks were aware of each other's existence, and although there was a certain degree of 'territoriality' on the part of the initiator of the London Group, Joseph Wilson, towards some members of the Carnegie project, the relation was one of cautious acceptance and some exchange of information.[22] Rather than opposing each other, the observations of the two networks can be considered two transfers of experience within information and publicity going from the League to the politicians and diplomats planning a new postwar international organization of which we shall see that, that of the London Group, became slightly more influential than the other in terms of information policy.

The London Report was authored by six former high officials of the Secretariat, who had had long careers in the Secretariat and represented smaller countries. The group did not want to risk being accused of acting as a purely British instrument, but deemed it would have a more legitimate claim if it represented a broader European counterweight to the postwar visions of the

United States.²³ Besides Drummond it included Greek Thanassis Aghnides of the former Disarmament Section, Norwegian Erik Colban of the Minorities Section, British Frank Walters, who had been deputy secretary general, British Joseph Wilson of the Central Section and Pelt, who was Dutch. The report addressed what the authors considered as the basic challenges facing an international administration: the organization of a secretariat, the question of international versus national allegiance, finances and so on.

In a chapter on 'external relations' and a more detailed appendix which addressed questions of information policy, Pelt's overall message was clear: A future information section should boost its efforts to pursue large-scale mass communication. His outline included offices dealing with news, publications, radio, films, pictures and exhibitions and lectures.²⁴ The League's section had included only three or four offices and although it pursued most of these activities as well, it films and broadcasting efforts took place on an experimental level. Pelt did not mention a 'liaison office' like the one that had existed in the Information Section. His omissions as much as what he included were informative as to what shift in policy he envisioned.

On top of this, the Dutchman reflected on the future target audience. The new information department, he thought,

> must seek to render interesting the undramatic as well as the dramatic aspects of international life. It must cater to the most varied public – the farmer in Nebraska, the shopkeeper in Lyons, the tractor-driver in a Soviet rural community. How this can best be done will vary from case to case, but it must be done in manner which is attractive and easily understandable to each group of readers, listeners or motion picture audiences.²⁵

The idea of a world public opinion was reappearing; Pelt still believed that the legitimacy of international organizations rested on an effort to inform and mobilize the public. However, he constructed a more diverse public than what had been imagined during the two decades of the League. More concretely, three themes could be extracted from his suggestions.

The first concerned 'size and technology'. Pelt was adamant the new organization ought to use new communications technologies to a greater extent than had the League and accordingly should be a better funded department. It should be equipped with long-wave broadcasting equipment to reach the geographical areas immediately around the transmitting point, not just distant countries. Consequently, the organization should control its own radio station and not have it hosted by a national government as had been the case in the League.²⁶

The second theme concerned qualifications of staff. Pelt expressed uneasiness about political journalists (despite being one himself), and argued that the section should enlist fewer of those and more 'communications-specialists'. He was referring to 'radio commentators, film experts, press photographers, exhibition-experts and professional lecturers'. This recommendation too suggested Pelt was trying to move beyond an elitist perception of the public, afraid as he was that journalists only catered to a foreign-affairs-focused and educated audience.[27]

Finally, the third theme concerned what Pelt referred to as freedom of expression. He argued that the section should be allowed to communicate in a livelier way than the old section – to place emphasis on some news and publish based on news value. He proposed in addition the establishment of a permanent joint agency of news agencies at the seat of the organization, responsible for disseminating 'everything' newsworthy going on under its auspices which would then leave more freedom for individual correspondents and for the section to strategize.[28] He was dismantling the 'taboo of propaganda'. On the contrary he emphasized its importance even stronger, complaining that in the 1920s the League had been 'to such an extent revolutionary that the new institution required active propaganda, although even at that time the use of the word was realized to be a drawback'. Instead he seemed to be arguing for a section which would be allowed to *diversify* its communication according to specific situations and targets.

Taken together, these themes are telling, not only to what some League officials hoped would be allowed in the future, but also to their verdict on the past. They indicate that a unique conceptualization of the public had dominated the interwar period. One could argue that during the first half of the twentieth century, the international sphere of life followed the sphere of national life in a process of democratization, which in turn brought a need for 'public mass justification' (in the words of Müller). The interwar period had been characterized by a cautious, elitist perception of the public. Although a trope was constructed of the power of the 'man in the street', widely different opinions coexisted on whether the uneducated, the illiterate and those not in some way associated with diplomatic life belonged to this public. Adrianus Pelt, on the other hand, was starting to argue the inclusion of literally everyone into the idea of the public – a farmer in Nebraska and a tractor-driver of a rural Soviet community.

Meanwhile, on the other side of the Atlantic, Sweetser, Gerig and Ranshofen-Wertheimer took part in the CEIP-conferences, the latter as secretary. The CEIP did not attribute as much importance to information policy as the London Group did. The conferences, which took place in New York City, were organized by Percy Corbett, a professor of law (and former short-termed translator at the League) and George A. Finch, a prominent lawyer and the assistant director of the CEIP's Law Division. The two meetings were held on 30 August 1942 and on 30 January 1943. Sweetser and Gerig took part in the first one, which had scheduled time for discussing information policy.[29] The aim was to 'discuss the administration and organizational problems with which those engaged in this international work had to cope and to make proposals for the future'.[30] Philip Jessup, director of the Law Division, chaired the meeting.[31] On the expected impact of the meetings, he stated to the participants: 'I think it is safe to say that all work of this kind that the Endowment has done has been able to proceed through the most immediate channels to those who are concerned with framing and putting into effect policy'.[32]

In this American forum, information and publicity took up only 4 of the 130 pages long proceedings that resulted from the meetings.[33] Seen in conjunction with Ranshofen-Wertheimer's book, which included a longer chapter on the subject, it appears the CEIP network did not give information policy high priority while not dismissing it altogether either. As with Pelt's recommendations, we may summarize its conclusions into three themes.

The first, echoing Pelt, was the freedom to diversify its message according to different national publics. The (anonymized) discussants regretted that the League had been hampered by a dogma of uniformity. When the discussant 'J' defended the work of the Information Section another discussant responded that 'J' was confusing the general work of the section with his own extraordinary work. This exchange was one among several indications that 'J' was Arthur Sweetser, since it was generally recognized that Sweetser had gone the extra mile to inform both the public and personal contacts and to use his extensive American liaison work to compensate for the dry uniformity of the section's communication. When the discussion turned to the use of propaganda and the way the fear of doing such a thing had hampered communication, a discussant remarked that the uniformity had been 'a drawback' to the section, because 'Something which might have seemed absolutely innocuous to the French Director of the Information Section would rouse a storm in countries like Germany or Hungary'.[34] Contrasted with the League's early years the former officials in the US forum seemed unconvinced of the compatibility of a universal internationalism with a world divided into nation states. Their misgivings were echoed in Ranshofen-Wertheimer's book.[35]

The second theme was the utility of public relations pursued together with private 'collaborating' organizations and individuals. Pelt had taken little interest in this. Ranshofen-Wertheimer argued its importance in his book, regretting that it had been termed 'a secondary task' of the section. At the meeting, when the chairman, suggested replacing the proceeding heading 'relations with the press' with 'public relations', 'J' supported this and remarked that a distinction should be made between 'the things that the new agency itself does by and for itself in the sense of its own publications and broadcasts, and the secondary things or material that it gets other people to do'. He was referring to what Sweetser (probably himself) had termed 'cooperative publicity' back in 1919. He argued that liaison with private groups was valuable and spoke warmly of the section's system of temporary collaboratots and the international conferences on press matters in 1927, 1932 and 1933, that in his view, belonged to the same category.[36] Assuming that 'J' was Sweetser it is remarkable that whereas he did not really acknowledge that the section had been too uniform in its communication, Ranshofen-Wertheimer agreed with him that cooperation with private groups was important. Thus, whereas Pelt, and therefore the London Group, felt the Information Section had been outdated in its audience targeting, Sweetser could not really see a problem in the old section's targeting on a narrow, influential layer of the public.

The third theme was the importance of new technologies, specifically radio, which, participants agreed, had not been prioritized properly by the League. 'J' remarked that the new agency needed a radio station (and not just a 'service') entirely under its control.[37] Ranshofen-Wertheimer integrated this criticism with one that echoed Pelt's, namely that journalists had dominated the League's old section and that its focus on the daily press had been exaggerated. The crux of this criticism was that *news* at the expense of *information* had kept the League focused on political news instead of on its technical, cultural and humanitarian work, which had received too little attention.[38]

Contrasted with the high-minded idealism of the post-Versailles period, the organizers at the CEIP seemed uninterested in the more principal visions underlying publicity and information – the idea of an open diplomacy. Their focus was on the practical aspects of information work. 'J' – Sweetser – pushed back against this. 'Mr. Chairman' he remarked, 'the heart of the problem is whether you are going to have open sessions or not throughout the whole agency. [. . .] I would be inclined to put the whole matter of publicity, the principle of publicity, ahead'.[39]

Overall the only difference that stands out between the two League evaluation networks was on the value of collaborating with private groups and individuals. Sweetser, and to some extent Ranshofen-Wertheimer, still saw this kind of work as a keystone in public legitimization. Pelt did not offer it any attention.

In March 1943, a few months after the last meeting of the CEIP, Pelt wrote to Sweetser, attaching a paper that largely corresponded to what would later constitute his contribution to the London Report. He asked Sweetser to respond with his comments to this blueprint as soon as possible.[40] In Sweetser's response letter from December 1943 (he took his time) he largely agreed with Pelt's outline:[41]

> I profoundly agree with you that the informational work of the League of Nations to follow this war will have to be organized on a far greater and broader basis than that which followed the last war. Indeed, when I look back to those early days when we were scrambling around in Piccadilly to draw the first embryonic outline on an absolutely virgin blackboard, I find it hard to believe that the world's technology in the field of information has developed to such an extraordinary degree as it has.[42]

Sweetser did make a few remarks that pointed to his temperament being slightly different from Pelt's when it came to how the relationship between an international organization and the public ought to function. He attributed value to some activities that Pelt felt were outdated, such as liaison with private groups. He also reflected that diversifying information would be good but would require 'a kind of super-man who just doesn't exist. He will [. . .] have to have the feel of all the regions and psychologies of the world'.[43] We cannot draw a dramatic contrast between an elitist Arthur Sweetser and a democratic-minded Adrianus Pelt. However, Sweetser clearly did seem to value discreet networking with prominent people more than Pelt, who in turn saw great opportunity in radio. Their attitudes may be said to have reflected their own respective experiences. Pelt directed the section after it had been reduced and its political responsibilities taken away from it. Sweetser had been encouraged to pursue lobbying and semi-diplomatic activities and, in fact, had not worked formally in the Information Section since his brief spell as director in 1933. As a politically minded journalist Sweetser never seemed to have cared much for professional categories and demarcations. It was not important what department undertook behind-the-scenes lobbying work between the League Secretariat and decision-makers, only that it was done.

Pelt changed very little based on Sweetser's comments. The changes he did make signalled his conviction that the attempts of the old section to compete with the diplomatic services of the Secretariat were outdated. In his draft for the plan, he wrote that the freedom of a future section must require from its officials 'a high sense of professional responsibility' and an 'absence of any ambition to play a secondary diplomatic fiddle'.⁴⁴ However, he removed the part about the fiddle before the final version of the text.

Planning for the UNDPI

In the summer of 1945 the League was still alive in Geneva under secretary general Seán Lester. Lord Robert Cecil had not yet put it to rest with his oft-cited words 'The League is dead – long live the United Nations'. That would not happen until April 1946.⁴⁵

During the spring and summer of 1945 Pelt and Sweetser both attended the UN Conference on International Organization at San Francisco. It must have felt to them like history was repeating itself on a bigger scale. The conference took place between April and June 1945, and the first General Assembly of the UN then convened in London in January 1946. The process of staffing and organizing the UN, including its Department of Public Information (UNDPI), took place during the fall between these two points in time.

The UN came into being as new global ideological blocs were emerging. Both sides of the Cold War divide would control seats in the UN Security Council, the new institution to take up the mantle from Council of the disgraced League. The fact that the Soviet Union was involved in planning the new organization resulted in a more complex organization phase, than had been the case with the League which rose out of British–French negotiations in 1919. Mark Mazower has shown how the founding of the UN was characterized by trade-offs between the two emerging superpowers, as well as insecurity about the implementation of the organization's legal components.⁴⁶ Furthermore, whereas the League's mission had initially been limited to providing a transparent diplomatic system of conflict-solution based on the principle of collective security, the UN ambition was broader. It would draw on a budget vastly bigger than the League's had ever been. Also, it would be just one (centrally positioned) among many international institutions, several with a socioeconomic focus, like the International Monetary Fund and the World Bank. In line with what had begun with the so-called Bruce Report in the last years of the League and continued into the Bretton Woods conference in 1944, such bodies were meant to facilitate a new and more crisis-resistant international economic and financial order.⁴⁷ Embedded into the new organization was also a much more ambitious continuation of the League's Intellectual Cooperation Organization, the specialized agency UNESCO.⁴⁸

Sweetser and Pelt were both in San Francisco as delegates of their own countries. In addition, they assumed the melancholy but interesting position as former League officials. They both had impressive resumés in international organization and were valued sources of experience. Their interests at this point were far broader than that of information policy, as illustrated by their respective subsequent careers, both as top advisers to the UN secretary general.

On 26 June 1945, in addition to signing the UN charter, the governments present in San Francisco also agreed to establish a Preparatory Commission for the UN. Convening in London, this commission would exist until the first General Assembly had elected a secretary general.[49] The following fall and winter period leading up to the General Assembly in London was an enlarged repetition of the planning period that had taken place in the spring of 1919. The Preparatory Commission instituted committees which in turn instituted advisory committees and sub-committees. These then prepared recommendations for the organization of the UN that could then be adopted by the first General Assembly, so that the person it elected secretary general could immediately take charge of a functioning organization.

One of these advisory committees was the Technical Advisory Committee on Information (TACI) established on 30 November by the Administrative and Budgetary Committee of the Preparatory Commission. On 21 December upon accepting the recommendations of the TACI, the Preparatory Commission instituted a sub-committee which was to study in greater detail the practical implementation of its recommendations.[50]

The silent League presence

The Technical Advisory Committee and its sub-committee held a total of twenty-nine meetings and eventually drafted the plan for the UN Department of Public Information. In both committees were former League officials, and these were consulted on a range of issues. However, the minute-takers of the committees downplayed the origins of the League veterans' experience in the records. The old Secretariat became 'anonymized' in the process.

The TACI had thirteen members, including delegates not only from the United States, The Soviet Union, France and Great Britain but also from smaller states. These included two former officials of the League Information Section were members: Pelt for the Netherlands and Frédéric Blondeel for Belgium. Blondeel had been among the last officials of the section remaining in Geneva, his presence requested by Pelt even after the emergency reductions during 1939.⁵¹ The practical value of these former officials was clear in that both sat in the sub-committee as well the 'mother' committee. Two former members of the section were thus directly involved in formulating the UN's future information policies and tasks. And there were more League veterans about. The sub-committee consulted Henry Cummings, who had steered the League's branch office in London. Cummings was now directing the Information Division of the United Nations Relief and Rehabilitation Administration (UNRRA). He advised the committees on his experience and on the workings of the League's branch offices.⁵² The provisional Public Information Service of the United Nations was directed by a former League translator, Vernon Duckworth-Barker, until the first General Assembly.⁵³ Finally, Arthur Sweetser watched the work of the committees closely, and probably advised them too, in an informal capacity, being as he was UN affiliated and with relevant experience. Almost all material relating to the TACI can be found today in his private papers, many of the documents streaked with his hand-written comments.⁵⁴

Although as we can see, former League officials were represented in the planning committees for the UNDPI, as mentioned, the fact of their League affiliation was mostly kept off the record. It was unsurprising that the League was not mentioned in Trygve Lie's inaugural address in February 1946 or in other official declarations made at the General Assembly. However, its absence in the confidential working papers for the UNDPI was striking. There was an indirect reference in a memo by Duckworth-Barker who brought up the League using its geographical metonym, 'Geneva' when he spoke of the press room there, which, he said, had been 'a god-send to the world's press'.⁵⁵ In the final report of the sub-committee to the secretary general presented on 13 February the League was completely absent. It stated that during its meetings, the sub-committee had heard 'both governmental and non-governmental experts' within information and publicity of various kinds.⁵⁶ League experience was valued but not advertised. However, this did not mean lessons were not drawn from its work.

League lessons

The UNDPI would include many more offices than the Information Section had boasted. Like other departments of the new Secretariat, it would have more leadership layers than had been the case in Geneva.⁵⁷ The report of the TACI, which the General Assembly voted into a resolution, officially founded the department. The resolution covered three themes: first, the organization of the new department; second, its overall purpose in relation to UN information policy; and third, its functions.

The department's director would report to an assistant secretary general for Public Information, and an Advisory Committee of media experts from a broad geographical span would oversee the demands made by the public for better information on the work of the organization. Although not the same thing, this ombudsman of the public (or at least of the press) may have been inspired by Pelt's idea of a joint agency of news agencies.[58] Other recommendations concerned coordination. The Economic and Social Council of the UN (ECOSOC) was instructed to coordinate its own information policy with the UNDPI. Finally, the establishment of a number of branch offices around the world were announced.[59]

The purpose of the old Information Section was largely reproduced in phrasing echoing Pelt's text from the London Report. The UNDPI would have the dual purpose of informing the public about the activities of the UN and informing the secretary general about its standing in public opinion. In language familiar to any League veteran it added that the UNDPI:

> should not engage in 'propaganda'. It should on its own initiative engage in positive informational activities that will supplement the services of existing agencies of information to the extent that these are insufficient to realize the purpose set forth above.[60]

Overall, the new department looked like the old, but there seemed to be some theoretical differences in its understanding of the public. The department reinstated the taboo of propaganda, perhaps even more forcefully than had been the case in the League. However, it did not frame its information activities as 'collaboration' with public opinion, nor said that it would be 'at the point of contact' with public opinion'. Thus, it planned for a more ambitious focus on dissemination of information at the expense of less direct interaction with the public in the form of liaison activities. Neutral information should be its main pillar, and its material should be distributed to national media and governmental information agencies, so that the department could work as a provider of supplementary facts. The resolution vaguely suggested that the department should be equipped in headquarters as well as in its branch offices, to follow trends in public opinion.[61]

The plan reinstated recognizable characteristics of the League's. The UN as such, not just its information department, should 'strive to establish, as a general policy, that the press, and other existing agencies of information, should be given the fullest possible direct access to the activities [. . .] of the organization'.

The famous Article 18 of the League's Covenant emerged as Article 102 of the UN charter. It promised that all treaties and international agreements should be registered and published by the Secretariat, but whereas the League had sworn that no treaty would be binding unless it was registered, the drafters of the UN charter were conscious not to overstate the point. The charter simply stated that no treaties that had not been registered could be invoked before any organs of the UN.[62] Although the implementation of such rules did not fall on the UNDPI they constituted, just like in the case of the Information Section, the firmament for the publicity and information strategy of the organization: The UN could not fight its cause with propaganda but could lay out its procedures and supplement them with facts, figures and information for the benefit of the public.

The department was to be charged with press relations, publications, radio, films, graphics and exhibitions, public liaison and a 'reference service'. Its radio station should be independent and equipped with all necessary wavelengths.[63] Radio, however, still presented a problem, just as it had in League days, because there was uncertainty about the acquiescence of member states to a powerful international radio station. The recommendation was therefore expressed in cautious phrasing.

Overall, the recommendations looked similar to Pelt's blueprint in the sense that all the functions he listed were included and then some. His highlighting of technology held a high priority in the UNDPI plan, despite the trouble about broadcasting. His points about qualifications of staff – that a new department should hire communications experts at the expense of political journalists – was addressed by the sub-committee report which stated that the department should include all kinds of specialists within the different media of communication.[64]

The degree to which Pelt's wish for a new department to be given the freedom to diversify information to different audiences had been integrated is more difficult to ascertain. The sub-committee's report said that the 'Information [. . .] issued by the Department should represent an authoritative record of UN policy and activities but it should be made clear on such material that it is not to be regarded as a legally binding official document'.[65] It was unclear what this changed, since documents issued by the old section, except press communiqués, had always carried a printed assurance that they were not official documents.

Another difference between the final plan for the department and Pelt's outline was the inclusion of 'public liaison' in its functions. Understood as liaison with private 'collaborators' this was the one activity of the old section that Pelt had virtually ignored. However, the committee described public liaison less idealistic and in more practical down-to-earth wording than had sometime been the case in the League days. It stated that the department should 'assist and encourage national information services, educational institutions and other governmental and non-governmental organizations of all kinds interested in spreading information about the United Nations'. For this, it should be well equipped with a reference service, lecturers, publications, films and so on.[66] The recommendations described a system for channelling information to researchers on request, yet it was not quite 'cooperative publicity' in the sense envisioned by the League, and it is worth contrasting the two approaches to civil society. Back in 1926, Pierre Comert's Information Section had described a 'liaison between the Secretariat in Geneva and an elite consisting of a few dozen hand-picked persons: parliamentarians, skilled journalists, politicians, public officials, and people from the financial world, academics, technicians or experts'.[67]

Lifting our gaze from all these details, we may compare the League's Information Section to the rising postwar information department. This makes the League's perception of public opinion emerge more clearly. In the most idealistic moments of the League days officials had conceptualized public opinion as something like a general mass of citizens, men and women, young and old, educated or uneducated, in all member states. However, the primary target of 'liaison' during the League years had been an elite, dominated by public officials, politicians, and academics. Its 'public' had existed in the halls of power at least as much as, if not more than, the streets of London, or, even less so, Montevideo. The sub-committee to the TACI mentioned nothing about UN collaboration with public officials, parliamentarians or academics but simply gave suggestions for how a desirable system for providing stakeholder, activists or other interest groups with information could be established.[68] The broadening of the audience indicated in the plans for the UNDPI did not just consist of a diminished elitism but also a more clear-cut focus on *dissemination* and less on *collaboration* with stakeholders, or 'collaborators', a favourite word in the old Information Section. There was no mention of partnering with national United Nations Associations (although they existed – Pelt would go on to become the secretary general of their World Federation).[69] The UN would speak to the public rather than collaborating with an exclusive selection of its members.

The UNDPI

The UNDPI existed for the same reason as the Information Section, namely because: 'the United Nations cannot achieve its goals unless the peoples of the world are fully informed of its aims and activities'.⁷⁰ The new department controlled 12 per cent of the total annual budget of the UN. The equivalent data for the League is not available, but the early Information Section was proportionally to the Secretariat, at least as well funded or better funded than the UNDPI, while the UNDPI got double the share of what the Information Section got during the latter's final years. In actual size, however, the UNDPI budget alone was bigger than the entire League Secretariat.⁷¹

The earliest UNDPI in 1946-7 gives the impression that an extensive expansion and professionalization of the setup had taken place in comparison to the experimental setup of the Information Section. This had become possible because of the size of the new department, which in turn reflected a new world order and the commitment of all Great Powers to the UN through its Security Council. The Information Section had been obliged to have its officials perform a multitude of tasks rather than specializing only in one type of work. Whereas the Information Section had included three or four 'offices' the UNDPI included six divisions (Press & Publications, Radio, Films and Visual Information, Headquarters Liaison, External Services and Reference and Research). Like the other seven departments of the new Secretariat the UNDPI was organized under an assistant secretary general (Chilean Benjamin Cohen). Below that level the departments were each headed by a principal director. For the UNDPI this was Norwegian Tor Gjesdal, a choice which illustrated that the recruitment dynamics of the new organization looked similar to that of the League in 1919, when so many officials were found among Allied delegations in Paris during the Peace Congress. Gjesdal had directed the Norwegian government-in-exile's Information Department and in the London of exiles would have met many former League people as well as future UN high officials.⁷²

Each division of a department was headed by its own director which made for eight leading officials of the UNDPI out of which there were no former officials of the Information Section. It appears that while former information officials were welcomed into the rest of the Secretariat they were not placed in the 'continuation' of their own office.⁷³ In terms of the highest officials, fresh eyes and a new start were asked for. Also, former League officials may not have been interested, moving on as many were, to other things.

In the *UN Yearbook* of 1946-7 the UNDPI echoed the confident communication of the early Information Section a quarter of a century earlier: It recounted that by 1947 the Press and Publications Division had accredited 800 journalists to cover permanently the UN – a number we know to be about double the peak number of the League at any time. Four and a half thousand press releases had been released – again, many times higher than the League's annual numbers at any point. Whereas we saw that the Information Section released a *Monthly Summary*, the UNDPI now published a weekly one. While the Information Section had broadcasted weekly to countries outside Europe, the UNDPI broadcasted daily to all parts of Europe and the United States and so on.[74] International communication, the high pace of which had already been commented upon by many in the interwar period, was speeding up.

The new department was positioned to cooperate much closer with the UNESCO than had been the case with the embryonic partnership between the Information Section and the Intellectual Cooperation Organization. The *Yearbook* explained that in the UN, international cooperation was not confined to political matters but encapsulated the 'widest possible fields for social progress and better standards of life in larger freedom. In this field specialized agencies as well as the United Nations have developed information services and have common interests'.[75]

Thus, the idea which had grown among League officials during its late years, that international organization encompassed much more than collective security was integrated into the backbone of the UNDPI. In order to make the public understand the breadth of UN agency the department planned and coordinated information campaigns with bodies such as the ECOSOC and the UNESCO.

The growing diversity of technology and integration into the rest of the UN's agencies called for an expanded infrastructure for addressing and interacting with the publics in the member states. Branch offices accordingly multiplied. The League's six branch offices had been a 'modest chain' in Arthur Sweetser's words and had occasionally been ignored, even by the League itself in descriptions of its work.[76] The Committee of Thirteen in 1930 called them 'liaison offices' each staffed with one official and in some cases a secretary – an experimental scheme in short.[77] By 1947, however, the UNDPI had established 'regional information centres' in nine cities with plans for four additional ones (in 1953 there would be eighteen),[78] and whereas four out of six of the League's branch offices had been located in Europe, the new scheme included centres in Mexico City, New Delhi, Rio de Janeiro, Shanghai, Washington, Cairo and Moscow. Sweetser's call to develop this branch of work 'far beyond what we had last time' had been adhered to but the setup in fact accommodated Adrianus Pelt's vision. The establishment of so many offices and the name 'information center' suggested a globalization of communications and an infrastructure better suited to diversify communication.

Despite the broadening of the target of public legitimization, some of the structural problems encountered by the League seemed to make their presence felt in the UN as well. When Robert Cory analysed the 'public information policy' of the early UN in 1953 it was clear the fundamental challenges of publicly promoting international organization were still very much alive. Cory compared the UNDPI and the UNESCO. He observed that the latter agency – which, in a radical break from the League, was given a bigger budget than the UNDPI – was becoming the most important stakeholder in the UN's public image.[79] However, Cory deemed the UNDPI was the hotbed of trouble, pointing out that the Soviet Union was constantly pressing for its reduction. This echoed Pitman Potter's discussion of the relation between the League's member states and the Information Section fifteen years prior. Cory tellingly asserted that the behaviour of the Soviet Union 'evidenced a distrust of the principles of public information rather than a mere concern for economy'. The UNESCO, he explained, steered clear of this distrust only because the USSR was not a member of the UNESCO. Thus, having the organization's most important legitimizer be a separate organization that not all UN member states were members of saved these policies from excessive scrutiny. However, the UNESCO too would later fall into disgrace – with the US government.[80] With tensions between the information department of the organization and its internal budgetary control organs, fuelled by political considerations in the Security Council and the General Assembly, history was repeating itself. In the early postwar UN, the department's nemesis was not called the Supervisory Commission but the Advisory Committee on Administrative and Budgetary Questions,[81] but the issue at hand was comparable to the old tensions that had riddled the Information Section.

At this point, there may be a growing suspicion that the inherent tensions of League information policy, about the mandate (who was the League?), its means (could it use propaganda?) and audience (who was the public?) are unsolvable. However, two of these three tensions do seem to have been approached differently by the UN than the League. Propaganda was no longer an unspoken 'taboo' but formally forbidden, and the target of the department was more clearly identified as a global mass audience to be reached through news media and radio, and not a carefully selected elite of influential 'collaborators'. Yet the third and perhaps central tension still loomed large: If a global intergovernmental organization was not a world government, then what was it, and why was its legitimacy continually deemed to depend upon the support of public opinion?

Conclusion

Veterans of the League influenced the public information setup of the early UN. In his proposals for future policy, Adrianus Pelt emphasized the value of new mass communications technology, of a bigger information department, of a continued abstention from 'propaganda activities' and of an insistence on the value of allowing the department to diversify its communication to different kinds of audiences. The Dutch former director was a member of the relevant UN-planning committees while Arthur Sweetser followed the process from outside but with privileged access to key decision-makers. What Pelt downplayed from the League experience was the idea that elites should be considered 'collaborators' in public legitimization and, related to that, the idea that national political elites were useful in the same way. In Pelt's view, semi-diplomatic activities should no longer be the business of the information department. It ought to know its place as a purely informative press department and in exchange it should expect to be generously funded.[82] On recalling the three tensions that have been used as a prism to understanding the challenges faced by the League, this signalled that Pelt was seeking to redefine (and broaden) the identity of the public while retaining the taboo of propaganda and the identification of a 'weak agency' for the international organization. Sweetser, on the other hand, appeared more satisfied with the elitist conceptualization of the public developed by Pierre Comert and himself. He too however, pushed most insistently for a better funded information department, something that he felt was overdue alone from the fact that the new organization enjoyed support from all the great postwar powers.

This enlargement was realized with the early UNDPI. It received better funding than the old section; it was seemingly more deeply integrated with the rest of the organization and became professionalized to a higher degree than the Information Section. Although this book falls short of studying the activities of the UNDPI after 1946, nothing in its setup indicated a return to the elite-oriented liaison efforts of the old Information Section and its uniquely narrow definition of the public. What neither Pelt nor Sweetser had envisioned was the rise of UNESCO as a superior platform for UN public legitimization through education and multicultural awareness. The UNESCO was better funded than the UNDPI and is much better known today, almost eight decades later. Further research may explain the origins of this new division of labour and its consequences for the public legitimization strategies of the UN.

Conclusion

In 1930, at a point which they would remember later as halfway through the lifetime of their workplace, officials of the Information Section described the League of Nations as 'the sum of public opinion'. This was an ambiguous way of expressing the organization's relation to its supposed life force. The suggestion that public opinion was somehow part of the organization's organism sounded powerful, but it may be understood as a watering-down of what they had been claiming in the past. To be precise it had replaced an idea of a united public that held the League accountable as a constituency and represented a 'moral force'. Contrasted with this image the League as the sum of public opinion sounded more like an apology for the emergence of internal disunity. Indeed, that statement reflected a moment of uncertainty in League thinking about its audiences. However, it still rested on the (perhaps wishful) thinking that the League was fuelled directly by public support, rather than simply operating on an uneasy mandate given to it by the governments of member states. The voice of the League of Nations, as it targeted the public with information, was therefore internationalism in practice. Its public communication came about as the result of a chorus of voices (in print, in speech or otherwise) of officials, many of whom were devoted to the liberal internationalist ideology imbued into the League since its founding in 1919.

These practical internationalists were not free to shape this voice as they saw fit, as they gradually realized, each according to his or her temper. From the very beginning, in the days of the provisional Secretariat in London their efforts to build an Information Section was closely watched and micromanaged by the office of the secretary general who imprinted on the minds of the officials a 'taboo of propaganda' reflecting his own cautiousness to secure for his Secretariat some degree of autonomy *vis-à-vis* the jealous member states. In the tense and unpredictable post-Versailles atmosphere that the League operated in, being accused of using propaganda, a weapon of war associated closely with the British war effort, was considered catastrophic. However, the secretary general allowed the Information Section of 1919–32 a key position in the Secretariat and allowed its director a close advisor-role to his own office. Later on, as the after-shakes of the American stock market crash and a composite of political crises hit Europe and Great Powers started to withdraw from the League, the Information Section faced mounting scepticism as to its purpose. Towards the end of the 1930s there were far fewer resources in the League and economies had to be made.

Between many intersecting factors including ideological convictions, cultural legacies of the First World War, personal characteristics, economics, Great Power politics, technological development and ongoing professionalization, this book has presented the strategies that the League of Nations employed, through its Information Section, to legitimize itself to the public 1919–40. Furthermore, it has evaluated the legacy of this work in the wartime planning phase that led to the founding of the United Nations, 1940–6 and its information department, the UNDPI. It has discussed which of the League experiences were emphasized and downplayed in the transition, and what change in strategy could be inferred from this development.

The challenges the League faced throughout all this can be described as working through a triangle of tensions which its officials were constantly confronted with. The first tension concerned *who* the public was that the League should address or mobilize. Did it consist of national or international publics, of narrow elites or the masses? Did it already support the League's cause, or must it be persuaded to do so? The second tension concerned internationalism and what the League *was*. Was it an independent agency, separate from its member states or simply a diplomatic framework representing their combined interests? The third concerned *how* the League could be promoted. Could aggressive propaganda be used, or only neutral, objective dissemination of facts? These tensions existed all through the League's lifetime and fluctuated in importance according to what else went on in international politics. This constant uncertainty meant that the League never established one single, monolithic public legitimization strategy. Instead, one can infer a number of more or less articulated strategies from the practices, prioritizations and communication of the Information Section and from this set one can discern some overall shifts in the way international bureaucrats thought about the public and how the journalists they appointed to speak the cause of internationalism disseminated this changing attitude. In the following I evaluate the trajectory of the League's public legitimization strategies throughout the whole period relating them to these three closely interrelated tensions. We begin with the most important one which concerned the identity of its audience, the public. Second, we discuss its negotiation of the League's identity. Third, we discuss its interaction with the concept of propaganda.

Finally, I ask how this story may be understood in conjunction with existing scholarly interpretations of League public information strategies.

Public opinion

The book shows that the interwar period saw two overlapping conceptualizations of the public collide with one replacing the other gradually during the 1930s. Investigating the strategies of the section has shed light on not only these in themselves but additionally on their preconditions – the prevailing understanding among League officials of the nature of the public. Thus, among League officials, a change in the perception of public opinion took place, which became visible only after the fall of the League. To tackle the constraints put on it, the section focused on mobilizing support for the organization in indirect ways, first by nurturing a close, almost symbiotic relationship with the Geneva press corps and the press in general, from which it regularly recruited new officials, and second by committing sympathetic semi-official circles and educated elites to its cause. To an extent and particularly during the period 1919–32, it came to identify these people, journalists and League-affiliated activists and interest groups, as *constituting* the public and their sentiments as constituting public opinion. However, towards the end of the League's existence the section's experiences and the depth of the crisis of legitimacy that had faced it during the 1930s had planted a realization among its officials that a more mass-oriented perception was a more appropriate way for an international organization to communicate. Sophisticated Westerners prone to taking an interest in international matters did not suffice as a target, especially when, as the section had bitterly learned, information strategies risked being cut no matter how cautiously it approached its mission.

The section never took much interest in defining its audience in concrete terms. The closest it came was to state in 1927 that its mission was to explain the work of the League to 'people from many different countries and classes', but it never elaborated on this plurality, and in practice it still predominantly aimed its publications at narrow, educated strata of what would today be called the public, whom it often perceived as its 'collaborators' in legitimizing the League. The first time the section discussed the public in depth, in 1930, it theorized that public opinion was 'not so much a collection of individual views' as 'perhaps a mass-feeling, partly emotional'.[1] This new note of uncertainty as to the rationality of the public paralleled ideas that were emerging at the time, notably the theory on public opinion by Walter Lippmann, who made an appearance at the beginning of this book as an observer of the League, and who had encouraged its leadership to appeal to the public. The idea of the masses and of the 'emotional public' brings to mind the role of journalism in the Information Section, a section which largely consisted of former foreign affairs correspondents. The rise of the League's Information policy and its reliance on foreign affairs journalists coincided with a formative period in the journalistic trade. The 1920 has been called a 'Golden Age' of foreign correspondence, but it was also a complicated time during which such influential and widely popular journalists were grappling with their responsibility as they discovered the fickleness and unpredictability of the public. Should journalists remain within the confines of striving for 'objectivity' or did the 'age of extremes' demand from them a role as guides and analysts? Such considerations were palpable among League officials, most of whom were former foreign correspondents.[2]

The fact that League officials steered clear of sharply defining public opinion but continued to argue that it was significant is a key point to be noted: through acts and 'speech acts', the League assured sceptical governments it was not trying to undermine national power, a manoeuvre that became possible because although it used the appeal regularly it never articulated it clearly enough to work as an actual constituency of the League that could disagree with member states. The League thus sought to capitalize on the pre-existing trope of the power of public opinion without entering dangerous waters by competing with national governments. This type of indirect legitimization could work in other ways as well. Many of the strategies employed by the section in its publications mimicked the authority of a state without ever outright comparing the League to one, thus capitalizing on statehood as a pre-existing source of legitimacy.

After the fall of the League, former officials of the Information Section had their chance to reflect on the assumptions on which they had based their strategies and reimagine what a new section could look like. The old section had been constrained in its options, and this had influenced the way it had imagined public legitimization. It prompted it to pursue it cautiously through its press services, behind the scenes through liaison with influential League sympathizers. Yet despite its prudence it had still been cut down in 1933. So, when a new organization with more resources and broader global support was rising, its former officials seized the opportunity to propose a powerful Information Section that would operate in the open and pursue mass communication using new technologies and communication specialists rather than operate behind the scenes. Accusations of propaganda, it was felt, would threaten the information section of an international organization no matter how it operated, and, thus, the cautious elite-strategy was considered to have been a mistake. The new emerging vision focused on *disseminating* information to the public rather than *collaborating* with carefully selected strata. Adrianus Pelt stated in his 1943 outline for a postwar Information Section that back in 1919 the old Information Section had corresponded 'almost perfectly to the then existing state of public opinion in the world',[3] but that now this state had changed. The rise of a proto-global mass society meant that collaboration with a few, influential people was vastly insufficient and a waste of resources. The postwar international public diplomacy would be bigger and more global, and it would aim at the whole public even if information officials were beginning to harbour scepticism about its rationality.

Internationalism

The section, through its size and centrality and the visions of its leading officials, was in effect an internationalist project. It represented an implementation of internationalist thought, yet at the same time it was always clearly organized in a way that reaffirmed *nations* and *national* interests as intrinsic to the League idea, thus countering any hypothesis that the Secretariat presented itself as an 'anti-national' institution. There were some exceptional examples in the earliest rhetoric of officials that framed the League as a 'world government', including one official's confidential assertion that 'as the League will be the center of world government so it must be the center of world political information'. However, such language was seldom used in the open, and even in confidential correspondence it was confined to the earliest years, just like the strategy of underscoring League 'action' was seen mainly between 1920 and 1921. Mirroring the Secretariat as a whole as it was organized by its first secretary general, the section was conceived as an international section answering only to the authority of the secretary general. However this did not prevent it from being subjected to an informal national hierarchy, and Comert explicitly thought of his section's multinational setup as the best way to ensure an anchoring in different national news media systems. Thus it simultaneously reaffirmed nations as the legitimate sources of political authority. This principle was reproduced in its news and publications too from the mid-1920s, when the section 'legitimized by proxy' borrowing ethos from national decision-makers and heads of state and thus underscored that the League drew its legitimacy from the community of nations it consisted of. After 1933 the section employed rhetorical strategies reminding the public that the League actually had no authority other than the collective authority of its member states. After the reduction of the section in 1933, and the ensuing period of political crises that hit the League, the question of whether the League represented an international authority started to look irrelevant. Its rhetorical strategies now hinted that the League rose above than the sum of its parts but never explicitly stated it, thus shielding the section from accusations of propaganda.

What development did the practised internationalism performed by the Information Section undergo during the League's existence? Even if the Secretariat was never a uniform actor with a streamlined set of ideals, what ideas did it empower or simply allow to exist and flourish within its walls? Let us consider Sandrine Kott's phrasing that international organizations rather than actors of internationalization are *sites* of such processes, where fruitful interactions between international bureaucracies and national goals may result in mutually beneficent outcomes.[4] Such a dynamic requires a degree of openness on the part of state actors whose goodwill form the basis of an international Secretariat and creativity from the officials who run the international machineries and whose cooperation with non-state actors and networked are often overlooked. Between 1919 and 1932 during the section's first director, overseen by the League's first secretary general, the Information Section embraced internationalism as an open-ended set of ideas, ranging from notions of world government to simply the lowering of tariffs and better understanding between nations. Pierre Comert, at the same time, was a pragmatist and represented his own government's positions in the Secretariat, yet he also worked well together with his highly idealist American colleague Arthur Sweetser. Together, they expanded the section's engagement with what they imagined as its most important audiences – international journalists and League of Nations association – and Comert defended the section's more radical voices, such as Konni Zilliacus, who argued that the League ought to work more closely together with socialist internationalists. After the League faced a crisis of legitimacy in 1932 the Secretariat could still theoretically be a site of internationalism, but it was a more restricted and less confident site. Following a challenge offered by Germany and Italy to the independence of the international Secretariat many of its functions became centralized under Joseph Avenol. This took away much of the Information Section's share in the unique autonomy among League officials that had been built at this time.[5] The lack of trust in private collaborators and the fear that the size of the Information Section should reflect poorly on the League diminished the degree to which the Secretariat was still a site where a liberal internationalism could thrive. The internationalist characteristics of the Information Section were slowly strangled by the spectre of propaganda.

Propaganda

In 1919 when Walter Lippmann had advised Raymond Fosdick to make 'publicity' the key function of the League, Lippmann was at the same time writing scathing articles about US war propaganda and about the lack of responsibility shown by the press in covering foreign affairs. Lippmann was deeply disillusioned about propaganda even though he had been involved in it himself – in April 1917 he had submitted a plan for how to conduct efficient US war propaganda overseas.[6] One may conclude from this seeming paradox that to people of Lippmann's training and generation (the same who worked in the League Secretariat) 'publicity' and 'propaganda' were simultaneously synonymous and two dramatically different things. When League officials felt that their methods approached what could be described as propaganda they would hesitate at the risk of making the League vulnerable or 'sink to the level' of its critics. However, they acknowledged that aggressive promotion was necessary to a degree. While the section distanced itself officially from propaganda its officials privately endorsed its use, particularly in the period immediately following the League's foundation. However, the hesitance described earlier steered the authors of the section's publications into subtlety and its officials in general into cautious behind-the-scenes activities. Even before 1933 its emphasis on 'cooperative publicity', collaboration with private sympathizers and pro-League groups was reinforced by a realization that genuine mass communication was near-impossible, because governments did not want a 'foreign' body to speak directly to their populations. The efforts to avoid resembling a propaganda department thus shaped the public legitimization strategies of the section throughout its existence.

Heidi Tworek, Martin Herzer and Jonas Brendebach have asked whether international organizations have been right to assume that the public wields Great Power and influence. They asserted that only when specific policy goals have been defined, as opposed to addressing the 'lofty [. . .] and vaguely moral category of a world public' has their communication been efficient.[7] Guessing at the real power of public opinion in foreign policy is beyond the scope of this book. There have been attempts by historians to grapple with this question, although in the case of the League only in passing, such as in Daniel Hucker's collection of (mostly nationally confined) case studies of the effect of public opinion on foreign policy.[8] However, despite not confronting this impact-question head-on, the book places the League's interaction with the idea of public opinion in its appropriate historical context. The most acute problem was not the nature of the public but the fear of being accused of making propaganda. Rather than a force to boost the everyday activities of the League, public opinion was considered a key rhetorical appeal to secure democratic legitimacy in international diplomacy, something its internationalist officials considered to be of vital importance after the unique experience of the war. The Secretariat was thus not shaken in its devotion to public opinion by the fact that its influence could not always be 'felt' on a day-to-day level. Its strategies focused on addressing what it deemed to be the public as efficiently as possible while desperately avoiding accusations that it was abusing its mandate. Thus, the book shows how the League instituted a large and well-staffed Information Section – arguably a waste of money had public opinion only been thought useful as a symbolic appeal. Officials, although shaken, continued to believe in the significance of the public all through the interwar period. While they rarely concretized how they identified it, they constructed it through their stated target groups in individual publications (parliamentarians, public officials, academics, journalists etc.) and in the way they initially organized the section to reflect public opinion through national liaison with private collaborators. In short, public opinion *was* important to the League – even after the reorganization of the Information Section in 1934 – but invoking it aggressively was seen as counterproductive. Part of the reason for this paradox was the several meanings of propaganda. Most dangerous was any communication that could be accused of favouring one member state's view over that of another, but even propaganda of a generic nature which simply celebrated the League as an abstract ideal and a framework for solving disputes was problematic because it cost money – and the money came from member states.

Member states were aware of the cost – and the potential – of propaganda. The interwar period was a time when many large Western powers – including Britain, France and the United States – began financing propaganda as part of their foreign services in peacetime. What might be considered crude use of war tactics in peacetime in reality reflected the need of modern states – liberal democratic and not so – to pursue what Müller has called public mass justification. After the experience of the Second World War (yet again) attached dark connotations to propaganda in the public mind, state bureaucracies would begin to refer to such activities as 'public diplomacy'.⁹ How do the League's information practices fit into this genealogy of propaganda? The short answer is that it fits neatly: the Information Section of the mid-1920s was an international microcosm of war-ridden Europe, and its officials (predominantly French, British, Italian and later German) arrived in Geneva with each their own, but quite similar, ambiguous feelings about the idea of publicly sponsored mass communication. They used the word 'propaganda' in internal correspondence, and its directors, in particular the first one, drew on the talents of officials who had worked within state propaganda – like George H. Mair, and in foreign ministry press offices. However, the book has clearly shown that according to the officials themselves – and their voices are of prime importance – the League's big challenge was not how to make good propaganda but how to avoid doing so. The fear of associating the League with the victors of the First World War by openly using 'propaganda methods' known from the war combined with a fervent belief that the League should be about transparency and open diplomacy make a study of the League information policies something different from a study of propaganda – almost a study of anti-propaganda.

The message from Geneva

The League's mistake, according to many researchers, was not that it expected too much from the public but that it misidentified it, focusing its information strategies on experts. This expert-focus reflected 'possible structural problems of communicating international affairs, which is detached from broader publics'.¹⁰ Tomoko Akami emphasized 'the League's inherent inability to reach the masses'.¹¹

However, we may ask whether it is precise to describe this inability of the Secretariat as 'inherent'. What role did the League's political context play? Certainly, as Akami points out, the League primarily aimed its public legitimization strategies at educated people. Nonetheless, since its communication aimed at enthusing its audience through aesthetic and moral appeals and since it consistently invoked public opinion, technical experts cannot be said to have exclusively constituted the target group. A more precise description of it would be a transnational civil society of educated League sympathizers of middle- to upper-class social standing, primarily in Europe and the United States. More importantly, Akami seems to distinguish somewhat the information policy of the League from the constraints within which it came about. Although the rise of nationalism plays an important role in her work she holds that rather than these phenomena it was the League's inherent inability to communicate with the public that led to a 'missed opportunity'. However, as this book has shown, the Information Section worked constantly to avoid confronting a number of tensions in its work, most notably its 'taboo of propaganda', and when it was reduced in 1933 it happened because even its cautious liaison with elites and its subtle legitimization in publications were seen as too aggressive. After the reorganization in 1933, the section did in fact continue some of its liaison with private collaborators, although its director would not bring the experience with him, perhaps understanding that such work aimed at too narrow a target. In short, liaison with elites was not the only way the section could imagine propagating the League, but it was one of the only ways its officials felt it was allowed to.

Laying aside the question of whether the elitism of the Information Section was a freely made choice or partly the result of tight constraints, it was at the centre of the League's public legitimization strategies. No single example of the priority given to semi-diplomatic activities was clearer than that of Arthur Sweetser which has also been discussed by Madeleine Herren and Isabella Löhr. They have argued that Sweetser represented a unique type of interwar agent who fused diplomacy and public information, operated between private and public institutions and facilitated communication through channels that would otherwise be closed – such as not only between the US Department of Justice and the League, but also between the many policy think tanks, philanthropic foundations and public institutions in wartime United States, leading up to the founding of the UN.[12] Sweetser certainly exemplified a type of unofficial diplomatic agent who seems to appear once vital lines of official communication close down, but at the same time his case was unique because of the peculiar position of the United States *vis-à-vis* the League. Sweetser's trajectory within the Secretariat mirrors the development of the Information Section he helped build: after its reduction in 1933 it was no longer justifiable to have him pursue semi-diplomatic activities on behalf of the League from within the Information Section, because it would have blurred the line between press relations and diplomacy which, by then, section had been explicitly discouraged from doing. Yet, at the same time Sweetser's activities were deemed to be of value to the Secretariat. He was therefore appointed 'Director without Section', while officials of the Information Section spent its last six impoverished years dreaming of a future in which greater resources would permit the pursuit of more ambitious public legitimization.

'The United Nations', wrote its former under secretary general for Special Political Affairs Brian Urquhart in his 1987 memoirs, 'is, and always has been, hopeless at public relations'.[13] International organizations are superstructures built on top of national governments. Such a body will probably always face dramatic challenges in forging coherent public communication. The confusing nature of its mandate often means that even when it is successful, credit will go to the national governments. But can broad, popular support for international organization ever be achieved and is it desirable? Does the 'moral force' of public opinion that internationalists have invoked since the League's days exist? This book gives no final answer to that question, but it shows that League officials consistently acted as if it did and that most continued to do so going into the postwar period. When, a century after the founding of the League, political scientist Ivan Krastev described the emergence of 'disloyal' elites in international agencies and the resistance they meet among their populations, he was first and foremost discussing a challenge connected to the fact that the European Union, as opposed to the League, is a supra-national institution with a much more direct accountability to the public. It was clear from the birth of the League that the officials of the Secretariat would never become entirely detached from national loyalties, and that the League would never be a world government. Nevertheless, this did not stop its officials from attempting to build a democratic legitimacy for it. The book has described a development in their strategies going from guarded neutral language, indirect rhetorical legitimization and cautious 'collaboration' with private, often elite sympathizers to a more confident postwar vision of broad, global interaction with a public that looked similar to how we define it today. The UN, it was seen, began to increasingly legitimize its project through educational, scientific and cultural activities rather than traditional propaganda or information work. International organizations certainly 'speak to us' in a different way today than they did a century ago. Nonetheless, they are still faced with the message from Geneva, namely the necessity of speaking credibly, consistently and authoritatively to the international public despite all the problems of legitimacy when political crises stand unaddressed and member governments are wavering in their commitment. Today, nationalist populism – an ideational complex that puts the people at its very centre – is on the rise all over the world. With this recent 'return of the nation', is it still possible for international organizations to pursue public mass justification? Ought they to rely on an international democratic legitimacy? And if so, how can this be built?

Notes

Introduction

1 E.g. Mark Mazower, *Governing the World – The History of an Idea 1815 to the Present* (New York: Penguin Books, 2012), 136.
2 Ibid., 125.
3 Mazower, *No Enchanted Palace – The End of Empire and the Ideological Origins of the United Nations* (Princeton: Princeton University Press, 2009), 38.
4 E.g. Peter Jackson, *Beyond the Balance of Power: France and the Politics of National Security in the Era of the First World War* (Cambridge: Cambridge University Press, 2013), 269.
5 Walter Lippmann, letter to Raymond B. Fosdick 15 August 1919, in Raymond Fosdick, *Letters on the League of Nations* (Princeton: Princeton University Press, 1966), 10.
6 Ibid., 12.
7 Farnaz Fassihi, 'U.N to Meet amid Growing Divisions and Demands from Global South', *The New York Times*, 18 September 2023.
8 Covenant of the League of Nations, in F. P Walters, *A History of the League of Nations* (London: The Royal Institute of International Affairs, 1954), 54.
9 Jan Werner-Müller, *Contesting Democracy – Political Ideas in Twentieth Century Europe* (New Haven: Yale University Press, 2013), 23.
10 Ivan Krastev, 'The Rise and Fall of European Meritocracy', *The New York Times*, 17 January 2017; The White House, 'Remarks by President Trump to the 74th Session of the United Nations General Assembly'. https://trumpwhitehouse.archives.gov/briefings-statements/remarks-president-trump-74th-session-united-nations-general-assembly/ (27 March 2023).
11 Susan Pedersen, 'Back to the League of Nations', *The American Historical Review* 112, no. 4 (2007): 1091–117, 1092. Among the scholars Petersen recounted, which worked with respectively peacekeeping, management of the end of empire and global governance were: Zara Steiner, *The Lights that Failed. European International History 1919-1933* (Oxford: Oxford University Press, 2007); Frederick S. Northedge, *The League of Nations: Its Life and Times, 1920-1946* (Leicester: Leicester University Press, 1986); Eric Hobsbawm, *The Age of Extremes – The Short Twentieth Century, 1914-1991* (London: Michael Joseph, 1994); Susan Pedersen, *The Guardians: The League of Nations and the Crisis of Empire* (Oxford:

Oxford University Press, 2015); Patricia Clavin, *Securing the World Economy: The Reinvention of the League of Nations, 1920-1946* (Oxford: Oxford University Press, 2013).

12 Pedersen, 'Back to the League of Nations', 1096–7; Daniel Laqua, 'Activism in the "Students" League of Nations': International Students Politics and the Confédération Internationale des Étudiants, 1919-1939', *English Historical Review* CXXXII, no. 556 (2017): 605–37; Laqua, 'Democratic Politics and the League of Nations: The Labour and Socialist International as a Protagonist of Interwar Internationalism', *Contemporary European History* 24, no. 2 (2015): 175–92; Anne-Isabelle Richard, 'Competition and Complementarity: Civil Society Networks and the Question of Decentralizing the League of Nations', *Journal of Global History* 7, no. 2 (2012): 233–56, 236; Thomas R. Davies, 'A Great Experiment of the League of Nations Era, International Nongovernmental Organizations, Global Governance, and Democracy Beyond the State', *Global Governance* 18 (2012): 405–23; Davies, 'Internationalism in a Divided World: The Experience of the International Federation of League of Nations Societies', *Peace and Change* 37, no. 2 (2012): 227–52. Helen McCarthy examined the activities of the British League of Nations Unions in context of the British interwar peace movement: McCarthy, *The British People and the League of Nations – Democracy, Citizenship and Internationalism, c. 1918-1948* (Manchester: Manchester University Press, 2011); Francisca de Haan, 'Writing Inter/transnational History: The Case of Women's Movements and Feminisms', in *Internationale Geschichte in Theorie und Praxis / International History in Theory and Practice*, ed. Barbara Haider-Wilson, William D. Godsey and Wolfgang Mueller (Vienna: Verlag der Österreichischen Akademie der Wissenschaften, 2017), 501–36, 517.

13 Simon Jackson and Alanna O'Malley, eds, *The Institution of International Order. From the League of Nations to the United Nations* (New York: Routledge, 2018), 4; Although in agreement with Jessica Reinisch's and David Brydan's call to 'rethink the European dimensions' of internationalism the book is neither wholly European nor global but focused on the world of Geneva and the work pursued there to establish global public relations. Brydan Reinisch, 'Introduction: Internationalists in European History', in *Internationalists in European History*, ed. Brydan Reinisch (London: Bloomsbury Academic, 2021), 10.

14 Arne Lorenz Gellrich, Erik Koenen and Stefanie Averbeck-Lietz, 'The Epistemic Project of Open Diplomacy and the League of Nations: Co-evolution between Diplomacy, PR and Journalism', *Corporate Communications: An International Journal* 24, no. 4 (2019); Erik Koenen, ed., *Communicating the League of Nations* (Geneva: United Nations Library Historical Series, 2024).

15 Egon Ranshofen-Wertheimer, *The International Secretariat – A Great Experiment in International Administration* (Washington, DC: Carnegie Endowment for

International Peace, 1945). See also Pitman B. Potter, 'League Publicity: Cause or Effect of League Failure?' *The Public Opinion Quarterly* 2, no. 10 (1983): 399–412; For case studies of various national groups and individuals of the Secretariat Christine Manigand, *Les Francais au Service de la Société des Nations* (Bern: Peter Lang, 2003); Kenneth Millen-Penn, 'From Liberal to Socialist Internationalism: Konni Zilliacus and the League of Nations, 1894-1939' (PhD thesis, New York: State University of New York, Department of History, 1993); Mary Kinnear, *Woman of the World: Mary McGeachy and International Cooperation* (Toronto: University of Toronto Press, 2004); Salvador de Madariaga, *Morning Without Noon* (Farnborough: Saxon House, 1973); Madeleine Herren and Isabella Löhr, 'Gipfeltreffen im Schatten der Weltpolitik: Arthur Sweetser und die Mediendiplomatie des Völkerbunds', *Zeitschrift für Geschichtswissenschaft* 62, no. 5 (2014): 411–24; Löhr Herren, 'Being International in Times of War: Arthur Sweetser and the Shifting of the League of Nations to the United Nations', *European Review of History* 25, no. 3–4 (2018): 535–52; Timo Holste, 'Tourists at the League of Nations: Conceptions of Internationalism around the Palais des Nations, 1925-1946', *New Global Studies* 10, no. 3 (2016): 307–44; David Allen, 'International Exhibitionism: The League of Nations at the New York World's Fair, 1939-1940', in *International Organizations and the Media in the Nineteenth Century and Twentieth Centuries. Exorbitant Expectations*, ed. Jonas Brendebach, Martin Herzer and Heidi Tworek (New York: Routledge, 2018); Tworek, 'Peace through Truth – The Press and Moral Disarmament Through the League of Nations', *Medien & Zeit* 25, no. 4 (2010): 16–28; Frank Beyersdorf, 'First Professional International: FIJ (1926-1940)', in *A History of the International Movement of Journalists. Professionalism vs Politics*, ed. Kaarle Nordenstreng, Ulf Jonas Björk, Frank Beyersdorf, Svennik Høyer and Epp Lauk (London: Palgrave, 2016); see also Carolyn N. Biltoft's book, which uses critical theory to interrogate the ways in which the League's pledge to create international information flows served both liberal and illiberal causes. Carolyn N. Biltoft, *A Violent Peace: Media, truth and power at the League of Nations* (London: University of Chicago Press, 2021).

16 Tomoko Akami, 'The Limits of Peace Propaganda: The Information Section of the League of Nations and its Tokyo Office', in *International Organizations and the Media*, ed. Brendebach et al., 86. See in particular Emil Eiby Seidenfaden, 'The League of Nations' Collaboration with an International Public 1919-1939', *Contemporary European History* 31 (2022): 268–380 and Seidenfaden, 'Legitimizing International Bureaucracy – Press and Information Work from the League of Nations to the UN', in *Organizing the 20th-Century World International Organizations and the Emergence of International Public Administration, 1920-1960s*, ed. Karen Gram-Skjoldager, Haakon A. Ikonomou and Torsten Kahlert (London: Bloomsbury, 2020).

17 This resonates with the assertion by media scholars Averbeck-Lietz et al. that the Information Section pursued an 'epistemic project of open diplomacy' that saw an international bureaucracy transversally committed to progressive ideas about transparency. However, this book shows that this would change towards the end of the League's lifetime. Gellrich, Koenen and Averbeck-Lietz, 'The Epistemic Project', 616.
18 E.g. Jackie Harrison and Stephanie Pukallus, 'The European Community's Public Communication Policy', *Contemporary European History* 24, no. 2 (2015): 223–51.
19 E.g. Linda Risso, *Propaganda and Intelligence in the Cold War. The NATO Information Service* (New York: Routledge, 2014).
20 E.g. Philip Taylor, *British Propaganda in the Twentieth Century – Selling Democracy* (Edinburgh: Edinburgh University Press, 1999); Didier Georgakakis, *La République contre la propagande: aux origins perdues de la communication d'État en France* (Paris: Economica, 2004).
21 Renaud Meltz, 'Lorsque le Quai d'Orsay dictait des articles: La fabrication de l'opinion publique dans l'entre-deux-guerres', *Relations Internationales* 2, no. 154 (2013): 33–50.
22 Klaus Kiran Patel's recently underscored the importance of studying 'the very practice of internationalism on the ground'. Patel, 'Afterword: On the Chances and Challenges of Populating Internationalism', in *Internationalists*, ed. Reinisch, 271.
23 Although examples of early inter-governmental cooperation, like the Hague conferences, had been 'media events' before this point. Maartje Abbenhuis, *The Hague Conferences and International Politics, 1898–1915* (London: Bloomsbury Academic, 2019).
24 A phrase used in the period to describe the general public. E. g Sweetser, *The League of Nations at Work* (New York: The Macmillan Company, 1920), 187.
25 Quentin Skinner, *Visions of Politics Vol 1: Regarding Method* (Cambridge: Cambridge University Press, 2002), 148, 150. Jan-Werner Müller has called on historians to mobilize Skinner's terminology with the aim of describing and understanding processes of 'what we might call mass justification (or mass legitimation)'. Müller, 'European Intellectual History as Contemporary History', *Journal of Contemporary History* 46, no. 3 (2011): 574–90, 588.
26 Ranshofen-Wertheimer, *The International Secretariat*, 201.
27 Keith Hamilton and Richard Langhorne, *The Practice of Diplomacy* (London: Routledge, 1995).
28 President Woodrow Wilson's Fourteen Points, 8 January 1918, *Yale University Law School – Avalon Project*. http://avalon.law.yale.edu/20th_century/wilson14.asp (24 May 2023).
29 Ludovic Tournés, *Philantropic Foundations at the League of Nations: An Americanized League?* (London: Routledge, 2022); Mazower, *Governing the World*, 137.

30 Covenant of the League of Nations, in Walters, *A History*, 54.
31 Ikonomou, 'The Administrative Anatomy of Failure: The League of Nations Disarmament Section, 1919-1925', *Contemporary European History* 30, no. 3 (2021): 321–34.
32 Kenneth Millen-Penn, 'Democratic Control, Public Opinion, and League Diplomacy', *World Affairs* 157, no. 4 (1995): 207–18, 207.
33 Mazower, *Governing the World*, 22.
34 Meltz, 'Lorsque le Quai d'Orsay', 33–4.
35 Edward Hallet Carr, *The Twenty Years Crisis 1919-1939* (London: Macmillan & Co Ltd. 1939), 31.
36 Stephen Wertheim suggested that such rebuttals miss the point that the concept was mainly used for its 'illocutionary power' – as a rhetorical appeal for legitimacy. However, the League nonetheless invested a substantial amount of resources and personnel in information and publicity, suggesting a genuine conviction that this was an important battleground. Wertheim, 'Reading the International Mind: International Public Opinion in Early Twentieth Century Anglo-American Thought', in *The Decisionist Imagination – Sovereignty, Social science and Democracy in the 20th Century*, ed. Daniel Bessner and Nicolas Guilhot (New York: Berghan, 2018), 27–63.
37 Michael Korzi, 'Lapsed Memory: The Roots of American Public Opinion Research', *Polity* 33, no. 1 (2000): 49–75, 54.
38 Sandrine Kott, 'Toward a Social History of International Organizations: The ILO and the Internationalisation of Western Social Expertise (1919-1949)', in *Internationalism, Imperialism and the Formation of the Contemporary World*, ed. Miguel B. Jeronimo and Jose P. Monteiro (London: Palgrave), 33–77.
39 Clavin, 'Introduction: Conceptualising Internationalism between the World Wars', in *Transnationalism Reconfigured: Transnational Ideas and Movements Between the World Wars*, ed. Daniel Laqua (New York: I.B. Tauris, 2011), 5–6; Sluga, *Internationalism in the Age of Nationalism* (Philadelphia: University of Pennsylvania Press, 2013). Clavin Sluga, 'Rethinking the History of Internationalism', in *Internationalisms. A Twentieth Century History*, ed. Clavin Sluga (Cambridge: Cambridge University Press, 2017), 3–14.
40 E.g. Clavin, 'Conceptualising Internationalism', xii.
41 Encyclopedia Britannica, 'Collective Security', *Encyclopedia Britannica*, 2018. https://www.britannica.com/topic/collective-security (10 December 2018). On national self-determination, see Erez Manela, *The Wilsonian Moment – Self-determination and the Historical Origins of Anticolonial Nationalism* (Oxford: Oxford University Press, 2009).
42 Carsten Holbraad, *Internationalism and Nationalism in European Political Thought* (London: Palgrave Macmillan, 2003).

43 Marco Moraes, 'Competing Internationalisms at the League of Nations Secretariat, 1933-1940', in *The League of Nations: Perspectives from the Present*, ed. Ikonomou and Gram-Skjoldager (Aarhus: Aarhus University Press, 2019). See also Madeleine Herren, 'Fascist Internationalism', in Clavin, *Internationalisms. A Twentieth-Century History*, 191–212.
44 Daniel Laqua, 'Internationalism', in European History Online (EGO), published by the Leibniz Institute of European History (IEG), Mainz 04 May 2021 http://www.ieg-ego.eu/laquad-2021-en (29 March 2023).
45 Taylor, *British Propaganda*, xii.
46 Paul, Jonathan Meller, 'The Development of Modern Propaganda in Britain, 1854–1902' (PhD thesis, Durham University, 2010); Risso, *Propaganda and Intelligence*, 8.
47 See Seidenfaden, 'Information Section', United Nations Library & Archives at Geneva Research Guide: League of Nations Secretariat. https://libraryresources.unog.ch/LONSecretariat/information (16 March 2023).
48 The book bases most of its analysis on material that provides an overview of the section's administrative history, concentrating on the activities that took place *in* Geneva, such as central Registry Files that originated in, or were tagged as pertinent to, the Information Section. Since such documents tell us little of how changes in organization or terms of reference were interpreted inside the section, they are supplemented by other files, such as minutes of the Secretariat Directors' Meetings 1919–40, personnel files of important officials and private papers of two of the three main agents in the United States.
49 Risso, *Propaganda and Intelligence*, 17.
50 Ikonomou, 'The Administrative Anatomy of Failure'.

Chapter 1

1 Sweetser, 'League of Nations Publicity', 27 May 1919, 272, R1332, LONA, 4.
2 Walters, *A History*, 33–6; Eric Drummond, 'The Secretariat of the League of Nations', *Public Administration* 9, no. 2 (1931): 228–35, 228. Initially, French Jean Monnet and American Fosdick were Deputy Secretaries General, but soon an Italian and a Japanese Undersecretary-General were appointed as well. For a discussion of this process, see Gram-Skjoldager and Ikonomou, 'The Construction of the League of Nations Secretariat. Formative Practices of Autonomy and Legitimacy in International Organizations', *The International History Review* 41, no. 2 (2019): 257–79.
3 Unknown author, 'Memorandum of Publicity by the Information Section', 21 July 1919, 419, R1332, LONA, 1; Drummond, 'The Secretariat', 231.
4 Fosdick, letter to the Secretary General, 14 July 1919, 305, R1332, LONA, 1.

5 Jean Monnet, letter to Pierre Comert, 7 July 1919, S745 (Pierre Comert Personnel File), LONA.
6 Warren F. Kuehl, *Biographical Dictionary of Internationalists* (Westport: Greenwood Press, 1983), 166.
7 Ibid., 166–7; Manigand, *Les Francais*, 67.
8 The same Monnet who would later play a key role in the founding of the European Coal and Steel Community.
9 Sweetser, *Roadside Glimpses of the Great War* (New York: The Macmillan Company, 1916).
10 Unknown author, 'World's Longest Serving International Civil Servant', 1946, Box 2, ASP, 2; Library of Congress, *Arthur Sweetser Papers – A Finding Aid to the Collection in the Library of Congress* (Washington, DC, Manuscript Division – L.O.C, 2013). http://hdl.loc.gov/loc.mss/eadmss.ms013059 (25 May 2023).
11 'Career in Secretariat – Contracts before Beginning of Continuous Service: Sweetser, Arthur', nd, S889, LONA.
12 Arthur Sweetser, letter to Pierre Comert, 16 May 1942, Box 30, Arthur Sweetser Papers, L.O.C (ASP henceforth).
13 Unknown author, 'Memorandum of Publicity', 21 July 1919; Drummond, letter to Comert, 11 December 1919, 2396, R1332, LONA.
14 E.g., Unknown author, 'Memorandum of Publicity', 21 July 1919.
15 Sub-Committee of Technical Advisory Committee on Information, 'Observations on Branch-Offices', 28 January 1946, Box 69, ASP, 2.
16 Secretariat of the League of Nations, 'Present Organization of the Secretariat: Information Section', in Commission des 13, *COM.13/1-15* (preparatory documents for the Committee charged with studying the organization of the Secretariat, the International Labor Organization and the Permanent Court of International Justice), LONA, 7; In 1921, the Assembly approved another such diplomatic representation-office for Latin America staffed with three officials. Ranshofen-Wertheimer, *The International Secretariat*, 188.
17 Secretariat of the League of Nations, 'Present organization of the Secretariat: Information Section', Commission des 13, 1930, 8.
18 Secretariat staff was divided into three divisions. First Division officials included the leadership of a section, the regular 'members of section' and certain counsellors. Most officials named in the book belonged to the First Division. Second Division officials included shorthand-typists, press readers, clerks and messengers as well as 'correspondents' who worked for the section outside Geneva. Third Division included service personnel of the League buildings. Ranshofen-Wertheimer, *The International Secretariat*, xvii; Raw data on all staff of the Secretariat courtesy of the League of Nations Search Engine project: Madeleine Herren et al., LONSEA – League of Nations Search Engine, Heidelberg/Basel, 2010–2017. http://www.lonsea.de/ (LONSEA data base henceforth).

19 Ranshofen-Wertheimer, *The International Secretariat*, 208.
20 Information Section, *The League of Nations and the Press*, International Press Exhibition in Cologne (Geneva, 1928), 10–11.
21 Commission d'enquete, C-E-20 'Report on the Information Section', 16 April 1921, in Secretariat de la Société des Nations – Commission d'enquete, *CE/1-27*, 1921, LONA, 2.
22 Talbot Imlay, *Clarence Streit and Twentieth-Century American Internationalism* (Cambridge: Cambridge University Press, 2023), 30–1.
23 Christian Delporte, 'Les journalistes dans l'entre-deux-guerres. Une identité en crise', *Vingtième Siècle, revue d'histoire*, no. 47 (1995): 158–75.
24 Stefanie Averbeck-Lietz, 'Discovering Open Diplomacy: The League of Nations' Information Section 1920-1932 and its External and Internal Communication', in *Communicating the League of Nations*, ed. Koenen.
25 Gellrich, Koenen and Averbeck-Lietz, 'The Epistemic Project', 610, 616.
26 Torsten Kahlert, 'Prosopography: Unlocking the Social World of International Organizations', in *Organizing*, ed. Gram-Skjoldager, Ikonomou and Kahlert, 65.
27 Ranshofen-Wertheimer, *The International Secretariat*, 208–9.
28 On the League's finances and their development, see Hannah Tyler, 'Breaking Even for the Future: The Financial History of the League of Nations 1919-1933', *Monde(s)* 1, no. 19 (2012): 119–38.
29 See: Gram-Skjoldager, 'Taming the Bureaucrats. The Supervisory Commission and Political Control of the Secretariat', in *The League of Nations: Perspectives*, ed. Gram-Skjoldager and Ikonomou, 40–51.
30 Ranshofen-Wertheimer, *The International Secretariat*, 226–7.
31 Kuehl, *Biographical Dictionary*, 167.
32 Information Section, *The League of Nations and the Press*, 10.
33 LONSEA data base.
34 Ibid.
35 Gram-Skjoldager and Ikonomou, 'The Construction'.
36 Ibid., 6.
37 Drummond, letter to Comert, 11 December 1919.
38 Commission d'enquete, 'Report on the Information Section', 1.
39 Sweetser, 'Memorandum to the Secretary-General', 22 August 1929, S889 (Arthur Sweetser Personnel File), LONA, 3.
40 Drummond, Letter to George Herbert Mair, 6 August 1919, S824 (George Mair Personnel file), LONA; Taylor, *British Propaganda*, 9–15.
41 Comert, letter to Drummond, 27 June 1929, S889, LONA, 25. Translated from French by author.
42 Comert, staff list to Eric Drummond, 8 December 1919, 2396, R1332, LONA.
43 Comert, letter to Drummond, 27 June 1929; Unknown author, 'Memorandum of Publicity', 21 July 1919, 1.

44 Unknown author, 'Salaries of the Information Section as of 1 January 1925', nd, S893 (Oscar Thorsing Personnel File), LONA.
45 Sweetser, untitled, fall 1919, Box 13, ASP, 3–4.
46 Madariaga, *Morning Without Noon*, 13.
47 Sweetser often articulated this zeal. E.g. when he went on a health-related leave in 1926: Sweetser, 'Farewell letter: Declaration of Faith', 1 February 1926, Box 14, ASP.
48 'Directeur attaché a la Haute Direction', See: LONA, *Répertoire Général, Fond du Secretariat, Section d'Information*, LONA, 320.
49 Staff Committee, 'Minutes of the Thirty fifth Meeting of the Staff Committee, held at 3.30 p.m. on Tuesday, 27 December 1921, in Mr. Colban's Room', 27 December 1921, S969, LONA.
50 Sweetser, 'Memorandum to the Secretary-General', 22 August 1929, 2; Mair, 'Memorandum on the League of Nations Publicity', nd, 1919, R1332, LONA; Comert, 'Secretariat de la ligue des nations – presse et publicité', 21 May 1919, R1332, LONA; Sweetser, 'League of Nations Publicity', 14 May 1919, R1332, LONA; Unknown author, 'Memorandum of Publicity', 21 July 1919.
51 Sweetser, 'Memorandum to the Secretary-General', 22 August 1929, 2.
52 Comert, 'Certificate as to Grant of Annual Increment', 23 November 1923, S889, LONA.
53 Susan Sweetser Clifford, *One Shining Hour* (Private Publication, 1990), 47.
54 'Career in Secretariat – Contracts before Beginning of Continuous Service: Sweetser, Arthur', nd, S889, LONA, 3.
55 Sweetser, *The League of Nations at Work*, 202–3.
56 Averbeck-Lietz, 'Discovering Open Diplomacy'.
57 Sweetser, diary entry, 20 December 1918, Box 1, ASP.
58 E.g. Manigand, *Les Francais*, 99.
59 Ibid., 70.
60 Comert, 'Article by M. Comert', 29 March 1921, *Minutes of the Directors' Meetings (MDM henceforth), 1921-1922*, LONA. Translated from French by the author.
61 Potter, 'League Publicity', 407. Potter interviewed several former officials including Drummond and Sweetser but not Comert.
62 Ibid., 411.
63 Information Section, *The League of Nations and the Press*, 10–11.
64 MDM, 13 August 1919, LONA, 3.
65 James Barros, *Office without Power* (Oxford: Clarendon, 1979), 394.
66 Several officials expressed deep regret over Comert's resignation. E. g Drummond, letter to Comert, 23 December 1932, S745, LONA.
67 Madariaga, *Morning without Noon*, 279.
68 Press cuttings, December 1932, Box 30, ASP.
69 Ibid.

70 E. g, in 1930: Secretariat of the League of Nations, *Ten Years of World-Co-operation* (London and Aylesbury: Hazel, Watson and Viney, 1930), 406–7; Ranshofen-Wertheimer, *The International Secretariat*, 409.
71 Ranshofen-Wertheimer, *The International Secretariat*, 203.
72 Gram-Skjoldager and Ikonomou, 'The Construction', 9; Secretariat of the League of Nations, Staff Regulations, 2nd edn, 1926, Annex VI: 'Publications, Lectures and Speeches by Members of the Secretariat. Abstention from Political Activities', 34631x, R1461, LONA, 57.
73 Commission d'enquete, 'Report on the Information Section', 2.
74 Fosdick, letter to the Secretary-General, 15 July 1919, 314, R1332, LONA, 1.
75 Sweetser, 'League of Nations Publicity', 27 May 1919, R1332, LONA, 1.
76 MDM, 21 April 1920, LONA, 2.
77 Potter, 'League Publicity', 408.
78 Ranshofen-Wertheimer, *The International Secretariat*, 203.

Chapter 2

1 Commission d'enquete, 'Report on the Information Section', 1.
2 League of Nations Assembly, *A.10.1933.X: Technical Concentration of the Activities of the League of Nations and Rationalisation of the Services of the Secretariat and the International Labour Office, Report by the Supervisory Commission to the Assembly July 20th, 1933*, LONA, 8.
3 The French report said 'milieux' which can mean 'social backgrounds', but the Secretariat translated it into 'classes:' Information Section, 'Report of the Information Section to the 8th Assembly', 1927, 1; Akami, 'The Limits', 73.
4 Sweetser, *The League of Nations at Work*, 201.
5 Secretariat of the League of Nations, *Ten Years*, 403.
6 Akami, 'Beyond the Formula of the Age of Reason: Experts, Social Sciences, and the Phonic Public in International Politics', in *The League of Nations: Perspectives*, ed. Ikonomou and Gram-Skjoldager, 161–72.
7 Potter, 'League Publicity', 410.
8 Risso, '"Enlightening Public Opinion": A Study of NATO's Information Policies between 1949 and 1959 based on Recently Declassified Documents', *Cold War History* 7, no. 1 (2007): 46.
9 On the PRESSA exhibition, see Stephanie Seul: '"Trägerin des europäischen Gemeinschaftsgedankens – lebendige Magna Charta des Friedens": Die politische Dimension der PRESSA Köln 1928 und ihr Widerhall in der zeitgenössischen deutschen und internationalen Presse', in *80 Jahre PRESSA, Internationale Presse-Ausstellung Köln 1928, und der jüdische Beitrag zum modernen Journalismus*, ed.

Susanne Marten-Finnis and Michael Nagel, vol. 1 (Bremen: edition lumière, 2012), 57–104.
10 Information Section, *The League of Nations and the Press*, 63.
11 Ranshofen-Wertheimer, *The International Secretariat*, 202.
12 Arne L. Gellrich and Erik Koenen, 'In Search of the Geneva Journalist', in *Communicating the League of Nations*, ed. Koenen.
13 Secretariat of the League of Nations, *Ten Years*, 406; Unknown author, 'Memorandum on the Work of the Information Section 1930-1931', nd, 1932, P191, Adrianus Pelt Papers (APP henceforth), LONA, 2.
14 Manigand, *Les Francais*, 95–6.
15 Today the *Palais Wilson* houses the United Nations High Commissariat for Human Rights.
16 Information Section, *The League of Nations and the Press*, 28–9.
17 Ranshofen-Wertheimer, *The International Secretariat*, 210–11; Information Section, *The League of Nations and the Press*, 28–9.
18 Information Section, *The League of Nations and the Press*, 62–3.
19 Ranshofen-Wertheimer, *The International Secretariat*, 204; Société des Nations, *A.21, 1932: Activités présentes du Secrétariat – et des organizations spéciales de la Société,'* Communiqué a l'Assemblée, au Conseil et aux Membres de la Société, Section Reorganization [. . .], P191, APP, 5; Yves Victor, Catherine Ghebali, *A repertoire of League of Nations Serial Documents, 1919-1947* (New York: Oceana Publications/CEIP, 1973), 121.
20 Commission d'enquete, 'Report on the Information Section', 5.
21 Information Section, 'Report of the Information Section to the 8th Assembly, 1927', 9. Between 1929 and 1932, the section distributed between 600 and 700 communiqués annually. This number probably included communiqués made during the Assembly. Société des Nations, *A.21, 1932: Activités présentes du Secrétariat*, 5.
22 League of Nations, *A.18.1937: The League of Nations and Modern Methods of Spreading Information Utilised in the Cause of Peace, (report by the secretary-general)*, September 1, 1937, LONA, 5.
23 Unknown author, 'Memorandum on the Work of the Information Section 1930–1931', 8.
24 Secretariat of the League of Nations, *Ten Years*, 412.
25 Ruth Sweetser on the work of her husband, cited in Arthur's diary: Sweetser, 'London, The Hague, Brussels, Geneva', 11 June 1920, Box 1, ASP, 1.
26 Maurice Hankey, letter to Drummond, 23 July 1919, 481, R1332, LONA, 1.
27 Fosdick, note: 'Publicity of Council Meetings', 25 July 1919, 481, R1332, LONA, 5.
28 Drummond, note: 'Publicity of Council Meetings', 28 July 1919, 481, R1332, LONA, 2.
29 Walters *A History*, 89–90.

30 Swedish Branting supported the German viewpoint in the discussion of the Saar question. M. Rault was the French chairman of the League-installed Saar Commission. MDM, 25 April 1923, 1923, LONA, 2.
31 MDM, 25 April 1923, 3–6.
32 MDM, 29 June 1921, 1921–2, 3.
33 Société des Nations, C.231. M.93: Document Préparatoires – Conference d'Experts des Presse, 11 May 1927, 6.
34 See also Nordenstreng and Tarja Seppä, '"Collaboration of the Press in the Organization of Peace" – The League of Nations as a Catalyst for Important Intellectual Trends', in *Communicating the League of Nations*, ed. Koenen.
35 Information Section, *Monthly Summary of the League of Nations* (*MS* henceforth), vol. II, no. 9, September 1922, LONA, 211.
36 League of Nations, '"Moral Disarmament" – Documentary material forwarded by the International Organization on Intellectual Co-operation', Conference document 98, 24 February 1932, LONA.
37 Société des Nations, Document Préparatoires, 11 May 1927, 6.
38 Sweetser, letter to Comert, 23 October 1952, Box 28, ASP.
39 Tworek, 'The Creation of European News: News Agency Cooperation in Interwar Europe', *Journalism Studies* 14, no. 5 (2013): 730–42, 734; Beyersdorf, 'First Professional International', 91.
40 Letter from Bureau Central des Agences Alliées to Drummond, 1 March, 1926, 49874, R1343, LONA.
41 Information Section, *The League of Nations and the Press*, 44–5.
42 Comert, letter to Sweetser, 17 April 1926, Box 30, ASP, 5.
43 Lord Burnham, letter to Adrianus Pelt, 26 February 1926, *Press & Communication*, P192, APP, 1.
44 Information Section, *The League of Nations and the Press*, 45–6; Ranshofen-Wertheimer, *The International Secretariat*, 213.
45 Beyersdorf, 'First Professional International', 91.
46 Société des Nations, Document Préparatoires, 11 May 1927, 20.
47 Information Section, *The League of Nations and the Press*, 45–7.
48 Ibid., 47–8.
49 Kaarle Nordenstreng and Seppä, 'Collaboration'.
50 Tworek, 'Peace through Truth', 16, 24.
51 Ibid., 26.
52 Beyersdorf, 'First Professional International'.
53 For a discussion focusing on these activities in the context of the in the League's information policies, see Seidenfaden, 'The League of Nations' Collaboration'.
54 Davies, 'A Great Experiment of the League of Nations Era', 411.
55 Sweetser, 'League of Nations Publicity', 2.
56 Ibid.

57 Bertram Pickard, 'The Greater League of Nations – A Brief Survey of the Nature and Development of Unofficial International Organizations', *Contemporary Review* 850, no. 150 (1936): 460–5, 465.
58 Committee to examine the organization of the Information Section, Annex to 'Note by Secretary General on the Commission de Controle – Réorganization de la Section d'Information', 21 September 1933, P191, APP, 3; Davies observed it was uncommon to distinguish between today's intergovernmental organizations (IGOs) and international non-governmental organizations (INGOs) and that 'the experience of the League of Nations in dealing with INGOs was consequently highly experimental.' Davies, 'A Great Experiment of the League of Nations Era', 408; Information Section, 'Memo on Liaison with International Organizations', 21 September 1933, P191, APP, 3.
59 Information Section, *The League of Nations – Its Constitution and Organization* (Geneva: 1926, revised edition) 40.
60 Jean-Jacques Renoliet, 'La genèse de l'institut international de Coopération intellectuelle', *Relations Internationales* 72 (1992): 387–98; Renoliet, *L'UNESCO oubliée. La Société des Nations et la coopération intellectuelle, 1919-1946* (Paris: Sorbonne, 1999); Laqua showed the mushrooming of League-associated bodies dealing with intellectual cooperation 1922-1930: Laqua, 'Activism in the "Students" League of Nations".
61 Pelt, 'Information Section – Liste des associations privée avec lesquelles la Section d'information est en rapport et analyse de chacune de ces liaisons', nd, 1933, P191, APP, 1–2.
62 Information Section, 'Report of the Information Section to the 8th Assembly, 1927', 16.
63 Sweetser, 'League of Nations Publicity', 3; Information Section, 'Draft. Questions', 14 August 1919, 743, R1332, LONA.
64 Drummond, note to Monnet, Fosdick, 14 August 1919, 743, R1332, LONA.
65 Ibid.
66 Comert, 'Associations Nationales – Bureau de liaison, Plan General', 20 August 1919, Box 13, ASP, 1.
67 McCarthy, 'Parties, Voluntary Associations, Democratic Politics in Interwar Britain', *The Historical Journal*, 50, no. 4 (2007): 893; Sluga, *Internationalism in the Age of Nationalism*, 71–2.
68 Ibid., 72.
69 Davies, 'Internationalism in a Divided World', 228.
70 Ibid., 234–5.
71 Letter from Shaikh Mushir Hosain Kidwal to Eric Drummond, 30 January 1920, 2849, R1332, LONA; letter from George Mair to Eric Drummond, 27 January 1920, 2849, R1332.
72 Davies, 'Internationalism in a Divided World', 227.
73 MDM, 10 December 1919, LONA, 4.

74 Davies, 'Internationalism in a Divided World', 429.
75 Special Circular 88, 11 November 1921, Société des Nations, *Special Circulars, 1921*, LONA, 3.
76 Drummond, letter to Jean Monnet, 23 June 1919, 992, R1332, LONA.
77 Radziwill, 'Women's Organizations', 17 May 1934, P191, APP.
78 LONSEA data base; Letter from Gabriele Radziwill to Drummond, 22 April 1931, S861 (Gabriele Radziwill Personnel File), LONA.
79 Secretariat, Special Circular 88, 2; E.g. Minutes of Information Section-meeting (MIS, henceforth), February 1934, P191, APP, LONA, 6; MIS, 8 May 1934; MIS, 22 February 1935.
80 Adrianius Pelt, 'Information Section – Liste des associations privée, 1933', 8.
81 Information Section, 'Representation du Secretariat aux divers congress, conferences etc. auxquels il a eté invité en 1924', 8 September 1924, 38568, R1600, LONA, 2.
82 Radziwill, 'Meeting of the International Federation of League of Nations Societies', 30 July 1926, 52102, R1336, LONA, 3.
83 Various files in: August 1927, 59564, R1336, LONA; Davies, 'Internationalism in a Divided World', 245; Ruyssen, 'La propagande pour la Société des Nations', in *Les Origines et l'œuvre de la Société des Nations vol II*, ed. Peter Munch (Copenhague: Rask-Ørstedfonden/Nordisk Forlag, 1924), 237–8.
84 See Myriam Piquet, 'Gender Distribution in the League of Nations', *The League of Nations: Perspectives*, ed. Ikonomou and Gram-Skjoldager, 62–73.
85 For a study of this relationship, seen from the perspective of the federation, see Richard, 'Between Publicity and Discretion: The International Federation of League of Nations Societies', in *Organizing*, ed. Gram-Skjoldager, Ikonomou and Kahlert, 148.
86 Mary Kinnear, *Woman of the World*, 59–60; McCarthy, *British People and the League of Nations*, 182.
87 Sluga, 'Women, Feminisms and Twentieth Century Internationalisms', in *Internationalisms. A Twentieth Century History*, 61–84.
88 E.g. Piquet, 'Gender Distribution', 63.
89 Kinnear, *Woman of the World*, 58–9.
90 See Benjamin Auberer, 'Murder, Intrigue, Sex and Internationalism – Novels about the League of Nations', in *The League of Nations: Perspectives*, ed. Ikonomou and Gram-Skjoldager.
91 Pelt, note to Comert: 'Suggestion pour l'etablissement d'un service radiophonique au sein de la section d'information', 12 December 1929, P192, APP.
92 On the list of organizations referred to as 'IIème Internationale, a mistake, since the Second International had merged into the Labour and Socialist International together with the Vienna International in 1923.
93 Millen-Penn, *From Liberal to Socialist Internationalism*, 158; MDM, 3 February 1926, 1926, LONA, 2–3; Iain Stewart, 'The French Press in Wartime London

1940-4: From the Politics of Exile to Inter-Allied Relations', *Journal of Contemporary History* 1, no. 21 (2022): 6; MDM, 3 February 1926, 1926, LONA.
94 For example the 'Union Fédérale des Associations Francaise de Blessés, Multilés, Reformés et anciens combattants de la Grande Guerre, de leurs Veuves, Orphelants et Ascendants', 1924, 35875, R1340.
95 Ibid.
96 Ludovic Tournés, 'La Philanthropie Americaine, La Société des Nations et la Coproduction d'un Ordre International (1919-1946)', *Relations Internationales* 3, no. 151 (2012): 25–36, 31–2.
97 Comert, 'Certificate as to Grant of annual Increment: José Plà', 10 August 1926, S856 (José Plà Personnel File), LONA; Plá, note for Comert, 'Temporary Collaborators', 9 December 1926, 53149, R1347, LONA, 2.
98 Secretariat of the League of Nations, *Ten Years*, 413.
99 Ranshofen-Wertheimer, *The International Secretariat*, 342.
100 Comert, 'Certificate as to Grant of Annual Increment: José Plà', 10 August 1926, S856, LONA.
101 Plà, 'Temporary Collaborators 1928', 11 January 1929, 901, R3297, LONA, 1.
102 Unknown author, Attachment to José Plà's, note 'Temporary Collaborators', 29 August 1931, 23004, R3297, LONA.
103 According to the LONSEA data base, the final list changed somewhat and forty-five arrived from twenty-seven countries.
104 Plá, note for Comert, 'Temporary Collaborators', 9 December 1926, 2.
105 Information Section, 'Report of the Information Section to the 8th Assembly, 1927', 18.
106 Secretariat of the League of Nations, *Ten Years*, 413.
107 A few collaborators were invited based on their hostility towards the League. For example, in 1930 the section invited Hans Hansen, editor in chief of the Danish right-wing newspaper *Jyllands-Posten*. Danish official Ludwig Krabbe argued that it would be good to invite a person who was sceptical towards the League. However, Hansen did not accept the invitation; Plà, note for Comert, 'Temporary Collaborators', 28 February 1930, 22585, R3297, LONA, 1.
108 Plá, note for Comert, 'Temporary Collaborators', 9 December 1926, 4.
109 Ibid.
110 Ranshofen-Wertheimer, *The International Secretariat*, 184–5.
111 Gram-Skjoldager and Ikonomou, 'The Construction', 15.
112 Ranshofen-Wertheimer, *The International Secretariat*, 185.
113 Mair, 'Memorandum on the League of Nations Publicity – Publicity during the Next Few Months [. . .]', 21 May 1919, 4.
114 Frank Beyersdorf, 'Credit or Chaos? The Austrian Stabilisation Programme of 1923 and the League of Nations', in *Transnationalism Reconfigured*, ed. Laqua, 135–58.
115 Barros, *Office without Power*, 394.

116 E.g. Sweetser organized various ad hoc League of Nations news dissemination services in collaboration with the World Peace Foundation: Letter from Denis P. Myers/World Peace Foundation to Arthur Sweetser, 13 August 1920, Box 35, ASP.
117 Letter from Fosdick to Sweetser, 27 July 1920, Box 31, ASP.
118 Comert, 'Certificate as to Grant of Annual Increment: Arthur Sweetser', 17 January 1928, S889, LONA.
119 Ibid.
120 Letter from Fosdick to Sweetser, 6 February 1924, Box 14, ASP, 3; Letter from Sweetser to Drummond, 28 February 1924, Box 14, ASP.
121 Löhr and Herren, 'Gipfeltreffen', 421.
122 Pensions schedule, nd, S889, LONA. During the year 1933 he was Acting Director of the section. See Chapter 4.
123 Sweetser, letter to Drummond, 23 January 1930, S889, LONA, 6.
124 Biltof, *A Violent Peace*, 9.

Chapter 3

1 Clavin, *Securing*.
2 Tyler, 'Breaking Even', 126–7.
3 Ranshofen-Wertheimer, *The International Secretariat*, 218; Confidential Circular 1, MDM, 10 March 1923, 5.
4 Ibid., 6.
5 Ranshofen-Wertheimer, *The International Secretariat*, 221.
6 Two caveats are necessary to establish when studying the Secretariat's news and information material: First, not all documents released by the Information Section targeted the broader public. The section produced press reviews for internal use in the Secretariat, the Council and the Assembly. Second, most documents published by the League were not published by the Information Section, as they were official documents of various kinds and not aimed at the broad public. Information Section, *The League of Nations and the Press*, 56, 58; League of Nations, *A.18.1937: The League of Nations and Modern Methods [. . .]*, 4.
7 Information Section, *The League of Nations and the Press*, 56.
8 Tyler, 'Breaking Even', 126.
9 Ranshofen-Wertheimer, *The International Secretariat*, 221.
10 Information Section, *The League of Nations and the Press*, 9.
11 Information Section, 'Report of the Information Section to the 8th Assembly, 1927', 10.
12 Information Section, *The League of Nations and the Press*, 58.
13 League of Nations, *A.18.1937: The League of Nations and Modern Methods*, 5.

14 Secretariat of the League of Nations, *Ten Years*, 405.
15 Ibid., v.
16 Ibid.
17 Comert, 'Article by M. Comert', 29 March 1921.
18 League of Nations, *A.18.1937: The League of Nations and Modern Methods*, 5.
19 Letter from Pierre Comert to Arthur Sweetser, 20 August 1924, Box 30, ASP, 2.
20 Sweetser, 'League of Nations Publicity', 27 May 1919, 1.
21 Nicholas Mulder, *The Economic Weapon – The Rise of Sanctions as a Tool of Modern War* (New Haven: Yale University Press, 2022); Walters, *A History*, 66, 81; Barros, *Office without Power*, 131.
22 Information Section, communiqué, 28 December 1920, *Communiqués de la Section d'Information*, LONA, 1.
23 Information Section, *MS*, April–May 1921, no. 1, LONA, 1.
24 For a contemporary discussion of this distinction, see Potter, 'Note on the Distinction between Political and Technical Questions', *Political Science Quarterly* 50, no. 2 (1935): 264–71.
25 Information Section, *MS*, April–May 1921, no. 1, 1.
26 Information Section, *MS*, no. 6, October 1921, 128.
27 Information Section, *MS*, no. 9, Annual 1921, 1.
28 Clavin, *Securing*.
29 Information Section, *MS*, Annual 1921, 207.
30 Victor and Ghebali, *A Repertoire*, 127.
31 Ibid., 8.
32 Ibid., 46.
33 Ibid.
34 Information Section, communiqué, 28 December 1920, 1.
35 Information Section, *MS*, no. 1, April–May 1921, 1.
36 League of Nations (Deuxième Assemblée de la Société des Nations), *La Société des Nations – Son activité par l'image* (Genève: Atar, 1921), 21.
37 Ibid.
38 Ibid., 57.
39 Information Section, *The League of Nations and the Press*, 63.
40 Walter Lippmann, *Public Opinion* (New York: Harcourt, Brace and Company, 1922).
41 Secretariat of the League of Nations, *Ten Years*, 399.
42 Ibid.
43 Ibid., 402, 405, 409, 411.
44 Ibid., 400.
45 Ibid., 403.
46 Ibid., 414.
47 Ibid., 399–400.

48 Information Section, *MS* VII, no. 5, May 1927, 130.
49 Information Section, *MS* VII, no. 9, September 1927, 306.
50 Information Section, *MS* VII, no. 12, December 1927, 340.
51 Information Section, *MS* VII, no. 7, July 1927, 233.
52 Information Section, *MS* VII, no. 5, May 1927, 129–30; Information Section, *MS* VII, no. 12, December 1927, 341–2; League of Nations, Information Section, *The League of Nations from Year to Year, 1926-1927* (Geneva, League of Nations Secretariat, 1927), 8.
53 Information Section, *MS* VII, no. 5, May 1927, 129–30.
54 Information Section, *The League of Nations – Its Constitution*, 45.
55 Ibid., 7.
56 Secretariat of the League of Nations, *Ten Years*, 401.
57 Anthony Best, Jussi M. Hanhimäki, Joseph A. Maiolo and Kirsten E. Schultze, *International History of the Twentieth Century and Beyond*, 3rd edn (London: Routledge, 2015), 57.
58 Clavin, *Securing*, 40.
59 Ibid., 52.
60 Ibid.
61 Secretariat of the League of Nations, *Ten Years*, 177.
62 Ibid., 178.
63 Ibid., 179.
64 Wolfram Kaiser and Johan Schot, *Writing the Rules for Europe – Experts, Cartels, and International Organizations* (New York: Palgrave Macmillan, 2014).
65 Secretariat of the League of Nations, *Ten Years*, 178, 179.
66 Moraes, 'Competing Internationalisms at the League of Nations Secretariat', 51–62.
67 Quinn Slobodian, *Globalists: The End of Empire and the Birth of Neoliberalism* (Cambridge, MA: Harvard University Press, 2018), 27–55.
68 Secretariat of the League of Nations, *Ten Years*, 179.
69 Lord Robert Cecil, *A Great Experiment – An Autobiography* (London: Jonathan Cape Ltd, 1941), 48–9.
70 Secretariat of the League of Nations, *Ten Years*, 1.
71 E.g. Mazower, *Governing the World*.
72 E.g. Sluga, *Internationalism in the Age of Nationalism*.
73 Secretariat of the League of Nations, *Ten Years*, 34.
74 Ibid., 33.

Chapter 4

1 MIS, 10 January 1934.
2 'Biography: Pelt, Adrien', nd, S852 (Adrian Pelt Personnel File), LONA; J. Bosmans, 'Adrianus Pelt', in *Biographical Dictionary of the Netherlands 1880-2000*.

http://resources.huygens.knaw.nl/bwn1880-2000/lemmata/bwn2/pelt (26 May 2023).
3   LONSEA data base; Bosmans.
4   Steiner, *The Lights that Failed*, 800.
5   Walters, *A History*, 768.
6   E.g. Steiner, *The Lights that Failed*, 812.
7   Ranshofen-Wertheimer, *The International Secretariat*, 28–9.
8   Committee of Thirteen, *A.16.1930: Committee of Enquiry on the Organisation of the Secretariat, the International Labour Office and the Registry of the Permanent Court of International Justice. Report of the Committee*, 1930, LONA, 30.
9   Barros, *Office without Power*.
10 Sweetser, letter to Drummond, 25 January 1932, Box 31, ASP.
11 Clavin, *Securing*, 35.
12 Barros, *Betrayal from within – Joseph Avenol, Secretary-General of the League of Nations, 1933-1940* (New Haven: Yale University Press, 1969), 3.
13 Société des Nations, Special Circular 54, 30 December 1933, LONA 1.
14 League of Nations, *A.10.1933.X: Technical Concentration of the Activities*, 1 (footnote).
15 'Financial Questions', in *Official Journal of the League of Nations* 14 (October 1933), 1181.
16 League of Nations, *A.10.1933.X: Technical Concentration of the Activities*, 8.
17 Ibid., 7.
18 Potter, *League Publicity*, 406–7.
19 Ibid., 406.
20 Ibid., 411.
21 Information Section, *The League of Nations and the Press*, 9.
22 MIS, 10 January 1934.
23 Averbeck-Lietz, 'Discovering Open Diplomacy', 30.
24 Lord Perth [Eric Drummond] et al., *The International Secretariat of the Future – Lessons by a Group of former Officials of the League of Nations* (London: Royal Institute of International Affairs/Oxford University Press, 1944), 61.
25 League of Nations, *A.18.1937: The League of Nations and Modern Methods*, 3.
26 Annex to 'C. C. 708. Commission de contrôle: Réorganisation de la Section d'Information. Note du Sécretaire generale', 21 September 1933, P191, APP, 3.
27 Ibid.
28 Ibid., 12.
29 League of Nations, *A.10.1933.X: Technical Concentration of the Activities*.
30 Ibid., 8.
31 Annex to 'C. C. 708', 21 September 1933, 21.
32 Ibid., 4.
33 Ibid., 3.

34 Special Circular 54, 30 December 1933, 1.
35 Robert H. Cory, 'Forging a Public Information Policy for the United Nations', *International Organization* 7, no. 2 (1953): 229–42, 233.
36 Annex to 'C. C. 708', 21 September 1933, 20.
37 Unknown author, 'Notes on the First Meeting of the Liaison Committee', 7 February 1934, P191, APP, 1.
38 Ranshofen-Wertheimer, *The International Secretariat*, 152–3.
39 Adrianus Pelt, 'To All Members of the Information Section', MIS, 26 February 1934.
40 MIS, 22 February 1934, 1.
41 Ibid.
42 Holste, 'Tourists at the League', 308.
43 MIS, 22 May 1936.
44 MIS, 26 May 1936.
45 Unknown author, 'Note on the Information Section', nd, P191, APP, 5.
46 Ranshofen-Wertheimer, *The International Secretariat*, 209.
47 Unknown author, 'Some Figures Illustrating the Activity of the Information Section in 1938', P191, APP, 1.
48 Annex to 'C. C. 708', 21 September 5; Société des Nations, *A.21, 1932: Activités présentes du Secrétariat*, 6.
49 MIS, 19 October 1934, 1.
50 League of Nations Secretariat, Standing Instructions no. 22, 1934, *Standing Instructions, 1934*, LONA.
51 Pelt, 'Section d'information – note pour les membres de la section – liste E', 1 July 1935, P191, APP.
52 E.g. Société des Nations, 'Circulaire Interieure', 43, 15 May 1940, LONA.
53 Pelt, 'Memorandum on the Reduction of Staff and the Reorganization of the Information Section', nd, P191, APP, LONA, 6.
54 Unknown author, 'International Federation of League of Nations Societies – Permanent Advisory Commission No. 1 – Education', 29 September 1934, 13877, R5177, LONA.
55 MIS, 15 May 1936; Unknown author, 'International Federation of League of Nations Societies', 29 September 1934.
56 MIS, 30 January 1934.
57 Plà, note to Sweetser, 26 May 1933, 3958, R5177, LONA.
58 Davies, 'A Great Experiment of the League of Nations Era', 417.
59 Plà, 'XIXème Assemblée Generale de l'Union Internationale des Associations pour la Société des Nations, (1935), report by Monsieur Plà', 19 June 1935, 17374, R5177, LONA, 7.
60 Note from Fritz Schnabel to Pelt, 5 September 1935, 17374, R5177, LONA.
61 E.g. Walters, *A History*, 721–39; Barros, *Betrayal*, 164–5.

62 Information Section, *MS* XIX, nos. 8–9, August–September 1939, 315.
63 Ibid.
64 E.g. Barros, *Betrayal*.
65 Unknown author, 'Bareme pour le calcul de la contribution volontaire des fonctionnaires', nd, P191, APP, 1.
66 Kinnear, *Woman of the World*, 57. Another example was more prominent: Rachel Crowdy led the Social Questions Section, although her title was never officially director but 'Chief of Section' similar to McGeachy's. Ranshofen-Wertheimer, *The International Secretariat*, 126; LONSEA database.
67 Sweetser was employed in the League until December 1942. Seán Lester, 'Statement by Acting Secretary-General', 16 May 1942, S889, LONA.
68 Holste, 'Tourists at the League'.
69 Allen, 'International Exhibitionism'.
70 Ibid., 106.

Chapter 5

1 Ranshofen-Wertheimer, *The International Secretariat*, 207.
2 League of Nations, *A.10.1933.X: Technical Concentration of the Activities*, 8. See also Pelle van Dijk, 'Internationalism on the Big Screen: Films on the League of Nations', *Studies in Communication Sciences* 23, no. 1 (2023): 62.
3 Information Section, 'Report of the Information Section to the 8th Assembly, 1927', 14.
4 Ranshofen-Wertheimer, *The International Secretariat*, 206–7.
5 Paul F. Douglas and Karl Bömer, 'The Press as a Factor in Modern International Relations', *The Annals of the American Academy of Political and Social Science* 162 (1932): 241–72, 251.
6 MIS, 18 January, 23 February and 16 March 1934.
7 League of Nations, *A.18.1937: The League of Nations and Modern Methods*, 6.
8 E.g. Ranshofen-Wertheimer, *The International Secretariat*, 205–6.
9 League of Nations, *A.18.1937: The League of Nations and Modern Methods*, 5.
10 The UN Audiovisual Library holds 30 clips of League film-material. https://www.unmultimedia.org/avlibrary/ Series: League of Nations (25 May 2023).
11 League of Nations, *A.18.1937: The League of Nations and Modern Methods*, 8.
12 UNESCO Archives database (AtOM), 'International Educational Cinematographic Institute (IECI)', *UNESCO Archives Catalogue*. https://atom.archives.unesco.org/international-educational-cinematographic-institute-ieci (25 May 2023).
13 'Regarding League of Nations: Films', UN-file *GIIB/3/1/25*, 15 December 1948, United Nations Library, Geneva.

14 Unknown author, Confidential note, 'Films on the League', 16 September 1936, P192, APP, 1–2.
15 Van Dijk, 'Internationalism on the Big Screen', 58.
16 Secretariat of the League of Nations, *Ten Years*, 411.
17 See Helle Strandgaard Jensen, Nikolai Schulz and Emil Eiby Seidenfaden, 'Film-splaining the League of Nations' in *The League of Nations: Perspectives*, 201–11.
18 Sweetser, *Diaries and Biographical Material 1913-1956: Manchuria*, Box 1, ASP.
19 League of Nations, *A.10.1933.X: Technical Concentration of the Activities*.
20 E. g Deuxieme Assemblée, *La Société des Nations*, 1921, discussed previously and *The League of Nations – A Pictorial Survey* (Geneva, 1929). Examples of pamphlets included *The League of Nations – Its Constitution and Organization*, 1923, 1926.
21 League of Nations, *A.10.1933.X: Technical Concentration of the Activities*, 8.
22 In a significant 1937 report the section proposed drastically increased resources within wireless equipment and films. It asked for a cinematographic budget sixteen times the size of the one it had. League of Nations, *A.18.1937: The League of Nations and Modern Methods*, 11.
23 Elisabetta Tollardo, 'International Experts or Fascist Envoys? Alberto Theodoli and Pietro Stoppani at the League of Nations', *New Global Studies* 10, no. 3 (2016): 283–306, 305.
24 See Jürgen Wilke, 'Cinematography as a Medium of Communication', in *Communicating the League of Nations*, ed. Koenen.
25 Unknown author, 'M. Bruccoleri/Note pour les membres de la section', 1 July 1935, P191, APP; LONSEA data base.
26 Walters, *A History*, 699.
27 Ghebali and Victor, *A Repertoire*, 125.
28 Information Section, *MS* XIV, no. 12, December 1934, 276.
29 Jürgen Osterhammel, 'Technical Co-operation between the League of Nations and China', *Modern Asian Studies* 13, no. 4 (1979): 661–80.
30 Information Section, communiqué, 7 November 1934, LONA, 1.
31 Information Section, communiqué, 17 October 1934, 1.
32 Ibid.
33 Information Section & Realist Film, *The League at Work*, Part 1 and 2, https://www.unmultimedia.org/avlibrary/asset/2082/2082355/ (26 May 2023).
34 For a systematic discussion of the specific film, see Strandgaard Jensen, Schulz and Seidenfaden, 'Film-splaining the League of Nations', 201–10.
35 Van Dijk, 'Internationalism on the Big Screen', 61.
36 Piquet, 'Gender Distribution', 67.
37 Information Section, *Petit Manuel de la Société des Nations* (Genève: Section d'Information, 1933), 72.
38 Information Section, *MS* VII, no. 12, December 1927, 340.
39 Information Section, *MS* XIV, no. 12, December 1934, 273.

40 Ibid., 274.
41 Information Section, communiqué, 8 March 1937, LONA, 1.
42 Information Section, *MS* XVIII, vol. 9, September 1938, 221.
43 Information Section, *MS* XVIII, vol. 12, December 1938, 301.
44 Information Section, *MS* XVII, no. 5, May 1937, 88.
45 E.g Mazower, *Governing the World*, 131–5.
46 Information Section, *MS* XVII, no. 12, December 1937, 297–8.
47 Ibid., 298.
48 See Mazower, *No Enchanted Palace*, for a discussion of Smuts' internationalism.
49 Information Section, *MS*XVII, no. 12, December 1937, 298.
50 Ibid., 300.
51 Information Section, *League of Nations Questions No. 9: The Refugees* (Geneva: Information Section, 1938), 8.
52 Information Section, *The Refugees*, 35.
53 Ibid., 39.
54 Ibid., 52.
55 E.g. Secretariat of the League of Nations, *Ten Years*, 410.
56 Tollardo, *Fascist Italy and the League of Nations 1922-35* (London: Palgrave Macmillan, 2016), 25.
57 Information Section, *MS* XIV, no. 1, January 1934, 2.
58 Information Section, *MS* XIV, no. 5, May 1934, 100.
59 Information Section, *MS* XIV, no. 9, September 1934, 230; Secretariat of the League of Nations, *Staff Regulations – Edition Issued in March 1933 and Incorporating Amendments in the Force on the Date of Issue* (Geneva, 1933), LONA, Article 2, Article 3.
60 Information Section, *MS* XIV, no. 9, September 1934, 199.
61 Information Section, *MS* XIV, no. 12, December 1934, 298.
62 Daniel Gorman, *The Emergence of International Society in the 1920s* (Cambridge: Cambridge University Press, 2012); Sluga, 'Women, Feminisms and Twentieth-Century Internationalisms', 61–84; Laqua, ed. *Internationalism Reconfigured*.
63 Brother of later UN Secretary General Dag Hammarskjöld.
64 Information Section, *MS* XVIII, no. 5, May 1937, 86; Information Section, *MS* XVIII, no. 7, July 1937, 146; Information Section, *MS* XVIII, no. 9, September 1937, 194.
65 Information Section, *MS* XVIII, no. 5, May 1937, 88.
66 Marco Ninno, 'A Modernist in Geneva: Le Corbusier and the Competition for the Palais des Nations', in *The League of Nations: Perspectives*, 246–55.
67 Information Section, *MS* XIV, no. 5, May 1934, 127.
68 Ibid.
69 Ibid.
70 Ibid., 128.
71 Allen, 'International Exhibitionism', 111.

72 Holste, 'Tourists at the League', 328.
73 Ibid., 332.
74 League of Nations, Information Section, *The League of Nations – A Vital Necessity in the Modern World, Addresses Delivered on the Occasion of the 100th Session of the Council* (Geneva, 1938), 2.
75 League of Nations, Information Section, *Petit Manuel de la Société des Nations,* 2nd edn (Genève: Section d'Information, 1934), 138.
76 League of Nations, Information Section, *Petit Manuel,* 1934, 175. Sweetser sent a sample of these very stamps to US president Franklin Roosevelt who replied with a thank-you-note in the summer of 1933: Letter from Franklin Delano Roosevelt to Sweetser, 3 July 1933, Box 34, ASP.
77 League of Nations, Information Section, *Petit Manuel,* 1934, opening page.
78 League of Nations, Information Section, *League of Nations – Its Secretariat and Buildings* (Geneva: Information Section of the League of Nations Secretariat, 1936), 5.
79 Sluga and Clavin, 'Rethinking', 7–9.
80 Sluga, *Internationalism in the Age of Nationalism.*
81 Steiner, *The Triumph of the Dark – European International History 1933-1939* (Oxford: Oxford University Press, 2013), 39.
82 World Economic Forum, Global Risk Report 2023. https://www.weforum.org/reports/global-risks-report-2023/digest (17 January 2023).

Chapter 6

1 Jane Mumby, 'Last Years of the Secretariat', League of Nations Secretariat – Research Guides at United Nations Library & Archives Geneva. https://libraryresources.unog.ch/LONSecretariat/secondwar (21 February 2023).
2 Mazower, *Governing the World,* 194.
3 With the help of his old collaborator Raymond Fosdick of the Rockefeller Foundation. Mazower, *Governing the World,* 192.
4 Gram-Skjoldager, Ikonomou and Torsten Kahlert have demonstrated the war migrations of Scandinavian League officials: A majority returned to national service, which in many cases meant exiled governmental agencies in London, and subsequently entered the UN system. Karen Gram-Skjoldager, Haakon A. Ikonomou and Torsten Kahlert, 'Scandinavians and the League of Nations Secretariat, 1919-1946', *Scandinavian Journal of History* 44, no. 4 (2019): 454–83.
5 Gram-Skjoldager, 'Drummond, Sir James Eric', in *IO BIO, Biographical Dictionary of Secretaries-General of International Organizations,* ed. Bob Reinalda, Kent J. Kille and Jaci Eisenberg. www.ru.nl/fm/iobio (23 January 2019).

6 'Témoignage de Pierre Comert', 29 June/6 July 1951, Archives Nationales de France, 72AJ/1909, 2.
7 Kuehl, *Biographical Dictionary*, 167; Sylvain Cornil, 'La Presse de la France Libre, 2013', *Fondation de la France Libre*. http://www.france-libre.net/presse-france-libre/#4 (6 November 2018).
8 Stewart, 'The French Press', 7–8.
9 Sweetser Clifford, *One Shining Hour*, 122.
10 Kuehl, *Biographical Dictionary*, 167.
11 Benjamin Auberer, 'Digesting the League of Nations Secretariat: Planning the International Secretariat of the Future 1941-1944', *New Global Studies* 10, no. 3 (2016): 393–426, 407.
12 Stewart, 'The French Press'; Julia Eichenberg, 'Crossroads in London on the Road to Nuremberg: The London International Assembly, Exile Governments and War Crimes', *Journal of the History of International Law* 24, no. 3 (2022): 334–53; Martin Conway and José Gotovitch, *Europe in Exile: European Exile Communities in Britain 1940-1945* (Oxford: Berghahn Books, 2001); Pavol Jakubec, 'Together and Alone in Allied London: Czechoslovak, Norwegian and Polish Governments-in-Exile, 1940–1945', *The International History Review* 42, no. 3 (2019): 477.
13 Auberer, 'Digesting the League', 409.
14 Letter from Philip Jessup to Sweetser 17 August 1942, *CEIP Records*, Box 210-211, Rare Books and Manuscript Library, Columbia University Libraries (RBM-CUL, henceforth).
15 Letter from Sweetser to Comert, 30 August 1947, Box 28, ASP, 1.
16 Letter from Comert to Sweetser, 11 August 1942, 2.
17 Giles Scott-Smith, 'Competing Internationalisms: The United States, Britain, and the Formation of the United Nations Information Organization during World War II', *International Journal for History, Culture and Modernity* 6, no. 1 (2019): 8.
18 Library of Congress, *Arthur Sweetser Papers – A Finding Aid to the Collection in the Library of Congress*. http://hdl.loc.gov/loc.mss/eadmss.ms013059 (26 May 2023).
19 Herren and Löhr, 'Being International in Times of War', 544.
20 Letter from Sweetser to Comert, 30 August 1947, 1.
21 Letter from Sweetser to Irvin Salomon, 11 November 1957, Box 34, ASP.
22 Auberer, 'Digesting the League', 412. Ranshofen-Wertheimer acknowledged the existence of, and his debt to, the London Group in his book. Ranshofen-Wertheimer, *The International Secretariat*, xiii.
23 E.g. Gram-Skjoldager and Ikonomou, 'The Construction', 12–14.
24 Lord Perth et al., *The International Secretariat of the Future*, 61–4.
25 Ibid., 36.
26 Ibid., 63.
27 Ibid., 61–2.
28 Ibid., 64.

29 Unknown author, 'List of Persons Invited to the Meeting at Washington 30 January 1943', *CEIP Records,* Box 210–11, Columbia University Library – Rare Books and Manuscript Collection; Letter from George Finch, to Sweetser, 6 April 1943, Box 30, ASP; CEIP, *Proceedings of the Exploratory Conference of the Experience of the League of Nations Secretariat, August 30th, 1942,* Box 244, Columbia RBM, 1; CEIP, *Proceedings of the Conference on Experience in International Administration, January 30th, 1943,* LONA.
30 CEIP, *Proceedings of the Exploratory Conference*, 1.
31 Auberer, 'Digesting the League', 412; Correspondence, Percy Corbett and George Finch, Box 210–11, Columbia RBM.
32 CEIP, *Proceedings of the Exploratory Conference*, 18.
33 Ibid., 115.
34 Ibid., 117.
35 Ranshofen-Wertheimer, *The International Secretariat*, 217.
36 Ibid., 118.
37 Ibid., 115.
38 Ibid., 215.
39 CEIP, *Proceedings of the Exploratory Conference*, 115.
40 Letter from Pelt to Sweetser, 10 March 1943.
41 Letter from Sweetser to Pelt, 2 December 1943, 3.
42 Letter from Sweetser to Pelt, 2 December 1943, Box 34, ASP, 2.
43 Ibid., 3.
44 Pelt, 'Outline of an Information Section in a post-war League of Nations Secretariat', attached to: Pelt, letter to Sweetser, 10 March 1943, 5.
45 Mazower, *Governing the World*, 211.
46 E.g. Ibid., 209–11.
47 E.g. Clavin, *Securing,* 306.
48 E.g. Akira Iryie, *Global Community. The Role of International Organizations in the Making of the Contemporary World* (Berkeley: University of California Press, 2002), 47.
49 United Nations Conference on International Organization, San Francisco, 'Interim arrangements concluded by the governments represented at the United Nations Conference on International Organization, 26 June, 1945'. http://research.un.org/ld.php?content_id=8048396 (26 May 2023).
50 Sub-Committee of the Technical Advisory Committee on Information, 'Report to the Secretary-General', 11 February 1946, Box 69, ASP, 1–2.
51 Pelt, 'Memorandum on the Reduction of Staff and the Reorganization of the Information Section', nd, 1939–40, 12.
52 Sub-Committee of Technical Advisory Committee on Information, 'Observations on Branch-Offices', 28 January 1946, 2; LONSEA data base; Kinnear, *Woman of the World,* 153.

53 Vernon Duckworth-Barker, 'Note on Organization of the Public Information Service', nd, Box 69, ASP.
54 Sub-committee of the Technical Advisory Committee on Information, 'Branch Offices' nd, Box 69, ASP.
55 Duckworth-Barker, 'Note on Organization of the Public Information Service', nd, 4.
56 Sub-committee of the Technical Advisory Committee on Information, 'Report to the Secretary-General', 11 February 1946, 2.
57 Formally, the UNDPI was instituted by General Assembly Resolution 13 (I) 'Organization of the Secretariat', the General Assembly approved the recommendations of the TACI, which were attached to the resolution as 'Annex 1'. General Assembly of the United Nations, 'Resolution 13 (I), 1 February 1946', *Resolutions adopted by the General Assembly during its First Session*. https://digitallibrary.un.org/record/228964?ln=en (26 May 2023).
58 Pelt had suggested a joint agency of the leading new agencies of the world to be represented at the seat of the new organization: Lord Perth et al., *The International Secretariat of the Future*, 62.
59 General Assembly of the United Nations, 'Resolution adopted by the General Assembly during the first part of its first session from 10 January to 14 February 1946 – Annex 1: Recommendations by the Technical Advisory Committee on Information concerning the policies, functions and organization of the Department of Public Information', *Advisory Committee on Information*, Box S-0540-0001-05, UN Archives, New York City.
60 Ibid., 1.
61 Ibid., 2.
62 United Nations, Charter of the United Nations, Chapter XVI: Miscellaneous Provisions, Article 102. https://www.un.org/en/about-us/un-charter/chapter-16 (26 May 2023).
63 General Assembly of the United Nations, 'Resolution Adopted by the General Assembly', 1.
64 Sub-committee of the Technical Advisory Committee on Information, 'Report to the Secretary-General', 11 February 1946, 4.
65 Ibid., 5.
66 General Assembly of the United Nations, 'Resolution Adopted by the General Assembly', 2.
67 Information Section, 'Report of the Information Section to the 8th Assembly', 1927, 16.
68 Sub-Committee of the Technical Advisory Committee on Information, 'Report to the Secretary-General', 11 February 1946, 23–4.
69 Press-cutting attached to: letter from Sweetser to Irvin Salomon, 11 November 1957.

70 General Assembly of the United Nations, 'Resolution Adopted by the General Assembly', 1.
71 Cory, 'Forging a Public Information Policy', 230; Brendebach, Herzer and Tworek, 'Introduction', in *International Organizations and the Media,* 12; Information Section, Budget 1939, nd, 1938, 33022, R5189, LONA.
72 Tor Gjesdal. Norsk Biografisk Leksikon. https://nbl.snl.no/Tor_Gjesdal (snl.no) (7 February 2023).
73 United Nations Department of Public Information, *Yearbook of the United Nations 1946-47* (New York: United Nations, 1947), 627, 657.
74 Ibid., 628.
75 Ibid., 629.
76 Sweetser, letter to Pelt, 2 December 1943, 3.
77 Committee of Thirteen, *COM.13/1-15*: 'Present Organization of the Secretariat: Information Section', 1930, 7.
78 Cory, 'Forging a Public Information Policy', 233.
79 Ibid.
80 E.g. Jonas Brendebach, 'Towards a New International Communication Order?' in *International Organizations and the Media in the Nineteenth Century and Twentieth Centuries. Exorbitant Expectations*, ed. Jonas Brendebach, Martin Herzer and Heidi Tworek (New York: Routledge, 2018), 160.
81 Cory, 'Forging a Public Information Policy', 235.
82 The shift can be argued to have reflected the UN's reinstatement of a 'conventionally defined diplomatic system' following the experimental interwar period and at the expense of network-driven transnational semi-diplomacy that Herren and Löhr saw as the trademark of Sweetser; Herren and Löhr, 'Being International in Times of War', 546–7.

Conclusion

1 Secretariat of the League of Nations, *Ten Years*, 399.
2 Imlay, *Clarence Streit*, 27–8; Eric Hobsbawm first baptized the time that began with the interwar period retrospectively 'the age of extremes'. Hobsbawm, *The Age of Extremes.*
3 Pelt, 'Outline of an Information Section', 10 March 1943, 1.
4 Kott, 'Toward a Social History'.
5 Gram-Skjoldager and Ikonomou, 'The Making of the International Civil Servant, 1920-1960', in *Organizing*, ed. Gram-Skjoldager, Kahlert and Ikonomou, 224–5.
6 Sue Curry Jansen, "The World's Greatest Adventure in Advertising': Walter Lippmann's Critique of Censorship and Propaganda', in *The Oxford Handbook*

of Propaganda Studies, Oxford Handbooks, ed. Jonathan Auerbach, and Russ Castronovo (2013; online edn, Oxford Academic, 3 March 2014). https://doi-org.ep.fjernadgang.kb.dk/10.1093/oxfordhb/9780199764419.013.003 (26 September 2023).
7   Brendebach, Herzer and Tworek, eds, 'Introduction', 1.
8   Daniel Hucker, *Public Opinion and Twentieth-Century Diplomacy. A Global Perspective* (London: Bloomsbury Academic, 2020).
9   Philip Taylor, *The Projection of Britain. British Overseas Publicity and Propaganda 1919-1939* (Cambridge: Cambridge University Press, 1981); Meltz, 'Lorsque le Quai d'Orsay'; Nicholas Cull, 'Roof for a House Divided: How U.S Propaganda Evolved into Public Diplomacy', in *The Oxford Handbook of Propaganda Studies*, ed. Jonathan Auerbach and Russ Castronovo (New York: Oxford University Press, 2013).
10 Akami, 'The Limits', 86.
11 Ibid.
12 Herren and Löhr, 'Gipfeltreffen'; Herren and Löhr, 'Being International in Times of War'.
13 Brian Urquhart, *A Life in Peace and War* (New York: W. W. Norton & Company, 1987), 196–7.

Bibliography

Published material

Abbenhuis, Maartje, *The Hague Conferences and International Politics, 1898–1915*. London: Bloomsbury Academic, 2019.

Akami, Tomoko, 'Beyond the Formula of the Age of Reason: Experts, Social Sciences, and the Phonic Public in International Politics', in *The League of Nations: Perspectives from the Present*, edited by Karen Gram-Skjoldager and Haakon A. Ikonomou, 161. Aarhus: Aarhus University Press, 2019.

Akami, Tomoko, 'The Limits of Peace Propaganda: The Information Section of the League of Nations and its Tokyo Office', in *International Organizations and the Media in the Nineteenth Century and Twentieth Centuries. Exorbitant Expectations*, edited by Jonas Brendebach, Martin Herzer and Heidi Tworek, 70. New York: Routledge, 2018.

Akira, Iryie, *Global Community. The Role of International Organizations in the Making of the Contemporary World*. Berkeley: University of California Press, 2002.

Allen, David, 'International Exhibitionism: The League of Nations at the New York World's Fair, 1939–1940', in *International Organizations and the Media in the Nineteenth Century and Twentieth Centuries. Exorbitant Expectations*, edited by Jonas Brendebach, Martin Herzer and Heidi Tworek, 91. New York: Routledge, 2018.

Auberer, Benjamin, 'Digesting the League of Nations Secretariat: Planning the International Secretariat of the Future 1941–1944', *New Global Studies* 10, no. 3 (2016): 393–426.

Auberer, Benjamin, 'Murder, Intrigue, Sex and Internationalism – Novels about the League of Nations', in *The League of Nations: Perspectives from the Present*, edited by Karen Gram-Skjoldager and Haakon A. Ikonomou, 211. Aarhus: Aarhus University Press, 2019.

Averbeck-Lietz, Stefanie, 'Discovering Open Diplomacy: The League of Nations' Information Section 1920–1932 and its External and Internal Communication', in *Communicating the League of Nations*, edited by Erik Koenen. Geneva: UNOG Library Historical Series, 2024.

Barros, James, *Betrayal from within – Joseph Avenol, Secretary-General of the League of Nations, 1933–1940*. New Haven: Yale University Press, 1969.

Barros, James, *Office Without Power*. Oxford: Clarendon, 1979.

Best, Anthony, Jussi M. Hanhimäki, Joseph A. Maiolo and Kirsten E. Schultze, *International History of the Twentieth Century and Beyond*, 3rd edn. London: Routledge, 2015.

Beyersdorf, Frank, 'Credit or Chaos? The Austrian Stabilisation Programme of 1923 and the League of Nations', in *Internationalism Reconfigured: Transnational Ideas and Movements between the World Wars*, edited by Daniel Laqua, 134. New York: I.B. Tauris, 2011.

Beyersdorf, Frank, 'First Professional International: FIJ (1926–1940)', in *A History of the International Movement of Journalists. Professionalism vs Politics*, edited by Kaarle Nordenstreng, Ulf Jonas Björk, Frank Beyersdorf, Svennik Høyer and Epp Lauk, 80. London: Palgrave, 2016.

Biltoft, Carolyn N., *A Violent Peace: Media, Truth and Power at the League of Nations*. London: University of Chicago Press, 2021.

Brendebach, Jonas, 'Towards a New International Communication Order?' in *International Organizations and the Media in the Nineteenth Century and Twentieth Centuries. Exorbitant Expectations*, edited by Jonas Brendebach, Martin Herzer and Heidi Tworek, 158. New York: Routledge, 2018.

Brendebach, Jonas, Martin Herzer and Heidi Tworek, 'Introduction', in *International Organizations and the Media in the Nineteenth Century and Twentieth Centuries. Exorbitant Expectations*, edited by Jonas Brendebach, Martin Herzer and Heidi Tworek, 1. New York: Routledge, 2018.

Carr, Edward Hallet, *The Twenty Years Crisis 1919–1939*. London: Macmillan & Co Ltd, 1939.

Cecil, Lord Robert, *A Great Experiment – An Autobiography*. London: Jonathan Cape Ltd, 1941.

Clavin, Patricia, 'Introduction: Conceptualising Internationalism between the World Wars', in *Internationalism Reconfigured: Transnational Ideas and Movements between the World Wars*, edited by Daniel Laqua, 1. New York: I.B. Tauris, 2011.

Clavin, Patricia, *Securing the World Economy: The Reinvention of the League of Nations, 1920–1946*. Oxford: Oxford University Press, 2013.

Clavin, Patricia and Glenda Sluga, 'Rethinking the History of Internationalism', in *Internationalisms. A Twentieth Century History*, edited by Patricia Clavin and Glenda Sluga, 3. Cambridge: Cambridge University Press, 2017.

Conway, Martin and José Gotovitch, eds, *Europe in Exile: European Exile Communities in Britain 1940-1945*, Oxford: Berghahn Books, 2001.

Cory, Robert H., 'Forging a Public Information Policy for the United Nations', *International Organization* 7, no. 2 (1953): 229–42.

Cull, Nicholas, 'Roof for a House Divided: How U.S Propaganda Evolved into Public Diplomacy', in *The Oxford Handbook of Propaganda Studies*, Oxford Handbooks, edited by Jonathan Auerbach and Russ Castronovo. 2013; online edn, Oxford Academic, 3 March 2014, https://doi-org.ep.fjernadgang.kb.dk/10.1093/oxfordhb/9780199764419.013.003 (26 September 2023).

Curry Jansen, Sue, '"The World's Greatest Adventure in Advertising": Walter Lippmann's Critique of Censorship and Propaganda', in *The Oxford Handbook of Propaganda Studies*, Oxford Handbooks, edited by Jonathan Auerbach and Russ Castronovo.

2013; online edn, Oxford Academic, 3 March 2014, https://doi-org.ep.fjernadgang.kb.dk/10.1093/oxfordhb/9780199764419.013.003 (26 September 2023).

Cutlip, Scott M., *The Unseen Power: Public Relations. A History*. Hillsdale: Lawrence Erlbaum Associates, 1994.

Davies, Thomas R., 'A Great Experiment of the League of Nations Era, International Nongovernmental Organizations, Global Governance, and Democracy Beyond the State', *Global Governance* 18 (2012): 405–23.

Davies, Thomas R., 'Internationalism in a Divided World: The Experience of the International Federation of League of Nations Societies', *Peace and Change* 37, no. 2 (2012): 227–52.

Delporte, Christian, 'Les journalistes dans l'entre-deux-guerres. Une identité en crise', *Vingtième Siècle, revue d'histoire* 47 (1995): 158–75.

Van Dijk, Pelle, 'Internationalism on the Big Screen: Films on the League of Nations', *Studies in Communication Sciences* 23, no. 1 (2023): 51–66.

Douglas, Paul F. and Karl Bömer, 'The Press as a Factor in Modern International Relations', *The Annals of the American Academy of Political and Social Science* 162 (1932): 241–72.

Drummond, Eric, 'The Secretariat of the League of Nations', *Public Administration* 9, no. 2 (1931): 228–35.

Fosdick, Raymond, *Letters on the League of Nations*. Princeton: Princeton University Press, 1966.

Gellrich, Arne Lorenz, Erik Koenen and Stefanie Averbeck-Lietz, 'The Epistemic Project of Open Diplomacy and the League of Nations: Co-evolution between Diplomacy, PR and Journalism', *Corporate Communications: An International Journal* 24, no. 4 (2019): 607–21.

Georgakakis, Didier, *La République contre la propagande: Aux origins perdues de la communication d'État en France*. Paris: Economica, 2004.

Gorman, Daniel, *The Emergence of International Society in the 1920s*. Cambridge: Cambridge University Press, 2012.

Gram-Skjoldager, Karen, 'Taming the Bureaucrats. The Supervisory Commission and Political Control of the Secretariat', in *The League of Nations: Perspectives from the Present*, edited by Karen Gram-Skjoldager and Haakon A. Ikonomou, 40. Aarhus: Aarhus University Press, 2019.

Gram-Skjoldager, Karen and Haakon A. Ikonomou, 'The Construction of the League of Nations Secretariat. Formative Practices of Autonomy and Legitimacy in International Organizations', *The International History Review* 41, no. 2 (2017): 1–23.

Gram-Skjoldager, Karen, Haakon A. Ikonomou and Torsten Kahlert, 'Scandinavians and the League of Nations Secretariat', *Scandinavian Journal of History* 44, no. 4 (2019): 454–83.

Haan, Francisca de, 'Writing Inter/transnational History: The Case of Women's Movements and Feminisms', in *Internationale Geschichte in Theorie und Praxis / International History in Theory and Practice*, edited by Barbara Haider-

Wilson, William D. Godsey and Wolfgang Mueller, 501–36. Vienna: Verlag der Österreichischen Akademie der Wissenschaften, 2017.

Hamilton, Keith and Richard Langhorne, *The Practice of Diplomacy*. London: Routledge, 1995.

Harrison, Jackie and Stephanie Pukallus, 'The European Community's Public Communication Policy', *Contemporary European History* 24, no. 2 (2015): 223–51.

Herren, Madeleine and Isabella Löhr, 'Being International in Times of War: Arthur Sweetser and the shifting of the League of Nations to the United Nations', *European Review of History* 25, no. 3–4 (2018): 535–52.

Herren, Madeleine and Isabella Löhr, 'Gipfeltreffen im Schatten der Weltpolitik: Arthur Sweetser und die Mediendiplomatie des Völkerbunds', *Zeitschrift für Geschichtswissenschaft* 62, no. 5 (2014): 411–24.

Hobsbawm, Eric, *The Age of Extremes – The Short Twentieth Century, 1914–1991*. London: Michael Joseph, 1994.

Holbraad, Carsten, *Internationalism and Nationalism in European Political Thought*. London: Palgrave Macmillan, 2003.

Holste, Timo, 'Tourists at the League of Nations: Conceptions of Internationalism around the Palais des Nations, 1925–1946', *New Global Studies* 10, no. 3 (2016): 307–44.

Hucker, Daniel, *Public Opinion and Twentieth-Century Diplomacy. A Global Perspective*. London: Bloomsbury Academic, 2020.

Ikonomou, Haakon A., 'The Administrative Anatomy of Failure: The League of Nations Disarmament Section, 1919–1925', *Contemporary European History* 30, no. 3 (2021): 321–34.

Imlay, Talbot, *Clarence Streit and Twentieth-Century American Internationalism*. Cambridge: Cambridge University Press, 2023.

Iryie, Akira, *Global Community. The Role of International Organizations in the Making of the Contemporary World*. Berkeley: University of California Press, 2002.

Jackson, Peter, *Beyond the Balance of Power: France and the Politics of National Security in the Era of the First World War*. Cambridge: Cambridge University Press, 2013.

Jackson, Simon and Alanna O'Malley, eds, *The Institution of International Order. From the League of Nations to the United Nations*. New York: Routledge, 2018.

Jacubec, Pavol, 'Together and Alone in Allied London: Czechoslovak, Norwegian and Polish Governments-in-Exile, 1940–1945', *The International History Review* 42, no. 3 (2019): 465–84.

Kahlert, Torsten, 'Prosopography: Unlocking the Social World of International Organizations', in *Organizing the 20th-Century World International Organizations and the Emergence of International Public Administration, 1920–1960s*, edited by Karen Gram-Skjoldager, Haakon A. Ikonomou and Torsten Kahlert. London: Bloomsbury Academic, 2020.

Kaiser, Wolfram and Johan Schot, *Writing the Rules for Europe – Experts, Cartels, and International Organizations*. New York: Palgrave Macmillan, 2014.

Kinnear, Mary, *Woman of the World: Mary McGeachy and International Cooperation*. Toronto: University of Toronto Press, 2004.

Koenen, Erik, ed., *Communicating the League of Nations*. Geneva: UNOG Library Historical Series, 2024.

Korzi, Michael, 'Lapsed Memory: The Roots of American Public Opinion Research', *Polity* 33, no. 1 (2000): 49–75.

Kott, Sandrine, 'Toward a Social History of International Organizations: The ILO and the Internationalisation of Western Social Expertise (1919–1949)', in *Internationalism, Imperialism and the Formation of the Contemporary World*, edited by Miguel B. Jeronimo and Jose P. Monteiro, 33–77. London: Palgrave.

Kuehl, Warren F., *Biographical Dictionary of Internationalists*. Westport: Greenwood Press, 1983.

Laqua, Daniel, 'Activism in the "Students' League of Nations": International Students Politics and the Confédération Internationale des Étudiants, 1919–1939', *English Historical Review* CXXXII, no. 556 (2017): 605–37.

Laqua, Daniel, 'Democratic Politics and the League of Nations: The Labour and Socialist International as a Protagonist of Interwar Internationalism', *Contemporary European History* 24, no. 2 (2015): 175–92.

League of Nations (Deuxième Assemblée de la Société des Nations), *La Société des Nations – Son activité par l'image*. Genève: Atar, 1921.

League of Nations, Information Section, *League of Nations. Its Secretariat and Buildings*. Geneva, 1936.

League of Nations, Information Section, *The League of Nations – Its Constitution and Organisation*. 2nd edn. Geneva: League of Nations Secretariat, 1926.

League of Nations, Information Section, *The League of Nations – A Pictorial Survey*. Geneva, 1929.

League of Nations, Information Section, *The League of Nations – A Vital Necessity in the Modern World. Addresses Delivered on the Occasion of the 100th Session of the Council*. Geneva, 1938.

League of Nations, Information Section, *The League of Nations and the Press*. International Press Exhibition, Cologne, Geneva, 1928.

League of Nations, Information Section, *The League of Nations from Year to Year, 1926-1927*. Geneva: League of Nations Secretariat, 1927.

League of Nations, Information Section, *League of Nations Questions No. 9: The Refugees*. Geneva, 1938.

League of Nations, Information Section, *Petit Manuel de la Société des Nations*. Genève, 1933.

League of Nations, Information Section, *Petit Manuel de la Société des Nations*. Genève, 1934.

League of Nations, Secretariat of the League of Nations, *Ten Years of World-Co-operation*. London and Aylesbury: Hazel, Watson & Viney Ltd, 1930.

Lippmann, Walter, *Public Opinion*. New York: Harcourt, Brace and Company, 1922.

Madariaga, Salvador de, *Morning Without Noon*. Farnborough: Saxon House, 1973.

Manela, Erez, *The Wilsonian Moment – Self-determination and the Historical Origins of Anticolonial Nationalism*. Oxford: Oxford University Press, 2009.

Manigand, Christine, *Les Francais au Service de la Société des Nations*. Bern: Peter Lang, 2003.

Mazower, Mark, *Governing the World – The History of an Idea 1815 to the Present*. New York: Penguin Books, 2012.

Mazower, Mark, *No Enchanted Palace – The End of Empire and the Ideological Origins of the United Nations*. Princeton: Princeton University Press, 2009.

McCarthy, Helen, *The British People and the League of Nations – Democracy, Citizenship and Internationalism, c. 1918–1948*. Manchester: Manchester University Press, 2011.

McCarthy, Helen, 'Parties, Voluntary Associations, Democratic Politics in Interwar Britain', *The Historical Journal* 50, no. 4 (2007): 891–912.

Meller, Paul Jonathan, 'The Development of Modern Propaganda in Britain, 1854–1902'. PhD thesis, Durham University, 2010.

Meltz, Renaud, 'Lorsque le Quai d'Orsay dictait des articles: La fabrication de l'opinion publique dans l'entre-deux-guerres', *Relations Internationales* 2, no. 154 (2013): 33–50.

Millen-Penn, Kenneth, 'Democratic Control, Public Opinion, and League Diplomacy', *World Affairs* 157, no. 4 (1995): 207–18.

Millen-Penn, Kenneth, 'From Liberal to Socialist Internationalism: Konni Zilliacus and the League of Nations, 1894–1939'. PhD thesis, State University of New York, Department of History, 1993.

Moraes, Marco, 'Competing Internationalisms at the League of Nations Secretariat, 1933–1940', in *The League of Nations: Perspectives from the Present*, edited by Karen Gram-Skjoldager and Haakon A. Ikonomou, 51. Aarhus: Aarhus University Press, 2019.

Mulder, Nicholas, *The Economic Weapon – The Rise of Sanctions as a Tool of Modern War*. New Haven: Yale University Press, 2022.

Ninno, Marco, 'A Modernist in Geneva: Le Corbusier and the Competition for the Palais des Nations', in *The League of Nations: Perspectives from the Present*, edited by Karen Gram-Skjoldager and Haakon A. Ikonomou, 246. Aarhus: Aarhus University Press, 2019.

Nordenstreng, Kaarle and Tarja Seppä, '"Collaboration of the Press in the Organisation of Peace" – The League of Nations as a Catalyst for Important Intellectual Trends', in *Communicating the League of Nations*, edited by Erik Koenen. Geneva: UNOG Library Historical Series, forthcoming.

Northedge, Frederick S., *The League of Nations: Its Life and Times, 1920–1946*. Leicester: Leicester University Press, 1986.

Osterhammel, Jürgen, 'Technical Co-operation between the League of Nations and China', *Modern Asian Studies* 13, no. 4 (1979): 661–80.

Pedersen, Susan, 'Back to the League of Nations', *The American Historical Review* 112, no. 4 (2007): 1091–117.

Pedersen, Susan, *The Guardians: The League of Nations and the Crisis of Empire*. Oxford: Oxford University Press, 2015.

Perth, Lord (Eric Drummond) et al., *The International Secretariat of the Future – Lessons by a Group of former Officials of the League of Nations*. London: Royal Institute of International Affairs/Oxford University Press, 1944.

Pickard, Bertram, 'The Greater League of Nations – A Brief Survey of the Nature and Development of Unofficial International Organizations', *Contemporary Review* 850, no. 150 (1936): 460–5.

Piquet, Myriam, 'Gender Distribution in the League of Nations', in *The League of Nations: Perspectives from the Present*, edited by Karen Gram-Skjoldager and Haakon A. Ikonomou, 62. Aarhus: Aarhus University Press, 2019.

Potter, Pitman B., 'League Publicity: Cause or Effect of League Failure?', *The Public Opinion Quarterly* 2, no. 10 (1938): 399–412.

Potter, Pitman B., 'Note on the Distinction between Political and Technical Questions', *Political Science Quarterly* 50, no. 2 (1935): 264–71.

Ranshofen-Wertheimer, Egon, *The International Secretariat – A Great Experiment in International Administration*. Washington, DC: Carnegie Endowment for International Peace, 1945.

Reinisch, Jessica and David Brydan, eds, *Internationalists in European History*. London: Bloomsbury Academic, 2021.

Renoliet, Jean-Jacques, 'La genèse de l'institut international de Coopération intellectuelle', *Relations Internationales* 72 (1992): 387–98.

Renoliet, Jean-Jacques, *L'UNESCO oubliée. La Société des Nations et la coopération intellectuelle, 1919–1946*. Paris: Sorbonne, 1999.

Richard, Anne-Isabelle, 'Between Publicity and Discretion: The International Federation of League of Nations Societies', in *Organizing the 20th-Century World International Organizations and the Emergence of International Public Administration, 1920–1960s*, edited by Karen Gram-Skjoldager, Haakon A. Ikonomou and Torsten Kahlert. London: Bloomsbury Academic, 2020.

Richard, Anne-Isabelle, 'Competition and complementarity: Civil society networks and the question of decentralizing the League of Nations', *Journal of Global History* 7, no. 2 (2012): 233–56.

Risso, Linda, '"Enlightening Public Opinion": A Study of NATO's Information Policies between 1949 and 1959 based on Recently Declassified Documents', *Cold War History* 7, no. 1 (2007): 45–74.

Risso, Linda, *Propaganda and Intelligence in the Cold War. The NATO Information Service*. New York: Routledge, 2014.

Ruyssen, Théodore, 'La propagande pour la Société des Nations', in *Les Origines et l'œuvre de la Société des Nations vol II*, edited by Peter Munch, 237–8. Copenhague: Rask-Ørstedfonden/Nordisk Forlag, 1924.

Scott-Smith, Giles, 'Competing Internationalisms: The United States, Britain, and the Formation of the United Nations Information Organization during World War II', *International Journal for History, Culture and Modernity* 6, no. 1 (2019).

Seidenfaden, Emil Eiby, 'The League of Nations' Collaboration with an International Public 1919–1939', *Contemporary European History* 31 (2022): 268–380.

Seidenfaden, Emil Eiby, 'Legitimizing International Bureaucracy – Press and Information Work from the League of Nations to the UN', in *Organizing the 20th-Century World International Organizations and the Emergence of International Public Administration, 1920–1960s*, edited by Karen Gram-Skjoldager, Haakon A. Ikonomou and Torsten Kahlert, 129. London: Bloomsbury, 2020.

Seidenfaden, Emil Eiby, Helle Strandgaard Jensen and Nikolai Schulz, 'Film-splaining the League of Nations', in *The League of Nations: Perspectives from the Present*, edited by Karen Gram-Skjoldager and Haakon A. Ikonomou, 201. Aarhus: Aarhus University Press, 2019.

Seul, Stephanie, '"Trägerin des europäischen Gemeinschaftsgedankens – lebendige Magna Charta des Friedens": Die politische Dimension der PRESSA Köln 1928 und ihr Widerhall in der zeitgenössischen deutschen und internationalen Presse', in *80 Jahre PRESSA, Internationale Presse-Ausstellung Köln 1928, und der jüdische Beitrag zum modernen Journalismus*, edited by Susanne Marten-Finnis and Michael Nagel, vol. 1, 57. Bremen: edition lumière, 2012.

Skinner, Quentin, *Visions of Politics Vol 1: Regarding Method*. Cambridge: Cambridge University Press, 2002.

Slobodian, Quinn, *Globalists: The End of Empire and the Birth of Neoliberalism*. Cambridge, MA: Harvard University Press, 2018.

Sluga, Glenda, *Internationalism in the Age of Nationalism*. Philadelphia: University of Pennsylvania Press, 2013.

Sluga, Glenda, 'Women, Feminisms and Twentieth Century Internationalisms', in *Internationalisms – A Twentieth Century History*, edited by Patricia Clavin and Glenda Sluga, 61–85. Cambridge: Cambridge University Press, 2017.

Steiner, Zara, *The Lights that Failed. European International History 1919–1933*. Oxford: Oxford University Press, 2007.

Steiner, Zara, *The Triumph of the Dark – European International History 1933–1939*. Oxford: Oxford University Press, 2013.

Stewart, Iain, 'The French Press in Wartime London 1940–4: From the Politics of Exile to Inter-Allied Relations', *Journal of Contemporary History* 58, no. 1 (2022): 1–21.

Sweetser, Arthur, *The League of Nations at Work*. New York: The Macmillan Company, 1920.

Sweetser, Arthur, *Roadside Glimpses of the Great War*. New York: The Macmillan Company, 1916.

Sweetser, Susan Clifford, *One Shining Hour*. Private Publication, 1990.

Taylor, Philip M., *British Propaganda in the Twentieth Century – Selling Democracy*. Edinburgh: Edinburgh University Press, 1999.

Taylor, Philip M., *The Projection of Britain. British Overseas Publicity and Propaganda 1919–1939*. Cambridge: Cambridge University Press, 1981.

Taylor, Philip M., 'Public Diplomacy and Strategic Communications', in *Routledge Handbook of Public Diplomacy*, edited by Nancy Snow and Philip M. Taylor, 12–16. New York: Routledge, 2009.

Tollardo, Elisabetta, *Fascist Italy and the League of Nations 1922–35*. London: Palgrave Macmillan, 2016.

Tollardo, Elisabetta, 'International Experts or Fascist Envoys? Alberto Theodoli and Pietro Stoppani at the League of Nations', *New Global Studies* 10, no. 3 (2016): 283–306.

Tournés, Ludovic, 'La Philanthropie Americaine, La Société des Nations et la Coproduction d'un Ordre International (1919–1946)', *Relations Internationales* 3, no. 151 (2012): 25–36.

Tournés, Ludovic, *Philanthropic foundations at the League of Nations: An Americanized League?* London: Routledge, 2022.

Tworek, Heidi, 'The Creation of European News: News Agency Cooperation in Interwar Europe', *Journalism Studies* 14, no. 5 (2013): 730–42.

Tworek, Heidi, 'Peace through Truth – The Press and Moral Disarmament through the League of Nations', *Medien & Zeit* 25, no. 4 (2010): 16–28.

Tyler, Hannah, 'Breaking Even for the Future: The Financial History of the League of Nations 1919–1933', *Monde(s)* 1, no. 19 (2012): 119–38.

United Nations Department of Public Information, *Yearbook of the United Nations 1946–47*. New York: United Nations, 1947.

Urquhart, Brian, *A Life in Peace and War*. New York: W. W Norton & Company, 1987.

Walters, Frank P., *A History of the League of Nations*. London: The Royal Institute of International Affairs, 1954.

Werner-Müller, Jan, *Contesting Democracy – Political Ideas in Twentieth Century Europe*. New Haven: Yale University Press, 2013.

Werner-Müller, Jan, 'European Intellectual History as Contemporary History', *Journal of Contemporary History* 46, no. 3 (2011): 574–90.

Wertheim, Stephen, 'Reading the International Mind: International Public Opinion in Early Twentieth Century Anglo-American Thought', in *The Decisionist Imagination – Sovereignty, Social Science and Democracy in the 20th Century*, edited by Daniel Bessner and Nicolas Guilhot. New York: Berghan Books, 2018.

Wilke, Jürgen, 'Cinematography as a Medium of Communication', in *Communicating the League of Nations*, edited by Erik Koenen. Geneva: UNOG Library Historical Series, forthcoming.

Online resources

Bosmans, J., 'Adrianus Pelt', *Biographical Dictionary of the Netherlands 1880–2000*, http://resources.huygens.knaw.nl/bwn1880-2000/ (06 November 2017).

Cornil, Sylvain, 'La Presse de la France Libre, 2013', *Fondation de la France Libre*, http://www.france-libre.net/presse-france-libre/#4 (06 November 2018).

Encyclopedia Britannica, 'Collective Security', *Encyclopedia Britannica*, 2018, https://www.britannica.com/topic/collective-security (10 December 2018).

Encyclopedia Britannica/Bruce Lannes-Smith, 'Propaganda', *Encyclopedia Britannica*, 2019, https://www.britannica.com/topic/propaganda (07 June 2017).

Gram-Skjoldager, Karen, 'Drummond, Sir James Eric', in *IO BIO, Biographical Dictionary of Secretaries-General of International Organizations*, edited by Bob Reinalda, Kent J. Kille and Jaci Eisenberg, www.ru.nl/fm/iobio (23 January 2019).

Hirsti, Reidar, 'Tor Gjesdal – Norsk biografisk leksikon', https://nbl.snl.no/Tor_Gjesdal (snl.no) (07 February 2023).

Ikonomou, Haakon, Yuan Chen, Obaida Hanteer and Jonas Tilsted, *Visualizing the League of Nations Secretariat – A Digital Research Tool*. Copenhagen: University of Copenhagen, 2023, https://visualeague-researchtool.com/ (2023 May 2022).

Laqua, Daniel, 'Internationalism', in European History Online (EGO), published by the Leibniz Institute of European History (IEG), Mainz, 04 May 2021, http://www.ieg-ego.eu/laquad-2021-en URN: urn:nbn:de:0159-2021032908 (29 March 20223).

Mumby, Jane, 'Last Years of the Secretariat', League of Nations Secretariat – Research Guides at United Nations Library & Archives Geneva, https://libraryresources.unog.ch/LONSecretariat/secondwar (21 February 2023).

Nationalism Working Group, European University Institute, 'Who We Are: Pelle van Dijk', *The Notebook of the Nationalism Working Group at the European University Institute*, https://nwg.hypotheses.org/credits/members/pelle-van-dijk (16 January 2019).

Seidenfaden, Emil, 'Information Section', United Nations Library & Archives at Geneva Research Guide: League of Nations Secretariat, https://libraryresources.unog.ch/LONSecretariat/information (16 March 2023).

UNESCO Archives database (AtOM), entry: 'International Educational Cinematographic Institute (IECI)', *UNESCO Archives Catalogue*, https://atom.archives.unesco.org/ (05 December 2018).

United Nations Archives at Geneva (UNOG), League of Nations Secretariat 1919–1946 (fond): Administration History, *United Nations Archives*, Catalogue, http://biblio-archive.unog.ch/detail.aspx?id=245 (04 November 2017).

White House, 'Remarks by President Trump to the 74th Session of the United Nations General Assembly', https://trumpwhitehouse.archives.gov/briefings-statements/remarks-president-trump-74th-session-united-nations-general-assembly/ (27 March 2023).

World Economic Forum, Global Risk Report 2023, https://www.weforum.org/reports/global-risks-report-2023/digest) (17 January 2023).

Media

Fassihi, Farnaz, 'U.N to Meet amid Growing Divisions and Demands from Global South', *The New York Times*, 18 September 2023.

Krastev, Ivan, 'The Rise and Fall of European Meritocracy', *The New York Times*, 17 January 2017.

Index

2023 UN General Assembly   3

Aghnides, Thanassis   138
Akami, Tomoko   5, 40, 161, 167 n.16
Allen, David   108, 127
Allied Shipping Control   82
Amador, M.R.   125
American isolationism   9
Ames, Herbert   47
Anderson, Benedict   130
Article 18 of the League's Covenant   147
Association Française pour la Société des Nations   54
Auberer, Benjamin   135
Avenol, Joseph   12, 14, 35, 82, 89, 92, 96, 97, 100, 101, 105, 106, 114, 116, 119, 124, 135, 158
Averbeck-Lietz, Stefanie   5, 24, 32, 42, 94, 166 n.14, 168 n.17, 172 n.24, 173 n.56, 183 n.23
Azcarate, Pablo de   97

Barros, James   35, 92
Beneš, Edvard   118
Bentham, Jeremy   10
Beyersdorf, Frank   49
Blondeel, Frédéric   102, 144
Brendebach, Jonas   159
Bretton Woods conference   137, 143
Briand, Aristide   127, 130
British-American partnership   133
British-French negotiations   143
British peace movement   54
Bruccoleri, Guiseppe   113
Bruce Report   143
Burnham, Lord   50

Carnegie Endowment for International Peace (CEIP)   57, 111, 112, 136, 139–41
Carr, E.H.   10

Cecil, Robert   9, 143
Chamberlain, Austen   127
Clavin, Patricia   11, 71, 81, 92
Colban, Erik   46, 138
collective security   3
Comert, Janet   32
Comert, Pierre   13, 19, 21–4, 26, 28–38, 41–3, 45–9, 51, 53–5, 57, 58, 60, 62, 63, 68, 69, 74, 89, 92, 94, 95, 99, 105, 113, 134–7, 148, 152, 157, 158, 178 n.91
commemorations   5, 124–7, 131
commission's four 'principles'   98
Committee for the Study of the Problem of Raw Materials   119
Committee of Thirteen   91, 125, 150
communications-specialists   139
communications technologies   16, 138, 152
'concert for peace'   2
Concert of Europe   2, 10
cooperative publicity   51–9, 97, 141, 148, 159
Corbett, Percy   140
Cory, Robert   151
Crowdy, Dame Rachel   117
Cummings, Henry   145

Davies, Thomas R.   51, 54
democratic legitimacy   19, 160, 163
Dijk, Pelle van   112
Disarmament Conference   9, 48, 90, 102, 103, 118, 119, 125
'division of labor' strategy   53
Drummond, Eric   20, 26–31, 34–7, 46, 49, 55, 60, 68, 71, 91, 92, 105, 126, 134, 135, 138, 172 n.37, 172 n.40, 172 n.43, 175 n.26, 175 n.28, 177 n.64, 177 n.71, 178 n.76, 188 n.5
Duckworth-Barker, Vernon   145
Dutch exile community   134

The Economic and Social Council of the
UN (ECOSOC)   146
*The Economic Interdependence of
States*   115
Eden, Anthony   116, 123, 124, 127, 130
'Edith-trilogy' (Moorhouse)   57
emotional public   156
Encyclopedia Britannica   169 n.41
*Essential Facts of the League of
Nations*   129
European crisis   90, 104, 123
European dictatorships   107
European economic cooperation   114
European imperialism   2
European politics   70
'The European Situation'   119

Finch, George A.   140
First World War   154
Fosdick, Raymond   3, 4, 21, 30, 36, 46,
53, 60, 61, 159, 170 n.2
foundational tensions of League   76
Free French movement   135
French exile community   135
French system of secretariat
correspondence   101

Gaumont-British Film Corporation   112
Gellrich, Arne Lorenz   5, 42, 166 n.14
Geneva press corps   24, 42, 44, 95, 102,
155
Gerig, Benjamin   24
Gjesdal, Tor   149
global economic crisis   16
Goebbels, Joseph   12
Gorman, Daniel   127
Gram-Skjoldager, Karen   27, 40, 59,
188 n.4, 188 n.5, 192 n.5
Great Depression   90
Great Powers   9, 30, 35, 39, 40, 45–7, 81,
85, 89, 94, 102, 114, 126, 149, 154,
159
Greek-Bulgarian dispute   84

Hammarskjöld, Åke   127
Hankey, Maurice   46
Hansen, Hans   179 n.107
Henderson, Arthur   125, 126
Herren, Madeleine   62, 137, 162

Herzer, Martin   159
High Commission for Refugees coming
from Germany   123
Hitler, Adolf   90, 100, 106, 118, 120, 122
Holbraad, Carsten   11
Holste, Timo   107, 128
Hucker, Daniel   160
Hull, Cordell   62
humanitarianism   123
human trafficking   117
Hymans, Paul   48

Ikonomou, H.A.   9, 27, 40, 59, 167 n.16,
188 n.4, 192 n.5
illocutionary power   169 n.36
Imlay, Talbot   23
Information Section, 1920–32, *see also
individual entries*
communiqués   44, 46
cooperative publicity   51–9
explanatory articles   44
group photo of   40, 41
management of press   48–51
moral disarmament   48–51
open diplomacy   58
press releases   44
public opinion   40, 44, 47, 50, 55, 58, 59
review of the press   42
secrecy   45–7
transparency   45–7
working with press   41–5
would-be diplomats   59–62
Information Section 1919–21, *see also
individual entries*
annual spending   26
branch offices   22
centrality of   24–6
citizenship of   27
epistemic project   24
First Division   27
foreign correspondents/foreign affairs
journalists   23
internationalism   31–5
international public opinion   28
levels of control   26
members of section   22–3
multinationalism   28
nationality   27
politics of nationality   26–31

propaganda 35–7
quality of staff 23
salary budget 24–6
staff appointments 24, 25
trustworthy information 21
Information Section 1933–40, *see also individual entries*
 Committee of Thirteen 91
 cooperative publicity 97
 development of size 95, 96
 eternal growth 93
 functions of 98, 99
 hierarchical work procedures 101
 instability of international situation 89
 line of demarcation 98
 lines of communication 104
 Minority Report 91, 92
 political liaison 98, 101
 Press Review 101
 propaganda 98
 publicity and information 103
 public opinion 91, 93–5
 reorganization scheme 92
 revisionist powers 91
 sacking of officials 93
 salaries and allowances of Secretariat 95, 96
 Standing Instruction 101
 status-quo powers 91
 technological revolution 95
 temporary collaborators 105
 war reparations schemes 90
 weakening of League's legitimacy 90
Intellectual Cooperation 48, 52, 82, 98–100, 111, 114, 131, 143, 150
Inter-Allied Information Committee (IAIC) 136
intergovernmental organizations (IGOs) 16, 177 n.58
International Bureaux Office 103
International Committee on Intellectual Cooperation 111
International Conference of Press Experts, 1927 42, 50, 62
international cooperation 16, 33, 40, 76, 82, 85, 102, 150
International Educational Cinematographic Institute (IECI) 113

International Federation for League of Nations Societies (IFLNS) 54–6, 104, 105, 108
International Institute for Intellectual Cooperation (IICI) 52
International Labor Conference 30
International Labour Organization 134
International Monetary Fund 143
International Non-Governmental Organizations (INGOs) 51, 177 n.58
international public opinion 26, 28, 42, 53, 54, 56, 77, 78
The International Secretariat (Ranshofen-Wertheimer) 137
international stability 2
International Union for Radio Broadcasting 57
Italy's invasion of Ethiopia 106

Jackson, Simon 166 n.13
Jansen, Sue Curry 192 n.6
Jessup, Philip 140

Kahlert, Torsten 24
Kaiser, Wolfram 82
Koenen, Erik 5, 42, 166 n.14
Kott, Sandrine 11, 158, 169 n.38
Krastev, Ivan 4, 163, 165 n.10
Kuehl, Warren 135

Labour and Socialist International (LSI) 57
Lange, Christian 55
Laqua, Daniel 127
leadership 14, 28, 38, 39, 64, 104, 145, 156, 171 n.18
The League at Work 112, 116, 123
The League from Year to Year 78, 80
League of Nations, *see also individual entries*
 Article 18 9
 challenges 7
 information policies 40
 and internationalism 11–12
 lines of communication 1
 Permanent Court of International Justice 2
 planning phase 21
 propaganda 6, 7, 12–13, 20

publicity work   21
public opinion   6, 8–11, 19, 27, 40
public relations   4
secretarial units   20
secretary general of   3
The League of Nations and the Press   75
'The League of Nations at Work,' 1920   75
The League of Nations – A Vital Necessity in the Modern World   129
The League of Nations: Its Constitution and Organization   80
League of Nations News Bureau   60
League of Nations Questions   113, 114, 122
The Economic Interdependence of States   115
League public information 1933–40
   audiovisual material   111
   commemorations   124–7, 131
   communiqué   115, 119
   crisis rhetoric   117–24
   film production   111
   homemade 'cinematographic films'   111
   intergovernmental framework   117
   international crisis   112
   The League at Work   112, 116
   League of Nations Questions   113, 114, 122
   League's line of defence   112
   limitation of dangerous narcotics   115
   Luce Films   111
   Monthly Summary   115, 118–20, 125–7
   pro-League film material   111–12
   public health and intellectual cooperation   114
   Radio Nations (see Radio Nations)
   Realist Film Unit   111
   regular information pamphlets   114
   retreat to aesthetics   112
   Summary of December   119, 120
   Summary of January   125
   technical cooperation programme   115
League public information material, 1919–32
   action and progress   69–73
   bureaucratic discourse   68
   communiqués   69, 70
   continuous flow of news   72

   factual information   68
   'flow of actual news'   69
   indirect legitimization   80–3
   La Société des Nations – son activité par l'image   71, 74
   Monthly Summary   67–9, 71, 78, 80
   moral force of public opinion   73–9
   officialdom   65
   publications   65–6
   target audiences   66–7
League's exhibition pavilion   107
League's 'mausoleum'   102
League's 'old' Secretariat   129
League's 'reinvention'   64, 82
League's Sales Department   65
legitimization by proxy   77
Lester, Seán   143
liaison activities   39, 65, 95, 100, 101, 103, 108, 146
Liaison Committee   100
liberal democracy   123
liberal internationalism   11–12, 90, 100, 108, 159
liberal internationalist ideology   153
Lie, Trygve   137, 145
Lippmann, Walter   3, 4, 10, 75, 156, 159
Locarno agreements   77, 85
Locarno equilibrium   81
Löhr, Isabella   62, 137, 162
London Group   134, 135, 137, 139, 141
'London of exiles'   135
London Report   135, 137, 142, 146
Lowell, Lawrence   10
loyalty   125
Luce Films   111

Madariaga, Salvador de   24
Madrid conference   50
Mair, George H.   29, 30, 32, 37, 54, 60, 63, 89, 161
Manchester Guardian   94
Manchuria Crisis   90, 112
mandates system   116, 120
Mantoux, Paul   41
mass democracy   4
Mazower, Mark   134, 143
McCarthy, Helen   54
McDonald, James   123
McGeachy, Mary   57, 107
Minority Report   91, 92

Monnet, Jean 21, 33, 35, 47, 53, 55, 60, 171 n.8
Mont Blanc Bridge, Geneva 74
Monthly Summary 67–9, 71, 78, 80, 106, 115, 118–20, 125, 126, 150
Moorhouse, Frank 57
Moraes, Marco 82, 170 n.43
moral disarmament 48, 50, 115
moral force of public opinion 73–9
Mulder, Nicholas 70
Müller, Jan-Werner 4
multinationalism 28
Mumby, Jane 188 n.1

Nansen, Fritiof 71, 122
Napoleonic France 2
national disagreements 14
nationalist populism 163
network diplomacy 137
news and publications 15, 114, 117, 124, 157
Neyman, Stanislas 101
Ninno, Marco 127
Noblemaire Report, 1921 36, 40
Nordenstreng, Kaarle 50

Office of War Information (OWI) 136
O'Malley, Alanna 166 n.13
open diplomacy 4, 5, 8, 34, 39, 45, 47, 48, 58, 100, 123, 141
Osuský, Štefan 92

The Pact of Locarno in 1925 39
Palais des Nations 102, 107, 108, 124, 127–9
Palais Wilson 42, 43
Paris Peace Conference 2, 20, 22, 89, 116
Patel, Klaus Kiran 168 n.22
Pax Romana 83
peace agreements 2
Peace Congress 149
Pedersen, Susan 5, 165 n.11, 166 n.12
Pelt, Adrianus 13, 16, 49, 57, 58, 60, 89, 92, 95, 107, 109, 112, 113, 133–5, 137–48, 150, 152, 157, 178 n.91, 191 n.58
Permanent Committees 45
Permanent Court of International Justice 2

Phillimore Committee 83
Pickard, Bertram 52
Plà, José 55, 57, 59, 104, 105
Polish-Lithuanian conflict/Polish-Lithuanian dispute 39, 73
political communication 8
political liaison 59, 60, 94, 95, 98, 101, 102, 108
Political Section 16, 59, 60, 98, 100–2
Potter, Pitman 34, 37, 41, 93, 94, 106, 151, 173 n.61
Pradt, Abbé de 10
pragmatism 47
Preparatory Commission 144
press associations 52, 102
professionalization of journalism 50, 51
public diplomacy 116, 134, 161
public legitimization 4, 5, 15, 16, 26, 40, 48, 85, 100, 102, 109, 114, 126, 141, 151, 152, 154, 156, 159, 161, 162
public mass justification 139, 160
Public Opinion (Lippman) 75
public speech 8

Quai d'Orsay 60, 134

Radio Nations 44, 105, 110, 113, 120
  information bulletins and lectures 111
  radio lectures 111
Radisics, Elemér de 103, 107
Radziwill, Gabriele 55–8, 104, 105
Ranshofen-Wertheimer, Egon 8, 9, 24, 36, 37, 42, 66, 101, 110, 136, 137, 139–41, 166 n.15, 189 n.22
Rappard, William 41
Reformation Hall of Geneva 43
The Refugees 122
Renoliet, Jean-Jacques 177 n.60
Risso, Linda 14, 41
Rockefeller, John D., Jr. 60, 78
Rockefeller Foundation 57
Roosevelt, Franklin 119, 136
Ruyssen, Théodore 55

The Saar Plebiscite (1935) 115
Saint-Pierre, Abbé de 83
Scandinavian League officials 188 n.4
Schot, Johan 82
Scialoja, Vittorio 125, 126

Scott-Smith, Giles   136
Second World War   1, 10, 12, 16, 89, 106, 133, 160
Secretariat's Staff Committee   31
secret diplomacy   8
semi-diplomatic liaison   15
The Settlement of Assyrians – A Work of Humanity and Appeasement   115
Seul, Stephanie   174 n.9
Skinner, Quentin   7, 8, 168 n.25
Slobodian, Quinn   83
Sluga, Glenda   11, 127, 130
Smuts, Jan   2, 120–4
Soviet Union   106, 114, 143, 144, 151
Spanish Civil War   120
Standing Instruction   101
Steiner, Zara   90
Stencek, Valentin   97
Stewart, Iain   189 n.12
strategic communication   5
Stresemann, Gustav   79, 127
Supervisory Commission   90, 92–5, 97–9, 101, 103, 107, 114, 151
Sweetser, Arthur   13, 19, 21, 22, 29–32, 36–8, 40–2, 45, 46, 49, 51, 53, 57, 60–3, 69, 72, 75, 89, 91, 92, 95, 97–100, 102, 105, 107, 108, 112, 113, 128, 133–7, 139–45, 150, 152, 158, 162, 170 n.1, 171 n.12, 172 n.39, 173 n.47, 173 n.50, 180 n.116, 181 n.19, 185 n.67, 188 n.76

taboo of propaganda   15, 63, 68, 83, 94, 124, 132, 139, 146, 152, 153, 162
Taylor, Philip M.   12
Technical Advisory Committee on Information (TACI)   144, 145, 148
technocratic internationalism   82
Temporary Mixed Commission on Armaments   47
Ten Years of World-Cooperation   75
'theory of publicity'   41

Theunis, Georges   77–9
Tollardo, Elisabetta   113
Tournés, Ludovic   168 n.29
Treaty of Versailles   2, 3, 9, 20, 22, 29, 69
Trump, Donald   4
Tworek, Heidi   49, 159
Tyler, Hannah   66

UN, including its Department of Public Information (UNDPI)   143–51, 154
United Nations Educational, Scientific and Cultural Organization (UNESCO)   99
United Nations Information Organization (UNIO)   136
United Nations Relief and Rehabilitation Administration-organization (UNRRA)   136–7, 145
Universal Khuddamul Ka'aba   54
Urquhart, Brian   163
US war propaganda   159
utilitarianism   10

van Dijk, Pelle   112, 116
Vicuna, Manuel   127

Weimar Constitution   81
Wertheim, Stephen   169 n.36
Wilson, Joseph   137
Wilson, Woodrow   2, 3, 8, 9, 11, 43, 61, 116, 130, 168 n.28
Wilsonianism   32
Wilsonian mission   24
World Economic Conference of 1933   90
World Peace Foundation   60
world public opinion   50, 79, 100, 134, 138

Yanez, Eliodoro   48

Zilliacus, Konni   57, 94, 158